The
Reference Shelf®

Propaganda & Misinformation

The Reference Shelf
Volume 92 • Number 2
H.W. Wilson
A Division of EBSCO Information Services, Inc.

Published by
GREY HOUSE PUBLISHING
Amenia, New York
2020

The Reference Shelf

Cover photo: istock

Copyright © 2020 by Grey House Publishing, Inc.

The Reference Shelf: Propaganda & Misinformation, published by Grey House Publishing, Inc., Amenia, NY, under exclusive license from EBSCO Information Services, Inc.

The books in this series contain reprints of articles, excerpts from books, addresses on current issues, and studies of social trends in the United States and other countries. There are six separately bound numbers in each volume, all of which are usually published in the same calendar year. Numbers one through five are each devoted to a single subject, providing background information and discussion from various points of view and concluding with an index and comprehensive bibliography that lists books, pamphlets, and articles on the subject. The final number of each volume is a collection of recent speeches. Books in the series may be purchased individually or on subscription.

All rights reserved. No part of this work may be used or reproduced in any manner whatsoever or transmitted in any form or by any means, electronic or mechanical, including photocopying, recording, or any information storage and retrieval system, without written permission from the copyright owner. For subscription information and permissions requests, contact Grey House Publishing, 4919 Route 22, PO Box 56, Amenia, NY 12501.

∞ The paper used in these volumes conforms to the American National Standard for Permanence of Paper for Printed Library Materials, Z39.48 1992 (R2009).

Publisher's Cataloging-In-Publication Data
(Prepared by The Donohue Group, Inc.)

Names: Grey House Publishing, Inc., compiler.
Title: Propaganda & misinformation / [compiled by Grey House Publishing].
Other Titles: Propaganda and misinformation | Reference shelf ; v. 92, no. 2.
Description: Amenia, New York : Grey House Publishing, 2020. | Includes bibliographical references and index.
Identifiers: ISBN 9781642656015 (v. 92, no. 2) | ISBN 9781642655995 (volume set)
Subjects: LCSH: Mass media and propaganda--United States. | Disinformation--United States. | Artificial intelligence--Social aspects--United States. | Government information--United States. | Hacktivism--United States. | LCGFT: Reference works.
Classification: LCC P96.P722 U55 2020 | DDC 303.3750973--dc23

Contents

Preface ix

1

The Story of Untruth

Defining Propaganda and Misinformation 3
The History of "Fake News" in America 8
Karen Yuan and Matt Peterson, *The Atlantic*

"Disinformation" Is the Word of the Year—And a Sign of What's to Come 11
Geoff Nunerg, *NPR*

How Woodrow Wilson's Propaganda Machine Changed American Journalism 13
Christopher B. Daly, *The Conversation*

What the Pope Gets Wrong about Fake News 17
Jack Shafer, *Politico*

Nineteenth-Century Nihilists Foretold Our Era 20
Robert Zaretsky, *Foreign Affairs*

A Short Guide to the History of "Fake News" and Disinformation 24
Julie Posetti and Alice Matthews, International Center for Journalists

2

Our Current Media Environment

Fake News, the Coronavirus, and the 2020 Election 47
NPR Poll: Majority of Americans Believe Trump Encourages
    Election Interference 53
Brett Neely, *NPR*

Trump's Favorite Tabloid Worried Its Saudi Propaganda
    Was as Bad as It Looked 56
Bess Levin, *Vanity Fair*

CNN vs. Fox: Why These Two Cable Networks Can't Stop
    Talking about Each Other 60
Paul Farhi, *The Washington Post*

Social Media Struggles to Counter Coronavirus Misinformation 63
Emily Birnbaum and Chris Mills Rodrigo, *The Hill*

Clinton Backer at Facebook Debunks Clinton Claims 67
James Freeman, *The Wall Street Journal*

The Propagandist and the Censor   70
Andrew Stuttaford, *National Review*

3

The Effects of Propaganda

The Subtle Influence of Misinformation   77
Why Do People Fall for Fake News?   82
Gordon Pennycook and David Rand, *The New York Times*

Why the Hysteria Around the "Fake News Epidemic" Is a Distraction   85
Cas Mudde, *The Guardian*

The Myth of the Echo Chamber   88
Elizabeth Dubois and Grant Blank, *The Conversation*

The Real Consequences of Fake News   91
Dominik Stecula, *The Conversation*

Echo Chambers May Not Be as Dangerous as You Think, New Study Finds   94
Science Daily

4

Big Tech and the New AI

AI, Bots, and Regulation   99
Not Your Father's Bots   104
Sarah Kreps and Miles McCain, *Foreign Affairs*

Google's Algorithm Isn't Biased, It's Just Not Human   107
Noam Cohen, *Wired*

Why the Fight Against Disinformation, Sham Accounts and Trolls Won't Be Any Easier in 2020   110
Alexandre S. Levine, Nancy Scola, Steven Overly and Cristiano Lima, *Politico*

The Information War Is On: Are We Ready for It?   115
Renee Diresta, *Wired*

Detecting Fake News at Its Source   119
Adam Conner-Simons, *MIT News*

We're Fighting Fake News AI Bots by Using More AI: That's a Mistake   122
Samuel Woolley, *MIT Technology Review*

How Social Networks Set the Limits of What We Can Say Online   128
Tarleton Gillespie, *Wired*

5

Navigating Misinformation

Ways to Combat Fake News	137
SPJ Code of Ethics Society of Professional Journalists	142
How to Help Kids Navigate Fake News and Misinformation Online Joanne Orlando, *The Conversation*	146
A College Reading List for the Post-Truth Era Michael T. Nietzel, *Forbes*	149
10 Journalism Brands Where You Find Real Facts Rather Than Alternative Facts Paul Glader, *Forbes*	152
Fact Checkers Say These Are the Best Fact-Checks They Did During This Decade Cristina Tardaguila, The Poynter Institute	157
Bibliography	161
Websites	167
Index	171

Preface

Negotiating the Truth

While concerns about propaganda and misinformation have been on the public radar since the beginning of the post-truth era, anxiety has been heightened by the upcoming 2020 presidential election, the world of "alternative facts," and our growing polarization. Media literacy has never been more important, as it becomes increasingly difficult to separate fact from the wealth of false information circling our media environment.

The spread of misinformation (which can be unwitting) and its intentional form, disinformation, has grown alongside mass communication, expanding in reach with the development of the printing press, radio, film, television, the internet, and social media. The last has allowed an unprecedented amount of information (or misinformation) to spread instantaneously.

Propaganda is defined as "the spreading of ideas, information, or rumor for the purpose of helping or injuring an institution, a cause or a person."[1] It can be traced back to at least the Roman Empire, when a political battle between Octavian and Mark Antony resulted in a very early instance of "fake news." Octavian disseminated what he claimed was Antony's last will, which specified, among other things, that large tracts of Roman territory would be left to his children with Cleopatra. Real or not, this document made Antony a traitor, and the Roman senate took away his right to command his armies.[2]

Historical moments of great social upheaval, like the sixteenth-century Reformation and the French and American revolutions of the eighteenth century, relied heavily on promulgating ideas. An increasingly literate population seeking political and social change was also more vulnerable to "mass persuasion." Governments recognized the importance of public opinion and created newspapers to gain a measure of social control. Propaganda reached new heights during World Wars I and II, as all involved countries hired writers, artists, and filmmakers to build support for their war efforts, portraying the other side as inhuman and evil. The Nazi propaganda machine opened the world's eyes to the horrors made possible by state-sponsored disinformation and censorship.[3]

Fake News and Free Speech

Is mis- or dis-information protected by the U.S. Constitution? The potential of false, exaggerated, or censored information to inform our policy debates and even who we choose as leaders has sparked controversy over the limits of free speech. Although several countries—including Singapore, Germany, Malaysia, France, and

Russia—have passed legislation combating fake news, efforts in the United States to curb intentional disinformation have thus far tended to be voluntary. The cure of regulating speech might be worse than the disease of false information. Some countries that have passed these laws are using them to quash political dissent. Russia labels anything that shows "blatant disrespect" for the state as fake news, and Malaysia's citizens face fines equal to hundreds of thousands of dollars and/or imprisonment for six years. Even Germany's novel approach of fining social media platforms for not removing offending posts within twenty-four hours has run into difficulties, as Facebook and Twitter are being overly cautious in response and blocking anything that might be interpreted as violating the new law.[4]

Senator and presidential candidate Elizabeth Warren, in her "Fighting Digital Disinformation" plan, "promises 'to create civil and criminal penalties for knowingly disseminating false information about when and how to vote in U.S. elections,'" according to a *Washington Examiner* article by Brad Polumbo. Although Polumbo acknowledges that these measures are designed to combat voter suppression, he voices concern that "government censorship will inevitably creep beyond just saying elections are on the wrong day . . . [and] stretch the definition of 'election misinformation' to include political predictions and commentary."[5]

In the absence of a regulatory solution to misinformation, the best approach is still an informed and skeptical public.

A Matter of Degree?

What makes our current media environment unique? Clearly the sheer volume of information and the speed with which it travels are important factors. But the internet has also taken the flow of information out of the hands of journalism's traditional gatekeepers, who arguably applied ethical standards to reporting. Some contend that this democratization of journalism has led to positive things like the Arab Spring revolutions. But it has also created polarization, a distrust of the media, and an increasing reliance on opinion and emotion—by media producers and their consumers alike—at the expense of fact. As *Medium* contributors Ed Madison and Ben DeJarnette note:

> Comment sections and digital aggregators like Reddit and Digg found themselves overrun by racist, sexist, and xenophobic internet trolls. Social media platforms wrote algorithms that bifurcated the web into insular filter bubbles. And opportunistic upstarts dressed up propaganda to look like real news, and then fed it to partisan news consumers who couldn't get enough.[6]

A 2018 study by the Rand Corporation, "Truth Decay," discusses four aspects of current public attitudes toward information: increasing disagreement about facts and their interpretation; a blurring of the line between fact and opinion; the increase in volume and so the influence of personal experience over fact; and declining trust in traditional sources of factual information. While acknowledging that some of these attitudes have been present in other historical periods of social upheaval—the Gilded Age, the Great Depression, and the Vietnam War era—the report finds differences in truth decay in our era. Similarities include some blurring of the line between fact and opinion as well as some distrust in institutions, but disagreement has historically centered around economic and social factors. What is not in evidence is "disagreement about basic and objective facts in areas where agreement was previously common and even unquestioned." The study credits cognitive bias, the rise of social media, the inability of the education system to keep up with the challenges of the new information system, and polarization as causes of truth decay.[7]

Alternative Facts

Although spinning events to present a party or a candidate in a favorable light is a longstanding tradition in politics, there has arguably never been as blatant a practitioner as President Donald Trump. The *Washington Post* has kept count of his false claims since he took office, and, although many statements are repeats, as of January 2020 the tally had risen to over 16,000.[8] Trump and his supporters regularly call any unfavorable reporting on the president—and there is plenty—fake news, and often retaliate with an "alternative" version of events. This antagonistic relationship with the media is one of the reasons for the escalation in concern about propaganda.

At what point does political spin cross over into something more sinister? Rutgers University journalism professor David Greenberg, who studies the relationship between presidents and the news, points out, "We don't expect our politicians to present the facts in a neutral, disinterested manner. We expect them to make their case for a particular position." He says of Trump in particular:

> Trump is in a difficult position. His appeal rests on being hostile to the whole system. It's a blustery, take-no-prisoners style. But while this propelled him to the presidency, it has also made him one of the most disliked politicians in American history. This paradox ties his hands. For him to moderate his message means risking the iconoclastic image he has cultivated. Yet I think that if he's ever to expand his appeal, he's going to have to work in another register.[9]

But Trump's attacks on the media also have real-world consequences. In addition to contributing to the general media-related angst, there has been a rise in threats against journalists since he took office. Following Trump's lead, some foreign leaders have used fake news to justify censoring, arresting, or assaulting journalists in their countries. In an interview with *New York Times* publisher A.G. Sulzberger, Trump said "I do notice that people are declaring more and more fake news, where they go, 'Fake news!'. . . I even see it in other countries. I don't necessarily attribute that to me. I think I can attribute the term to me. I think I was the one that started using it, I would say." Trump went on to talk about his perceived unfair treatment by the mainstream media: "But I think I get it really bad. I mean, let's face it, this is at a level that nobody's ever seen before."[10]

Is Propaganda Ever Justified?

Influential advertising pioneer Edward Bernays—often referred to as the "father of public relations"—believed propaganda was an unavoidable part of society. His work with the controversial Creel Committee during World War I convinced him of the importance of shaping public opinion in a way he believed was beneficial to society. He said of the experience, "The impact words and pictures made on the minds of men throughout Europe made a deep impression on me. I recognized that they had been powerful factors in helping win the war."[11] In the 1947 article "The Engineering of Consent," Bernays describes a media environment that may seem similar to ours:

> Words hammer continually at the eyes and ears of America. The United States has become a small room in which a single whisper is magnified thousands of times.

He goes on to assert, "We must recognize the significance of modern communications not only as a highly visible organized mechanical web but as a potent force for social good or possible evil."[12] Despite his declared intentions, Bernays engaged in some highly effective but morally questionable campaigns—convincing women that smoking was part of their liberation, and working with the United Fruit Company in connection with the CIA-orchestrated takeover of the Guatemalan government in 1954. And even though Bernays was Jewish, his methods were used by Joseph Goebbels to craft Adolf Hitler's public image. Bernays recounted in his 1965 autobiography, "They were using my books as the basis for a destructive campaign against the Jews of Germany. This shocked me, but I know any human activity can be used for social purposes or misused for antisocial ones."[13]

In the early 2010s, the United States government and other countries attempted to address al-Qaeda's successful web-based recruitment efforts to join its global *jihad* with a counternarrative as a way to combat terrorism. The largely unsuccessful effort ironically developed into a narrative of its own for justifying domestic nationalistic extremist policies that is ongoing to this day.[14]

The Role of Technology

In the wake of the 2016 election, Facebook came under scrutiny for its role in proliferating fake news that benefitted Donald Trump's campaign. Although the company does not describe itself as a media company, many of its users get the majority of their news and information from the platform, making it a de facto editorial gatekeeper. Facebook and other social media platforms have increased efforts to combat misinformation using both technology and human moderators. But critics contend that not enough resources are dedicated to an endeavor that could conflict with advertising revenue and also that there is not enough transparency in how tech companies make decisions.[15]

As Madison and DeJarnette state, "The reality is that sensationalism and partisanship are not bugs in Facebook's platform so much as features of the machine—a machine that works best when audiences become glued to their screens, no matter what brings them there."[16]

Technological developments geared toward combating disinformation include a machine-learning system that can determine the credibility of a media outlet. The system's developers—MIT's Computer Science and Artificial Intelligence Lab and the Qatar Computing Research Institute—claim that on the basis of language analysis the system can determine if a site is trustworthy by analyzing 150 articles. This could be an improvement over the slow process of checking individual facts.[17] However, new artificial intelligence systems are designed to generate reports that sound credible, at high speed and low cost, and could prove undetectable.[18]

Is Everything Propaganda?

The work of Italian scholar Umberto Eco often highlighted the dangers of over-interpretation and "behindology" (from the Italian *dietrologia*), or of constantly searching for the meaning behind apparent truth and assuming conspiracies at every turn.[19] Educators have expressed similar concerns about teaching propaganda. In response to materials distributed to schools and libraries in the 1930s by the Institute for Propaganda Analysis, some teachers worried that exposing propaganda techniques would increase cynicism and alienation. One teacher questioned whether the IPA curriculum—which still surfaces in media literacy literature—might "simply promote an attitude of generalized cynicism, a feeling that you can't trust any newspaper, any radio commentator, any political speaker?" The trick, according to IPA head of operations Clyde Miller, is to not respond negatively to propaganda but to analyze it carefully, taking into account one's personal biases and world view.[20] The alternative is to be manipulated by someone else's words and political agenda. As political theorist Hannah Arendt warned in a 1967 *New Yorker* article:

> The result of a consistent and total substitution of lies for factual truth is not that the lies will now be accepted as truth, and the truth be defamed as lies, but that the sense by which we take our bearings in the real world . . . is being destroyed.[21]

Works Used

Arendt, Hannah. "Truth and Politics." *New Yorker*. Feb 18, 1967. https://www.newyorker.com/magazine/1967/02/25/truth-and-politics.

Bernays, Edward. "The Engineering of Consent." First published Mar 1, 1947. https://journals.sagepub.com/doi/10.1177/000271624725000116.

Branson, Ken. "President Trump and the Art of Spin." *Rutgers Today*, Feb 23, 2017. https://news.rutgers.edu/qa/president-trump-and-art-spin/20170222#.XksT-mIpKiM8.

Conner-Simons, Adam. "Detecting Fake News at Its Source." MIT Computer Science and Artificial Intelligence Lab (CSAIL). Oct 4, 2018. http://news.mit.edu/2018/mit-csail-machine-learning-system-detects-fake-news-from-source-1004.

Grynbaum, Michael M. "Trump Discusses Claims of 'Fake News,' and Their Impact, with New York Times Publisher." *New York Times*. Feb 1, 2019. https://

www.nytimes.com/2019/02/01/business/media/donald-trump-interview-news-media.html?campaignId=7JFJX.

Gunderman, Richard. "The Manipulation of the American Mind: Edward Bernays and the Birth of Public Relations." *The Conversation*. July 9, 2015. https://theconversation.com/the-manipulation-of-the-american-mind-edward-bernays-and-the-birth-of-public-relations-44393.

Hung Ng, Sik, and Fei Deng. "Language and Power." *Oxford Research Encyclopedia of Communication*. Aug 2017. https://oxfordre.com/communication/view/10.1093/acrefore/9780190228613.001.0001/acrefore-9780190228613-e-436.

Kavanagh, Jennifer, and Michael D. Rich. "Truth Decay An Initial Exploration of the Diminishing Role of Facts and Analysis in American Public Life." Santa Monica, CA: RAND Corporation, 2018. https://www.rand.org/pubs/research_reports/RR2314.html.

Kessler, Glenn, Salvador Rizzo, and Meg Kelly. "President Trump Made 16,241 False or Misleading Claims in His First Three Years." *Washington Post*. Jan 20, 2020. https://www.washingtonpost.com/politics/2020/01/20/president-trump-made-16241-false-or-misleading-claims-his-first-three-years/.

Kreps, Sarah and Miles McCain. "Not Your Father's Bots: AI Is Making Fake News Look Real." *Foreign Affairs*. Aug 2, 2019. https://www.foreignaffairs.com/articles/2019-08-02/not-your-fathers-bots.

MacDonald, Eve. "The Fake News That Sealed the Fate of Antony and Cleopatra." *The Conversation*. Jan 13, 2017. https://theconversation.com/the-fake-news-that-sealed-the-fate-of-antony-and-cleopatra-71287.

Madison, Ed, and Ben DeJarnette. "Journalism's Gatekeepers Lost Control of Their Gates." *Medium*. June 21, 2017. https://medium.com/s/how-journalism-became-a-dirty-word/journalisms-gatekeepers-lost-control-of-their-gates-8548f1bec0a3.

Polumbo, Brad. "Criminalizing Free Speech Online? Elizabeth Warren Has a Plan for That.' *Washington Examiner*. Jan 29, 2020. https://www.washingtonexaminer.com/opinion/elizabeth-warren-unveils-dystopian-fighting-disinformation-plan-criminalizing-free-speech-online.

Schetzer, Alana. "Governments Are Making Fake News a Crime—But It Could Stifle Free Speech." *The Conversation*. July 7, 2019. https://theconversation.com/governments-are-making-fake-news-a-crime-but-it-could-stifle-free-speech-117654.

Smith, B.L. 'Propaganda Analysis and the Science of Democracy." *Public Opinion Quarterly*, vol. 5, no. 2 (1941): 250–59. Quoted in Hobbs, Renee, and Sandra McGee. "Teaching about Propaganda: An Examination of the Historical Roots of Media Literacy." *Journal of Media Literacy Education*, vol. 6, no. 2, 56–67. https://digitalcommons.uri.edu/jmle/vol6/iss2/5/.

Sullivan, Margaret. "Facebook's Role in Trump's Win Is Clear: No Matter What Mark Zuckerberg Says." *Washington Post*. Sept 7, 2017. https://www.washingtonpost.com/lifestyle/style/facebooks-role-in-trumps-win-is-clear-no-matter-what-mark-zuckerberg-says/2017/09/07/b5006c1c-93c7-11e7-89fa-bb822a46da5b_story.html.

Thomson, Ian. "Umberto Eco Obituary." *The Guardian*. Feb 20, 2016. https://www.theguardian.com/books/2016/feb/20/umberto-eco-obituary.

Tye, Larry. *The Father of Spin*. New York: Henry Holt, 1998. https://www.google.com/books/edition/The_Father_of_Spin/GarJLYMm3A0C?hl=en&gbpv=1&printsec=frontcover.

U.S. Holocaust Memorial Museum. "What Is Propaganda?" https://www.ushmm.org/propaganda/resources/.

Webster's dictionary. https://www.merriam-webster.com/dictionary/propaganda.

Notes

1. Webster's dictionary, https://www.merriam-webster.com/dictionary/propaganda.
2. MacDonald, "The Fake News That Sealed the Fate of Antony and Cleopatra."
3. U.S. Holocaust Memorial Museum, "What Is Propaganda?"
4. Schetzer, "Governments Are Making Fake News a Crime—But It Could Stifle Free Speech."
5. Polumbo, "Criminalizing Free Speech Online? Elizabeth Warren Has a Plan for That."
6. Madison and DeJarnette, "Journalism's Gatekeepers Lost Control of Their Gates."
7. Kavanagh and Rich, "Truth Decay: An Initial Exploration of the Diminishing Role of Facts and Analysis in American Public Life."
8. Kessler, Rizzo, and Kelly. "President Trump Made 16,241 False or Misleading Claims in His First Three Years."
9. Branson, "President Trump and the Art of Spin."
10. Grynbaum, "Trump Discusses Claims of 'Fake News' and Their Impact, with New York Times Publisher."
11. Tye, *The Father of Spin*, p. 22.
12. Bernays, "The Engineering of Consent."
13. Gunderman, "The Manipulation of the American Mind: Edward Bernays and the Birth of Public Relations."
14. Hung Ng and Deng, "Language and Power."
15. Sullivan, "Facebook's Role in Trump's Win Is Clear: No Matter What Mark Zuckerberg Says."
16. Madison and DeJarnette, "Journalism's Gatekeepers Lost Control of Their Gates."
17. Conner-Simons, "Detecting Fake News at Its Source."
18. Kreps and McCain, "Not Your Father's Bots: AI Is Making Fake News Look Real."
19. Thomson, "Umberto Eco Obituary."
20. Smith, "Propaganda Analysis and the Science of Democracy," p. 250.
21. Arendt, "Truth and Politics."

1
The Story of Untruth

This iconic image was created for the Creel Committee during World War I. By James Montgomery Flagg, United States Library of Congress Prints and Photographs Division, via Wikimedia.

Defining Propaganda and Misinformation

Propaganda, currently defined as "information, especially of a biased or misleading nature, used to promote or publicize a particular political cause or point of view, originates from Pope Gregory XV's 1622 missionary organization, the *Congregatio de propaganda fide* ("Congregation for propagating the faith"),[1] and was—and still can be—considered a neutral term. For instance, public health campaigns, like those for AIDS or vaccinations, are forms of propaganda in its simplest form—information that is spread or promoted.

Propaganda and War

Although war propaganda is as old as war itself, the First World War marked the first time major governments attempted to manage the information being promoted. The ways in which information was disseminated also increased at this time—including newspapers, speeches, films, photographs, posters, books, and cartoons. As words and images were sent out to the public to create support for the war, governments passed laws to keep information judged harmful to the war effort from being circulated.

U.S. President Woodrow Wilson created the Committee on Public Information (CPI) by executive order a week after Congress declared war in April 1917. The model that Wilson established in interacting with the press and the public during wartime had far-reaching effects, and has been used by many U.S. presidents since to control public opinion and thus, create a sense of national mission. The CPI (a.k.a. the Creel committee after chairman George Creel) was organized like a modern public relations department and relied heavily on populist journalism and advertising techniques. Creel referred to the CPI as a "'vast enterprise in salesmanship, the world's greatest adventure in advertising,'" and his methods are often criticized as deceptive and manipulative. CPI volunteer Edward L. Bernays, a nephew of Sigmund Freud who employed psychological methods to sway public opinion, believed his efforts were necessary, stating: "'The conscious and intelligent manipulation of the organized habits and opinions of the masses is an important element in democratic society. . . . Propaganda is the executive arm of the invisible government.'" Several units were created to write speeches, produce film reels and artwork, and monitor the domestic and foreign press. The Speaking Division of the CPI alone employed 75,000 specialists. The Division of Pictorial Publicity produced the iconic image of "Uncle Sam" pointing his finger and declaring "I WANT YOU FOR U.S. ARMY!"[2] The "Four-Minute Men" (intentionally conjuring the "Minute Men" of the Revolution) were volunteers giving short speeches at public venues throughout the country that lasted no longer than the time it would take to change a film reel. As in Great Britain and France, the U.S. government assumed broad powers over the press, passing the Espionage Act of June 1917 and the Sedition Act of May 1918, both of which made it a crime to criticize the war effort or the U.S. government.

In any discussion of propaganda, Nazi Germany holds a central place. In contrast to the Allies, during WWI, the German government openly subsidized its own news agency and radio news service. Some of its major newspapers were government-controlled. German propaganda efforts were mostly begun, and eventually dominated, by the military. At the start of the war all of Germany except Bavaria was placed under control of army commanders under a state-of-siege law. The German army issued and enforced directives to the press, and controlled the filming of fighting on the front. Several divisions eventually came under the control of the supreme command of the German army, the Oberste Heeresleitung (OHL).[3]

When the Nazis seized power in 1933, Adolf Hitler created the Reich Ministry of Public Enlightenment and Propaganda under the direction of Joseph Goebbels. According to Hitler, the purpose of propaganda "'is not to make an objective study of the truth, in so far as it favors the enemy, and then set it before the masses with academic fairness; its task is to serve our own right, always and unflinchingly.'" As the Allies did, the Nazis used art, music, theater, radio, and films to spread their message. Building on real and perceived anti-German prejudice in territories that had been ceded to east European nations after WWI, Nazi propaganda focused on race consciousness among ethnic Germans and on convincing major European powers that Nazi Germany was making understandable demands for concessions. Jews were portrayed as subhuman, parasitic, and in control of the Allied powers in a conspiracy to provoke war. Propaganda created tolerance for violence, and acceptance of legal measures, against Jews, such as relocation and the Nuremberg Race Laws, which stripped basic citizenship rights from an ever-broadening population. Increasing exhortations to achieve racial purity led to the "Final Solution"—the mass murder of European Jews. Nazi officials compelled prisoners who were later executed to send postcards to relatives stating that they were living in good conditions. In June 1944 the Germans allowed the International Red Cross to inspect a sanitized camp-ghetto, Theresienstadt, which had been created to quiet any reservations of ethnic Germans questioning the deportation of German and Austrian Jews.[4]

Propaganda efforts similar to those employed by Wilson in WWI and Franklin D. Roosevelt in WWII have been part of every major U.S. conflict, including the Vietnam War in the 1960s, the invasion of Afghanistan in 2001 following the 9/11 attacks on the Twin Towers, and the Iraq War in 2003. Although it is necessary in times of war to withhold information, from the public and press, that might endanger military personnel or operations, what is less clear are justifications for campaigns to begin or enter into a war in the first place.

Fake News and Propaganda

Misinformation can be anything from well-meaning but inaccurate medical advice, like the antivaxxer campaign, to lengthy descriptions of extraterrestrial life on the moon. A century before Orson Welles broadcast "The War of the Worlds" on CBS radio, the *New York Sun* in 1835 published "The Great Moon Hoax," a series of six articles that featured unicorns, two-legged beavers, and winged humanoids that had been "discovered" on the moon by a prominent astronomer of the day. Most likely it was meant as satire; in any event, sales of the paper shot up and a team of scientists from Yale University traveled to New York in search of the source documents.[5] In an interesting twist, recent evidence suggests that the "panic" reported in newspapers after Welles's broadcast may have been exaggerated in order to discredit radio as a source of news.[6]

While a belief in unicorns and aliens might arguably be harmless, medical misinformation—governments are currently battling false facts about the coronavirus—can lead to physical harm or even death. Misinformation is usually not spread with the intention to deceive, and can even be sent to friends as an example of something ludicrous or amusing. The end result, however, is the same: questionable information spreads, quickly and to many. Syracuse University professor Whitney Phillips explains that people fall for hoaxes in part because of how we process information; if a story fits with our worldview and appears to have a coherent narrative, we often make snap decisions on its credibility, choosing to share on social media what a quick Google search will often prove false.[7]

Organized campaigns deliberately disseminating misinformation, such as corporate-sponsored materials casting doubt on the health effects of tobacco and vaping, or denying climate change, can have devastating effects. These offensives are more accurately described as "disinformation" and "fake news."

Soviet dictator Josef Stalin is credited with coining the term "dezinformatsiya." According to Romanian secret police defector Ion Mihai Pacepa, Stalin wanted a French-sounding word to root its origins in the West. Predating the 2016 Russian interference in the U.S. election, suspected Soviet disinformation efforts include a 1980s story that the United States developed the AIDs virus as a biological weapon that spread to 50 countries, and that the CIA was involved in the assassination of John F. Kennedy. The United States government has also engaged in planting newspaper articles, including those in Muslim countries about Soviet "invasion day celebrations" after the Soviet invasion of Afghanistan.[8]

In an attempt to define our current media environment, *Quartz* contributor Gideon Lichfield lists how 20th-century propaganda techniques and 21st-century technology have resulted in "propaganda on steroids": echo chambers (consumers only consulting news sources that agree with a particular world view); alternative news sources (well-financed news operations with a strong agenda); fake news (sensational content created as click bait); online swarms (the mobilization of vast groups of people to troll opponents' online content); bots (automated social media accounts used to amplify or quash messages); and psychological profiling and target advertising (efforts by major tech companies like Facebook to influence users' moods or even voting habits). Lichfield compares President Donald Trump's Twitter account to a one-man alternative news source that can "change the news cycle, determine what gets attention and what doesn't, force media to chase stories they might otherwise ignore and neglect those they should be paying attention to."9

In addition to taking into account our own bias, we have to ascertain the possible agendas of information sources. Technological factors such as bots will continue to distort information and its importance and are becoming harder to detect with advances in artificial intelligence. Ferreting out the truth in our ever-more-complicated media environment is a daunting, but important, task.

Works Used

Badsey, Stephen. "Propaganda: Media in War Politics." International Encyclopedia of the First World War. https://encyclopedia.1914-1918-online.net/article/propaganda_media_in_war_politics.

Daly, Christopher B. "How Woodrow Wilson's Propaganda Machine Changed American Journalism." *The Conversation*. Apr 27, 2017. https://theconversation.com/how-woodrow-wilsons-propaganda-machine-changed-american-journalism-76270.

Fox, Jo. "World War One Atrocity Propaganda." British Library. https://www.bl.uk/world-war-one/videos/world-war-one-atrocity-propaganda.

"'The Great Moon Hoax' Is Published in the *New York Sun*." History.com. https://www.history.com/this-day-in-history/the-great-moon-hoax.

Lichfield, Gideon. "21st-Century Propaganda: A Guide to Interpreting and Confronting the Dark Arts of Persuasion." *Quartz*. May 13, 2017. https://qz.com/978548/introducing-our-obsession-with-propaganda/.

Martineau, Paris. "Why People Keep Falling for Viral Hoaxes." *Wired*. Aug 22, 2019. https://www.wired.com/story/why-people-keep-falling-viral-hoaxes/.

Memmot, Mark. "75 Years Ago, 'War of the Worlds' Started a Panic. Or Did It?" *NPR*. Oct 30, 2013. https://www.npr.org/sections/thetwo-way/2013/10/30/241797346/75-years-ago-war-of-the-worlds-started-a-panic-or-did-it.

"Nazi Propaganda." Holocaust Encyclopedia, U.S. Holocaust Memorial Museum. https://encyclopedia.ushmm.org/content/en/article/nazi-propaganda.

"Powers of Persuasion." National Archives. https://www.archives.gov/exhibits/powers-of-persuasion.

Taylor, Adam. "Before 'Fake News,' There Was Soviet 'Disinformation.'" *Washington Post*. Nov 26, 2016. https://www.washingtonpost.com/news/worldviews/wp/2016/11/26/before-fake-news-there-was-soviet-disinformation/.

"U.S. Congress Passes Espionage Act." History.com. https://www.history.com/this-day-in-history/u-s-congress-passes-espionage-act.

Webster's Dictionary. "Propaganda." https://www.merriam-webster.com/dictionary/propaganda.

Notes

1. Webster's Dictionary.
2. Daly, Christopher. "How Woodrow Wilson's Propaganda Machine Changed American Journalism."
3. Badsey, "Propaganda: Media in War Politics."
4. "Nazi Propaganda." Holocaust Museum.
5. "'The Great Moon Hoax' Is Published in the *New York Sun*."
6. Memmot, "75 Years Ago, 'War of the Worlds' Started a Panic. Or Did It?"
7. Martineau, "Why People Keep Falling for Viral Hoaxes."
8. Taylor, "Before 'Fake News,' There Was Soviet 'Disinformation.'"
9. Lichfield, "21st-Century Propaganda: A Guide to Interpreting and Confronting the Dark Arts of Persuasion."

The History of "Fake News" in America

By Karen Yuan and Matt Peterson
The Atlantic, January 9, 2018

Fake news is old news in America—it's been part of news traditions since the political propaganda created during the American Revolution. "Fake news has existed as long as American journalism has been around," said Jacob Soll, a professor of history at University of Southern California, who described a world history of fake news in an article for Politico. "It's the rise of objective news that is something different. The idea of objective journalism only really came about in the early 20th century."

In fact, looking at the history of journalism in America, "real news" appears to be more novel than fake news. The prevalence of fake news today is not the result of a slide from truth to fiction but rather a testament to how real news is something of a novelty in American journalism.

Fake news can mean a lot of different things: In the Trumpian sense, it's best understood as hoaxes or misleading and erroneous reporting. For Soll, fake news is yellow journalism—sensationalist stories that often have a political bent. In the beginning, Soll said, "fake news was how you sell papers: sightings of things that didn't happen and two-headed whales." He recounted the example of Ben Franklin, the Founding Father who is remembered as a truth-seeking scientist. He was also a newspaper editor and printer, however, and his newspapers fabricated stories in the colonies about King George III allying with murderous Indians. Those stories influenced popular animosity toward the king.

By the 1800s, yellow journalism had become a mainstream business model for newspapers. "Americans excelled at it. America had its own particular genre of tabloid news," Soll said. The publisher William Randolph Hearst built a media empire out of tabloids in the Gilded Age. "The 19th century saw the birth of the journalism baron. That's why Hearst has Hearst Castle in California—he made that kind of money." Hearst, who helped instigate the Spanish-American War by publishing false stories about Spain's persecution of the Cuban people, famously told a correspondent in Cuba, "You furnish the pictures, I'll furnish the war."

Yellow journalism may have been good business, but some of its critics saw through it. I found one of the earliest instances of the phrase in an article in *The Sun* from September 3, 1892, which charged its competitor the *New York World* with "manufacturing news in its own office … Of all unfortunate and foolish things a newspaper may do, that of destroying public confidence in itself is most unfortunate and most foolish, and it can accomplish this end in no other way more quickly or more completely than in the matter of 'fake' news."

From *The Atlantic*, January 9 © 2018. Reprinted with permission. All rights reserved.

"The line between news and propaganda was always thin until the birth of the objective newspaper," Soll said, one of which was the *New York Times*. In the late 19th century, publisher Adolph Ochs aimed for the paper to be the antithesis of peers like the *World*. "It was for a funny reason—to sell papers to people who wanted solid information so they could invest money with it," Soll said. But it was part of a broader movement toward objective, fact-based news. "The Hearst model exhausted Americans who wanted something not sensationalist."

> **Fake news is "yellow journalism"—sensational stories that often have a political bent.**

In the 20th century, journalistic conventions as we recognize them today emerged. News organizations began to professionalize and regulate the way they reported news. Objective news was crystallized by journalistic practices in the '60s and '70s, especially during seminal moments like the coverage of Watergate and the Pentagon Papers. "People loved leaked news, which seemed much more real because it had been leaked," said Soll.

Today, technology is enabling fake news just as it did in the 18th century. Rashes of contemporary yellow journalism have appeared online recently in the form of, for example, sensationalist partisan news sites operated by teenagers looking to make cash. Back then, mass printing technology let publishers like Franklin thrive. The internet today plays a similar role, according to Soll. "It's cheap. Web is problematic because it gives you news cheaply … you got that in the 18th century with the explosion of cheap pamphlets filled with crazy stories." At the time, pamphlets spread news even wider than traditional news placards on the street, which often featured false headlines.

For Soll, it's not only the ease of distribution but also the nature of the stories themselves that define, both then and now, yellow journalism. Much of fake news in the 19th century was political in nature. Anti-Catholic newspapers in Philadelphia made false claims in 1844 that Irishmen stole bibles from schools, influencing violent attacks on Catholic churches in the area. Today's fake news is a "more politicized version of Hearst," Soll said. "Telling stories that whip up racial and economic fear is a version of yellow journalism." Fake news that incites prejudice has precedent. "Fake news of this sort is often calculated to produce international ill-feeling," wrote the author of an essay on "fake journalism" in the 1898 political anthology *The Arena*.

The history of fake news in America is the history of news in America. But how does real news thrive when fake news has such a head start and an accommodating medium? "You can't go down rabbit hole with placards but you can go down the rabbit hole with the web," Soll said. "And that's what's really scary."

Print Citations

CMS: Yuan, Karen, and Matt Peterson. "The History of 'Fake News' in America." In *The Reference Shelf: Propaganda & Misinformation,* edited by Annette Calzone, 8–10. Amenia, NY: Grey House Publishing, 2020.

MLA: Yuan, Karen, and Matt Peterson. "The History of 'Fake News' in America." *The Reference Shelf: Propaganda & Misinformation,* edited by Annette Calzone, Grey House Publishing, 2020, pp. 8–10.

APA: Yuan, K., & Peterson, M. (2020). The history of "fake news" in America. In Annette Calzone (Ed.), *The reference shelf: Propaganda & misinformation* (pp. 8–10). Amenia, NY: Grey House Publishing.

"Disinformation" Is the Word of the Year—
And a Sign of What's to Come

By Geoff Nunerg
NPR, December 30, 2019

As always, this year's word of the year candidates came from all over. There were the viral memes like "OK, boomer" and "weird flex, but OK," but they won't endure any longer than earlier years' candidates like FOMO and "manbun." "Quid pro quo" had a moment, but the jury's still out on that one. And a surge in dictionary lookups led *Merriam-Webster* to pick nonbinary "they."

My choice of "disinformation" needs some explaining. It isn't a new word—just one of the family of names we give to the malignancies that contaminate the public discourse, along with "propaganda," and in particular "misinformation" and "fake news." Each of those last two was chosen as word of the year by some dictionary or organization in 2017.

But over the past couple of years "disinformation" has been on a tear—it's 10 times as common in media headlines as it was five years ago, to the point where it's nudged its siblings aside. That rise suggests a basic shift in focus: What most troubles us now isn't just the plague of deceptive information on the Internet, but the organized campaigns that are spreading the infection.

Most of those headlines concerned the Russians. There was their weaponization of social media during the 2016 elections, which the *New York Times* called "the Pearl Harbor of the social media age," and the fears it will be repeated next year. There were also the stories about their interference in recent elections in the U.K., Italy and other nations. And most recently, there was the Russians' success in planting the conspiracy theory that it was Ukraine rather than Russia that interfered in our 2016 elections, despite it being debunked by U.S. intelligence agencies.

Disinformation is as old as human conflict—in the fifth century B.C.E., the great Chinese military theoretician Sun Tzu wrote that all warfare is based on deception. But the Russians can take credit for inventing the word itself. The term "dezinformatsiya" was reputedly coined by no less than Josef Stalin in the 1920s as the name of the section of the KGB tasked with deceiving enemies and influencing public opinion. Over the decades, that unit disseminated rumors by means of forgeries, moles, front organizations, fake defections and sympathetic fellow travelers, which, by the way, is another term that was translated from Russian. The Soviets put out that Pope Pius XII was a Nazi sympathizer and that the CIA had assassinated John F. Kennedy and invented the AIDS virus.

From *NPR*, December 30 © 2019. Reprinted with permission. All rights reserved.

"Dezinformatsiya" was anglicized to "disinformation" during the Cold War era and extended to Western intelligence operations. The characters in John le Carré's spy novels are always talking about planting disinformation to deceive the KGB, using the same clandestine techniques the Soviets did. But the advent of social media created a new field of play and a new panoply of tools for diffusing and amplifying disinformation: trolls and troll farms, bots, hacked accounts and microtargeting.

The Russians weren't the only ones to see the possibilities. In a recent report called the Global Disinformation Order, the Oxford Internet Institute identified organized social media campaigns in 70 nations. Authoritarian regimes use social media domestically to discredit political opponents. A dozen or so nations, such as Russia, China, Iran, Pakistan and Saudi Arabia, use it to influence opinion in foreign nations.

> **Authoritarian regimes use social media domestically to discredit political opponents.**

Dictionaries typically define "disinformation" as the dissemination of deliberately false information, and modern disinformation campaigns all make use of the mendacious techniques we associate with the Orwellian propaganda of the totalitarian states of the last century. They generate a deluge of deceptive narratives that some describe as the "firehose of falsehoods" concocted to glorify a leader or a cause or to malign their enemies. But these campaigns are not all lies. They're also aimed at sharpening tribal divisions and sowing confusion or apathy, and a lot of their effort goes to building out networks of followers. And for those purposes, a true report or even a benign cat photo can sometimes be just as effective as a blatant falsehood. You have to win friends to influence people.

Print Citations

CMS: Nunerg, Geoff. "'Disinformation' Is the Word of the Year—And a Sign of What's to Come." In *The Reference Shelf: The Reference Shelf: Propaganda & Misinformation*, edited by Annette Calzone, 11–12. Amenia, NY: Grey House Publishing, 2020.

MLA: Nunerg, Geoff. "'Disinformation' Is the Word of the Year—And a Sign of What's to Come." *The Reference Shelf: Propaganda & Misinformation*, edited by Annette Calzone, Grey House Publishing, 2020, pp. 11–12.

APA: Nunerg, G. (2020). "Disinformation" is the word of the year—And a sign of what's to come. In Annette Calzone (Ed.), *The reference shelf: Propaganda & misinformation* (pp. 11–12). Amenia, NY: Grey House Publishing.

How Woodrow Wilson's Propaganda Machine Changed American Journalism

By Christopher B. Daly
The Conversation, April 27, 2017

When the United States declared war on Germany 100 years ago, the impact on the news business was swift and dramatic.

In its crusade to "make the world safe for democracy," the Wilson administration took immediate steps at home to curtail one of the pillars of democracy—press freedom—by implementing a plan to control, manipulate and censor all news coverage, on a scale never seen in U.S. history.

Following the lead of the Germans and British, Wilson elevated propaganda and censorship to strategic elements of all-out war. Even before the U.S. entered the war, Wilson had expressed the expectation that his fellow Americans would show what he considered "loyalty."

Immediately upon entering the war, the Wilson administration brought the most modern management techniques to bear in the area of government-press relations. Wilson started one of the earliest uses of government propaganda. He waged a campaign of intimidation and outright suppression against those ethnic and socialist papers that continued to oppose the war. Taken together, these wartime measures added up to an unprecedented assault on press freedom.

I study the history of American journalism, but before I started researching this episode, I had thought that the government's efforts to control the press began with President Roosevelt during WWII. What I discovered is that Wilson was the pioneer of a system that persists to this day.

All Americans have a stake in getting the truth in wartime. A warning from the WWI era, widely attributed to Sen. Hiram Johnson, puts the issue starkly: "The first casualty when war comes is truth."

Mobilizing for War

Within a week of Congress declaring war, on April 13, 1917, Wilson issued an executive order creating a new federal agency that would put the government in the business of actively shaping press coverage.

That agency was the Committee on Public Information, which would take on the task of explaining to millions of young men being drafted into military service—and to the millions of other Americans who had so recently supported neutrality—why they should now support war.

The new agency—which journalist Stephen Ponder called "the nation's first ministry of information"—was usually referred to as the Creel Committee for its chairman, George Creel, who had been a journalist before the war. From the start, the CPI was "a veritable magnet" for political progressives of all stripes—intellectuals, muckrakers, even some socialists—all sharing a sense of the threat to democracy posed by German militarism. Idealistic journalists like S.S. McClure and Ida Tarbell signed on, joining others who shared their belief in Wilson's crusade to make the world safe for democracy.

At the time, most Americans got their news through newspapers, which were flourishing in the years just before the rise of radio and the invention of the weekly news magazine. In New York City, according to my research, nearly two dozen papers were published every day—in English alone—while dozens of weeklies served ethnic audiences.

Starting from scratch, Creel organized the CPI into several divisions using the full array of communications.

The Speaking Division recruited 75,000 specialists who became known as "Four-Minute Men" for their ability to lay out Wilson's war aims in short speeches.

The Film Division produced newsreels intended to rally support by showing images in movie theaters that emphasized the heroism of the Allies and the barbarism of the Germans.

The Foreign Language Newspaper Division kept an eye on the hundreds of weekly and daily U.S. newspapers published in languages other than English.

Another CPI unit secured free advertising space in American publications to promote campaigns aimed at selling war bonds, recruiting new soldiers, stimulating patriotism and reinforcing the message that the nation was involved in a great crusade against a bloodthirsty, antidemocratic enemy.

Some of the advertising showed off the work of another CPI unit. The Division of Pictorial Publicity was led by a group of volunteer artists and illustrators. Their output included some of the most enduring images of this period, including the portrait by James Montgomery Flagg of a vigorous Uncle Sam, declaring, "I WANT YOU FOR THE U.S. ARMY!"

Other ads showed cruel "Huns" with blood dripping from their pointed teeth, hinting that Germans were guilty of bestial attacks on defenseless women and children. "Such a civilization is not fit to live," one ad concluded.

Creel denied that his committee's work amounted to propaganda, but he acknowledged that he was engaged in a battle of perceptions. "The war was not fought in France alone," he wrote in 1920, after it was all over, describing the CPI as "a plain publicity proposition, a vast enterprise in salesmanship, the world's greatest adventure in advertising."

Buried in Paper

For most journalists, the bulk of their contact with the CPI was through its News Division, which became a veritable engine of propaganda on a par with similar government operations in Germany and England but of a sort previously unknown in the United States.

In the brief year and a half of its existence, the CPI's News Division set out to shape the coverage of the war in U.S. newspapers and magazines. One technique was to bury journalists in paper, creating and distributing some 6,000 press releases—or, on average, handing out more than 10 a day.

> **After stimulating the demand for news while artificially restraining the supply, the government stepped into the resulting vacuum and provided a vast number of official stories that looked like news.**

The whole operation took advantage of a fact of journalistic life. In times of war, readers hunger for news and newspapers attempt to meet that demand. But at the same time, the government was taking other steps to restrict reporters' access to soldiers, generals, munitions-makers and others involved in the struggle. So, after stimulating the demand for news while artificially restraining the supply, the government stepped into the resulting vacuum and provided a vast number of official stories that looked like news.

Most editors found the supply irresistible. These government-written offerings appeared in at least 20,000 newspaper columns each week, by one estimate, at a cost to taxpayers of only US$76,000.

In addition, the CPI issued a set of voluntary "guidelines" for U.S. newspapers, to help those patriotic editors who wanted to support the war effort (with the implication that those editors who did not follow the guidelines were less patriotic than those who did).

The CPI News Division then went a step further, creating something new in the American experience: a daily newspaper published by the government itself. Unlike the "partisan press" of the 19th century, the Wilson-era Official Bulletin was entirely a governmental publication, sent out each day and posted in every military installation and post office as well as in many other government offices. In some respects, it is the closest the United States has come to a paper like the Soviet Union's *Pravda* or China's *People's Daily*.

The CPI was, in short, a vast effort in propaganda. The committee built upon the pioneering efforts of public relations man Ivy Lee and others, developing the young field of public relations to new heights. The CPI hired a sizable fraction of all the Americans who had any experience in this new field, and it trained many more.

One of the young recruits was Edward L. Bernays, a nephew of Sigmund Freud and a pioneer in theorizing about human thoughts and emotions. Bernays volunteered for the CPI and threw himself into the work. His outlook—a mixture of idealism about the cause of spreading democracy and cynicism about the methods involved—was typical of many at the agency.

"The conscious and intelligent manipulation of the organized habits and opinions of the masses is an important element in democratic society," Bernays wrote a few years after the war. "Propaganda is the executive arm of the invisible government."

All in all, the CPI proved quite effective in using advertising and PR to instill nationalistic feelings in Americans. Indeed, many veterans of the CPI's campaign of persuasion went into careers in advertising during the 1920s.

The full bundle of techniques pioneered by Wilson during the Great War were updated and used by later presidents when they sent U.S. forces into battle. Now, as the Trump administration begins to engage in military operations abroad, the American experience in WWI provides some timely warnings: The news media and all U.S. citizens should demand not propaganda, but accurate information in times of hostilities, and the government should never be allowed to equate dissent with disloyalty.

Print Citations

CMS: Daly, Christopher B. "How Woodrow Wilson's Propaganda Machine Changed American Journalism." In *The Reference Shelf: Propaganda & Misinformation*, edited by Annette Calzone, 13–16. Amenia, NY: Grey House Publishing, 2020.

MLA: Daly, Christopher B. "How Woodrow Wilson's Propaganda Machine Changed American Journalism." *The Reference Shelf: Propaganda & Misinformation,* edited by Annette Calzone, Grey House Publishing, 2020, pp. 13–16.

APA: Daly, C.B. (2020). How Woodrow Wilson's propaganda machine changed American journalism (2020). In Annette Calzone (Ed.), *The reference shelf: Propaganda & misinformation* (pp. 13–16). Amenia, NY: Grey House Publishing.

What the Pope Gets Wrong about Fake News

By Jack Shafer
Politico, January 24, 2018

I thought I had a deal with the Vatican. Its popes would run Vatican City, provide spiritual guidance to the faithful, appoint bishops and cardinals, issue encyclicals and explore exotic locations in their Popemobiles. Meanwhile, I would oversee press criticism.

This arrangement has worked extraordinarily well over the decades. But today, Pope Francis veered from his lane into mine at a high rate of speed by releasing a naïve bit of press-crit titled "The Truth Will Set You Free: Fake News and Journalism for Peace." In it, he diagnosed the causes of fake news and prescribed his cure. The nerve of that guy! Do I step on his turf by officiating at beatification and canonization ceremonies?

His Holiness gets off to a fine start by defining fake news as "disinformation." This neatly separates him from our blockhead president, who regards any criticism of him or any news stories that don't praise him as fake. Then, the pope squanders this advantage. He fails to provide one example of fake news to illustrate his thesis, leaving it to his congregations' imagination whether he's talking about Pizzagate, alleged no-go zones in the Netherlands or the charges of massive voter fraud in the 2016 election. Fake news, the pope maintains, exists because evil-doers have willed it into existence.

I'm not kidding. In a belabored parable, Francis compares the promulgation of fake news to the acts of treachery and temptation performed by Satan when he took the form of a serpent and whispered his untruths to Adam and Eve in the Garden of Eden. In the pope's view, fake news is primarily a supply-side thing, created by those with a "thirst for power." Consumers of fake news, he holds, are "victims" and "unwilling accomplices" whose "instantaneous emotions like anxiety, contempt, anger and frustration" make them easy targets of exploitation.

Who possesses the courage to tell the pope that he's skating on thin ice by presenting himself as a dispeler of disinformation or even an impartial guide to the truth? Surely Francis knows nonbelievers regard the good news he preaches about God sending his son to Earth to redeem humanity as a bouquet of fake news, engineered to exploit the emotionally vulnerable the same way he thinks fake news does. The Catholic Church's celebration of miracles and apparitions and its promise of life everlasting to the devout subtract from whatever authority the pope might have adjudicating fake news from true.

From *Politico*, January 24 © 2018. Reprinted with permission. All rights reserved.

More to the point, the pope's grounding in journalistic history—how do we phrase this delicately without antagonizing Bill Donohue of the Catholic League?—stinks. Writing in Politico in 2016, Jacob Soll traced fake news back to the advent of print 500 years ago, when publishers printed "spectacular stories of sea monsters and witches" and "made claims that sinners were responsible for natural disasters." As I wrote, the American press in the 1800s overflowed with hoaxes, stunts, pranks and hogwash such that our era looks tame in comparison. Fake news slithers into print and onto the Web not because bad people want to take advantage of good people. It endures because there's a demand for it, a demand that has little to do with the rise of social media, as the pope seems to believe is the case.

> **Fake news slithers into print and onto the Web not because bad people want to take advantage of good people. It endures because there's a demand for it.**

Historian Heidi Tworek notes that the pope gets it completely wrong when he places the responsibility for eradicating fake news on the shoulders of journalists. As she points out to me, it's not journalists who are spreading disinformation and falsehoods, so how exactly can it be their responsibility to stop fake news? "Ironically, by having high standards (e.g., corrections), [journalists] can be played by Trump, who seizes on every mistake and failure to live up to high journalistic standards as evidence of 'fake news,'" Tworek says.

Proving that he missed the "public journalism" (aka "civic journalism") boomlet of the late 1990s, led by James Fallows and Jay Rosen, the pope calls for the creation of a "journalism of peace." Created by people for people, the pope's journalism of peace would be "less concentrated on breaking news than on exploring the underlying causes of conflicts" and more "committed to pointing out alternatives to the escalation of shouting matches and verbal violence." I would never say never to the pope's vision, but based on this sketch he thinks journalists should transform themselves into social workers.

After reading Pope Francis' musing on fake news and journalism, I had to ask myself: Doesn't the Vatican have a rewrite desk where it vets and punches up his copy? At the very least, the pope should have called on St. Francis de Sales, the patron saint of writers and journalists, to intervene on his behalf. Although St. Francis wasn't exactly a fount of hot copy, as his guide to the devout life proves, he possessed the tenacity of a real news hawk. When the Calvinists he attempted to convert back to Catholicism slammed doors in his face or threw rocks at him, he soldiered on, slipping the doctrinal pamphlets he'd written under their doors.

The pope's intentions are good, but the idea that even he can snuff out fake news is a little grandiose. As the parable of the snake shows, it's hard to keep us humans from sharing forbidden fruit. According to legend, the last word St. Francis ever uttered was "humility." Dare I suggest the pontiff heed this sage advice?

Print Citations

CMS: Shafer, Jack. "What the Pope Gets Wrong about Fake News." In *The Reference Shelf: Propaganda & Misinformation,* edited by Annette Calzone, 17–19. Amenia, NY: Grey House Publishing, 2020.

MLA: Shafer, Jack. "What the Pope Gets Wrong about Fake News." *The Reference Shelf: Propaganda & Misinformation,* edited by Annette Calzone, Grey House Publishing, 2020, pp. 17–19.

APA: Shafer, J. (2020). What the pope gets wrong about fake news. In Annette Calzone (Ed.), *The reference shelf: Propaganda & misinformation* (pp. 17–19). Amenia, NY: Grey House Publishing.

Nineteenth-Century Nihilists Foretold Our Era

By Robert Zaretsky
Foreign Affairs, September 6, 2019

Most historians view the French Revolution as the source of the ideologies that have shaped the modern and postmodern eras. For any ism—from liberalism, conservatism, and communism to nationalism, totalitarianism, and anarchism—historians can make the case that it springs from the cascade of events that began in 1789. An ism that usually fails to make the list, however, is one that now seems to be on the tip of every pundit's pen—namely, nihilism.

In one of the odder footnotes to the revolution, the Baron de Cloots, Jean-Baptiste du Val-de-Grâce—better known by his pen name, Anacharsis Cloots, if not by his chosen title as "Orator of the Human Race"—embraced the term "nihilism." Determined that the fledgling French Republic be truly secular, Cloots insisted that its citizens avoid all reference to God. Even atheists, he warned, by their denial of God's existence keep God's name alive. For this reason, he intoned, the "republic of the rights of man is strictly speaking neither theist nor atheist, but nihilist."

While the aspiring nihilist did not live long enough to realize his hope for establishing a republic on the moon—Cloots literally lost his head during the Terror—the term he introduced has enjoyed a long and varied life. Indeed, it is now experiencing something of a renaissance. Even the most casual consumer of news keeps stumbling across the term, especially when it comes to the theater of American politics. Rather like neighboring tribes that, according to anthropologists, accuse each other of engaging in cannibalism, our political parties denounce each other for engaging in nihilism. Victor Davis Hanson of the Hoover Institution disparages the "new nihilism" of the Democratic Party, while Alex Pareene of the *New Republic* decries the Senate majority leader, Mitch McConnell, as the "nihilist in chief." A Google search of "Trump" and "nihilism" sparks well more than half a million hits, crowding the screen from both sides of the political spectrum: the conservative columnist Ross Douthat reserves "nihilist in chief" for the president, while the liberal columnist E. J. Dionne, as if nihilism alone were not bad enough, castigates Trump for his "incoherent nihilism."

Yet we must not conclude that nihilism is in the eye of the belittler. "Fascism," for example, has long been treated as a rhetorical rod for bashing others over the head—such that we forget that the word refers to a clear and uncompromising conception of political and social life. So, too, with nihilism, though on a grander scale. With the bicentenary of Fyodor Dostoyevsky's birthday just around the corner—the Russian government, academic institutions, and global organizations such as

---

From *Foreign Affairs*, September 6 © 2019. Reprinted with permission. All rights reserved.

UNESCO are well into planning the celebrations for 2021—where better to turn for a grasp of a notion so elusive yet so vital?

To be sure, Dostoyevsky neither coined the term nor gave it currency. The word was loosely applied to semiclandestine student groups in mid-nineteenth-century Russia, at one another's throats over strategy but united in their determination to overthrow the repressive tsarist state. The publication of Ivan Turgenev's *Fathers and Children* in 1862 firmly entrenched the term in the popular imagination. The novel's charismatic protagonist, Evgeny Vasilich Bazarov, embodies a heroic conception of nihilism. When asked just who or what is a nihilist, Bazarov proudly replies: "We act on the basis of what we recognize as useful. . . . Nowadays the most useful thing of all is rejection—we reject." When his shocked interlocutor insists that the construction of a better world is also important, Bazarov cuts him short: "That's not for us to do. . . . First, the ground must be cleared."

Appalled by the terrorist activities of the young nihilists on whom Turgenev based Bazarov, Dostoyevsky transformed their political doctrine into something much larger and more dreadful. In his later novels, ranging from *Crime and Punishment* through *The Devils* to *The Brothers Karamazov*, Dostoyevsky suggested that the true specter haunting Europe was not communism but nihilism. It was an ism unlike any other insofar as it held that the carcass of the past was not worth preserving, the misery of the present demanded that one act, and the promise of the future permitted one to do whatever was necessary to bring it about. Whereas Turgenev's Bazarov made pronouncements, Dostoyevsky's Raskolnikov made plans and acted upon them.

Dostoyevsky drew nihilism from the realms of politics and ethics into that of metaphysics. If everything we have thought is a tale told by an idiot, if everything we have done amounts to a hill of beans, we find ourselves unmoored not just from morality but from the possibility of meaning itself. Everything is permitted, as Ivan Karamazov declares, when you believe in nothing and hold nothing to be important. Whereas the political nihilism that hovers over the characters in *Fathers and Children* disavows political and social institutions, the metaphysical nihilism that hounds the actors in The Brothers Karamazov disavows existence itself.

Dostoyevsky and Nietzsche offered prescriptions along with their descriptions of our common predicament.

In order to grasp the relevance of this claim for our own era, we need to glance at the work of the man whose reading of Dostoyevsky led to the definition of nihilism with which we still grapple. In 1887, Friedrich Nietzsche excitedly wrote to a friend about a discovery he had just made: "I knew nothing about Dostoyevsky until a few weeks ago. . . . The instinct of affinity (or what shall I call it?) spoke to me instantaneously—my joy was beyond bounds." As Nietzsche perceived, the Russian novelist had not just blasted political nihilism but also detonated the enlightened foundations, built with the mortar of reason and means of technology, into smithereens.

That same year, while still reading Dostoyevsky, Nietzsche posed the $64,000 question: "What does nihilism mean?" Nietzsche being Nietzsche, he already had the answer, one he emblazoned in italics: "*That the highest values devaluate themselves." By "values," Nietzsche means nothing less than truth and reason. The acid of reason, by dissolving every belief we ever held, ultimately dissolves itself. It seems to abandon us in a cosmic dead end, leaving us with a dismal consolation prize—the paradoxical affirmation that "there is simply no true world." What this offers someone who is dying for meaning, of course, is what an empty glass offers someone who is dying of thirst.

But Dostoyevsky and Nietzsche offered prescriptions along with their descriptions of our common predicament. For the former, the answer was religious faith—and not just any religion, but specifically Eastern Orthodox Christianity—while for the latter, the answer was aesthetic faith, or the belief that art alone could impose meaning on the world.

But for many of us today, these answers come up short. We live in a world that bears an uncanny resemblance to the one foreseen by Dostoyevsky and Nietzsche. It is steeped in claims and counterclaims of fake news and steered by a president who has made more than 12,000 false claims since entering office. In our world, presidential advisers have graduated from deriding "reality-based communities" to deciding that "alternative facts" are all the facts we need. Ours is a world where the claims of objective truth hardly resonate amid the clamor of tribal truths.

Even so, the nihilist is not to be confused with the narcissist or fabulist, the hired gun or hanger-on. On the contrary, a nihilist offers a kind of constancy and hope. "A nihilist is a man who judges of the world as it is that it ought not to be," Nietzsche declared, "and of the world as it ought to be that it does not exist." Though this observation runs against the interpretive grain of most Nietzscheans, it suggests that a nihilist—Nietzsche described himself, after all, as the "first perfect European nihilist"—takes the full measure of the situation, plumbs its significance, and searches for an answer. Moreover, and again unlike the narcissist, Nietzsche's nihilist seeks to overcome that situation by mastering, not by cosseting, the self.

> **The acid of reason, by dissolving every belief we ever had, ultimately dissolves itself.**

Neither Dostoyevsky nor Nietzsche pretended to be a political theorist. One suspects, though, that if they had, they would have thought twice before dismissing the ideals of modern democracies. We are witness to a political world shorn of the values that Dostoyevsky declared useless without God and that Nietzsche pronounced dead along with God. If our current situation is as dire as many believe, we might leave to others the task of sorting out the status of God and instead wager on the values of the world as it once was and again needs to be.

Print Citations

CMS: Zaretsky, Robert. "Nineteenth-Century Nihilists Foretold Our Era." In *The Reference Shelf: Propaganda & Misinformation,* edited by Annette Calzone, 20–23. Amenia, NY: Grey House Publishing, 2020.

MLA: Zaretsky, Robert. "Nineteenth-Century Nihilists Foretold Our Era." *The Reference Shelf: Propaganda & Misinformation,* edited by Annette Calzone, Grey House Publishing, 2020, pp. 20–23.

APA: Zaretsky, R. (2020). Nineteenth-century nihilists foretold our era. In Annette Calzone (Ed.), *The reference shelf: Propaganda & misinformation* (pp. 20–23). Amenia, NY: Grey House Publishing.

A Short Guide to the History of "Fake News" and Disinformation

By Julie Posetti and Alice Matthews
International Center for Journalists, July 23, 2018

Synopsis

Information fabrication is not new. As *Guardian* columnist Natalie Nougayrède has observed: "The use of propaganda is ancient, but never before has there been the technology to so effectively disseminate it".[1] So, it is important to understand the historical context when examining and reporting on contemporary manifestations of what has been termed a 21st-century 'information disorder'[2].

Misinformation, disinformation and propaganda have been features of human communication since at least the Roman times when Antony met Cleopatra. Octavian waged a propaganda campaign against Antony that was designed to smear his reputation. This took the form of "short, sharp slogans written upon coins in the style of archaic Tweets."[3] These slogans painted Antony as a womaniser and a drunk, implying he had become Cleopatra's puppet, having been corrupted by his affair with her. Octavian became Augustus, the first Roman Emperor and "fake news had allowed Octavian to hack the republican system once and for all."[4]

The invention of the Gutenberg printing press in 1493 dramatically amplified the dissemination of disinformation and misinformation, and it ultimately delivered the first-large scale news hoax—'The Great Moon Hoax' of 1835[5]. The *New York Sun* published six articles about the discovery of life on the moon, complete with illustrations of humanoid bat-creatures and bearded blue unicorns. Conflicts, regime change, and catastrophes then became markers for the dissemination of disinformation.

As one-to-many communications developed in the 20th century, especially with the advent of radio and television, satirical news evolved, sometimes being mistaken as the real thing in news consumers' minds. Finally, as this guide illustrates, the arrival of the internet in the late 20th century, followed by social media in the 21st century, dramatically multiplied the risks of misinformation, disinformation, propaganda and hoaxes. Both errors and fraudulent content now go viral through peer-to-peer distribution (many-to-many communication)[6], while news satire is regularly misunderstood and re-shared as straight news by unwitting social media users[7]. We now inhabit a world with computational propaganda, state-sponsored 'sock-puppet networks', troll armies[8], and technology that can mimic legitimate news websites

From International Center for Journalists, July 23 © 2018. Reprinted with permission. All rights reserved.

and seamlessly manipulate audio and video to create synthetic representations of any number of sources. In this environment, where trust becomes polarised around what "news" aligns with their views, many news consumers feel entitled to choose or create their own 'facts'. Combined, these developments present an unprecedented threat level that can drown out journalism, as well as contaminate it with the implication that there is nothing to distinguish it from false and fraudulent information more broadly.

> **Contemporary manifestations of disinformation and misinformation are mainly evident in social media systems—with grave risks to authentic journalism and to open societies more broadly.**

This learning module designed to be used by journalists, journalism trainers and educators (along with their students) provides historical context for the analysis of the 21st century 'fake news' crisis. Relevant case studies and a timeline are designed to better inform users about the causes and consequences of 'information disorder'—from harassment of journalists by 'troll armies' to the manipulation of elections and diplomatic crises. While news media have historically been caught up in disinformation and misinformation, including through news hoaxes, this is not regarded as legitimate in the dominant contemporary paradigm across different news media. This explains in part why contemporary manifestations of disinformation and misinformation are mainly evident in social media systems—with grave risks to authentic journalism and to open societies more broadly.

The current crisis includes the 'weaponisation' of information by many governments, as well as abuse by an industry of public relations companies often under contract to political entities and actors. This risks an 'arms race' of disinformation efforts, which is arguably a recipe for mutually assured contamination of information environments in general as well as high potential blowback. Where disinformation campaigns have been exposed, the result has been major damage to the actors involved—both the implementing agencies and their political clients (see the cases of Bell-Pottinger and Cambridge Analytica below).

Propaganda, Hoaxes and Satire as Historical Features of the Communications Ecology

A selected timeline of 'Information Disorder' through the ages [9]

Circa 44 BC—Mark Antony smear campaign
Octavian's propaganda campaign against Antony deployed Twitter-worthy slogans etched onto coins to smear Antony's reputation.

Circa 1450–Gutenberg printing press invented
Invented 'facts' took off at the same time that news began to circulate widely in Europe, enabled by the printing press[10]

1835–The Great Moon Hoax
The *New York Sun* published six articles about the discovery of (non-existent) life on the moon, claiming to recount the findings of astronomer Sir John Herschel.[11]

1899-1902–The Boer War
Propaganda perpetuated "the Boer" stereotype during this conflict in South Africa. It was popularised by the British Army to sway British public opinion to support an unpopular war.[12]

1914-1918–World War I Propaganda played a crucial part in the recruitment effort, appealing to nationalism and patriotism: "Your country needs YOU"; "Daddy, what did YOU do in the Great War?"[13]

1917–The German corpse factory British propaganda focused on demonising enemy Germans during World War I. In 1917, the *Times* and the *Daily Mail* printed articles claiming that due to a fat shortage in Germany, resulting from the British naval blockade, the German forces were using the corpses of their own soldiers to boil down for fats, bone meal, and pig food. This had implications during World War II, when early reports of Holocaust atrocities emerged. The disinformation contained within news stories in 1917 is said to have caused the accurate reports of Nazi atrocities to be doubted when they first appeared[14]

1917–The Russian Revolution Russian Revolution-era propaganda emerges; one strategy involved using the Russian rail network to target 'large audiences' with catchy slogans and punchy colour.[15]

1933–Reich Ministry of Public Enlightenment and Propaganda established With the rise of Nazism, Joseph Goebbels established the Reich Ministry of Public Enlightenment and Propaganda to spread Nazi messages of hatred-inciting violence against Jews, using all mediums—including theatre and the press. "Nazi propaganda was…essential to motivating those who implemented the mass murder of the European Jews and of other victims of the Nazi regime. It also served to secure the acquiescence of millions of others—as bystanders—to racially targeted persecution and mass murder."[16]

1938–War of the Worlds radio drama The War of the Worlds radio drama in the USA fooled many unwitting listeners into believing that Earth was being attacked, foreshadowing 21st-century responses to news satire. "No one involved with War of the Worlds expected to deceive any listeners, because they all found the story too silly and improbable to ever be taken seriously."[17]

1939-1945–World War II Edward Herzstein, in his book *The War that Hitler Won* (1978), described the Nazi propaganda campaign as "the most infamous propaganda campaign in history."[18] The Nazis demonised and persecuted Jews so effectively that atrocities were committed with popular support and Holocaust denialism continues in the 21st century.

1955-75–The Vietnam War
U.S. briefings on the war staged at the end of every day at a Saigon hotel were dubbed "Five O'clock Follies".[19] The US propaganda campaign, sometimes called the "Optimism Campaign"[20], employed the 'domino theory' as a fear tactic to suppress opposition to the war[21]—if one country came under communist influence or control, its neighbouring countries would soon follow.

1965–30th September Movement, Indonesia Members of Indonesia's armed forces assassinated six high-ranking Indonesian Army generals. The head of the army's strategic military reserve command, General Suharto, accused the Communist Party of the coup attempt and took over as the military's de facto leader. In the months that followed, Suharto's forces executed at least half a million people for association with communism. Suharto's military dictatorship "made wildly inaccurate anti-communist propaganda a cornerstone of its legitimacy and ruled Indonesia with US support until 1988".[22]

1947-1991–The Cold War During this period, international broadcasting was harnessed to influence populations to take sides. [23] [24]

1972-1990s–South Africa's propaganda war South Africa's apartheid government sponsored a sophisticated, secret, global propaganda and lobbying campaign to win support for, and counter opposition against, its apartheid policies. It targeted key opinion formers in Western capitals and was spearheaded by government minister Eschel Rhoodie. The campaign was exposed by local investigative reporters in the late 1970s but continued into the early 1990s.[25]

1983 – April Fools interview The Associated Press reporter Fred Bayles interviewed pop culture historian and Boston University Professor Joseph Boskin, who tried to tell him the origins of April Fools were murky. Bayles kept pushing, so Boskin "created a story" about a jester who became king. Boskin expected Bayles would catch on, but the story was published—the news hoax succeeded.[26]

1996–*The Daily Show* begins The news satire and self-described 'fake news' TV programme kicked off in the USA, giving way to the rise of satirical news as a genre that became "some sort of corrective to, and substitute for, mainstream journalism".[27]

1998–*The Onion* begins publishing online The USA-based news satire website started publishing online, with many of its stories later mistakenly taken as fact, as "fake news takes over Facebook feeds".[28] In 2012, it published the story 'Kim

Jong-Un Named *The Onion*'s Sexiest Man Alive For 2012'. The Chinese Communist Party's *People's Daily* fell for it and reported on his new title,[29] as did the *Korean Times*.[30] #NotTheOnion became a commonly used hashtag to denote accurate stories that were parody-worthy.

2003-2011–The Iraq War
In the run-up to the 2003 US-led coalition invasion of Iraq, as part of the post-9/11 'War on Terror', the *New York Times* published a series of articles including an account in 2001 that was "never independently verified" of a camp where "biological weapons were produced". Reporter Judith Miller's articles containing misinformation about weapons of mass destruction[31] are said to be among those that had "the greatest consequences for America" and were cited by Bush administration officials as one of the reasons to go to war with Iraq[32]. It has been argued that the *New York Times* "presented the notion of Iraqi weapons of mass destruction as fact".[33] This episode became known as 'Weapons of Mass Distraction'. Debate continues about the newspaper's predisposition at the time to believe its sources without sufficient due diligence and thereby open itself up to manipulation by purveyors of disinformation.

A former Iraqi diplomat, Muhammed Saeed al-Sahhaf, was Saddam Hussein's Information Minister during the war. His propaganda tactics were so colourful that he was treated like a parody, becoming known as 'Comical Ali' and 'Baghdad Bob' among Western media because of wildly inaccurate claims he made about the conflict. For example, he was filmed denying US tanks were in Baghdad even as they were seen rolling across the city behind him while he did a TV interview.[34]

2004–The New York Times issues apology over reporting of weapons of mass destruction "Editors at several levels who should have been challenging reporters and pressing for more skepticism were perhaps too intent on rushing scoops into the paper. Accounts of Iraqi defectors were not always weighed against their strong desire to have Saddam Hussein ousted." This was the reflective critique of the *New York Times*' editorial board about the paper's coverage of 'weapons of mass destruction'. "We consider the story of Iraq's weapons, and of the pattern of misinformation, to be unfinished business. And we fully intend to continue aggressive reporting aimed at setting the record straight."[35]

2005–*The Colbert Report* begins The satirical late-night television talk programme headed by a fictional anchorman began. The "striking emergence" of such shows in the USA has been called a "long-term generational phenomenon".[36] The show's impact on politics, along with other 'fake news' programmes like the *Daily Show*, goes further than other satirical shows like *Saturday Night Live*, by blurring the lines between real and fake coverage, making satire less obvious: "much of what passes for serious coverage…has become a simulation of reality".[37]

2010–Egyptian State-run newspaper doctors photo of world leaders to place Egypt's President front and centre The newspaper Al-Ahram 'photoshopped' a picture of world leaders en-route to the opening of a session of Middle East peace talks in order to place then Egyptian President Hosni Mubarak at the front of the pack. In the undoctored image, he was in fact trailing behind the heads of state of the US, Palestine and Israel. The manipulation was revealed by an Egyptian blogger.[38]

2011–Syrian Civil War (ongoing) An information war was waged alongside armed hostilities in Syria as adversaries spread misinformation via social media and other digital channels in order to discredit one another. A spokesperson for the International Committee of the Red Cross (ICRC) in Syria, described an atmosphere of "information chaos".[39] Following incoming US President Donald Trump's deployment of the term 'fake news' in 2016, Syrian President Bashar Assad said "we are living in a fake news era"[40] in response to 2017 Amnesty International report[41] of a "calculated campaign of extrajudicial execution" in a Syrian prison. The report claimed that between 2011 and 2015 up to 13,000 people opposed to Assad's government were secretly hanged. In April 2017, President Assad said reports of a chemical attack that killed 89 people were "100 percent fabrications".[42] He suggested that photographs showing children who had died in the attack on a rebel-held town were staged, describing the entire incident as "fabricated" and "unconvincing."[43] However, collaborative forensic reporting by The New York Times fact-checked Assad's claim that the incident was 'fabricated', concluding that the Syrian government had dropped a chlorine bomb on an apartment building.[44]

2013–Australian media outlets publish fake press release In a cautionary tale of the "perils of speed before accuracy," several media outlets in Australia published a hoax press release saying the ANZ bank was withdrawing $1.2 billion in funding from Whitehaven Coal's flagship mine project.[45] The press release appearing to be from ANZ bank was written by anti-coal campaigner Jonathan Moylan and directed media to a real executive. Moylan replaced the executive's phone number with his own.[46] Share prices in Whitehaven Coal plunged by 6%, wiping $300 million off the company's value.[47]

2014–Russia and Ukraine Reports emerged of the Internet Research Agency (based in St Petersburg)[48] as conflict in Ukraine escalated. Former workers told *The Guardian* of being "paid to flood forums and social with anti-Western and pro-Kremlin comments"[49] and BuzzFeed cited leaked documents revealing workloads of "troll armies". According to these sources, on an average working day, the hired 'footsoldiers' were to post on news articles 50 times. Each blogger was to maintain six Facebook accounts, publishing at least three posts a day and discussing the news in groups at least twice a day. By the end of the first month, they were expected to have won 500 subscribers and get at least five posts on each item a day. On Twitter, the bloggers were expected to manage ten accounts with up to 2,000 followers and tweet 50 times a day.[50] The "Stop Fake"[51] centre was formed in Ukraine, (and had spread to more European countries by 2018).

2015–Egyptian TV anchor portrays video game footage as evidence of Russian action in Syria A TV news anchor is criticised for airing incorrect information, after he went to air praising Russian intervention in Syria as superior to US efforts: "Yes, this is the Russian army, this is Russian weaponry, this is [Vladimir] Putin. Yes, they are countering terrorism, truly countering it. Now you will see a terrifying video, terrifying." But the footage was sourced to a five-year-old YouTube upload from a Russian video game.[52]

2016–Polls United States: In the days immediately before and after the US election, "people shared nearly as much 'fake news' as real news on Twitter."[53] One particular 'fake news' story circulating around the time of the election outlined a supposed child abuse-ring allegedly led by Hillary Clinton, running out of a pizza restaurant called Comet Ping Pong.[54] It led one man to 'self-investigate' by firing an assault rifle inside the restaurant.[55] Additionally, Facebook says an operation, likely based in Russia, spent US $100,000 on thousands of U.S. ads on the social network over a two-year period, which included the election.[56] A *New York Times* investigation, and research from cybersecurity firm FireEye, said that Russian operators made Facebook and Twitter profiles of "fake Americans" and used Twitter bots to post "anti-Clinton" messages.[57]

Brexit: A large-scale analysis of social media in the lead up to Brexit showed that "not only were there twice as many Brexit supporters on Instagram, but they were also five times more active than Remain activists."[58] Similar patterns emerged on Twitter. Foreign accounts were reported to have sent "hundreds of thousands of pro-leave tweets on polling day."[59][60]

Philippines: Rappler.com deployed investigative journalism to identify and counter State-sponsored disinformation campaigns following the 2016 Philippines election.[61] Their method included 'big data analysis', fact-checking and debunking deceptive social media content,[62] exposing 'sock-puppet' networks. CEO and Editor in Chief Maria Ressa and many of her staff continue to be subjected to unrelenting online harassment linked to the State[63].

2016-2017–Troll farms and 'fake news'-for-profit As the US election approached in 2016, international media reports revealed a profitable troll farm run by teenagers in the small town of Veles in the Former Yugoslav Republic of Macedonia. It was discovered that over 100 pro-Trump websites pushing fabricated news were registered in Veles, with one operator earning US$16,000 in the final three months of the campaign[64]. The content included viral fake stories about the Pope endorsing candidate Donald Trump and the 'imminent indictment' of Democratic Presidential hopeful Hillary Clinton. The operators of the fake news sites profited significantly from automated advertising engines (e.g. Google AdSense) tracking their sensationally false content. In the final weeks of the election campaign President Obama talked at length about the "digital gold rush" experienced by Veles' fake news' farm.[65]

Hyperpartisan 'news' sites that deal in misinformation for profit are also prevalent in the USA. In 2017, a BuzzFeed investigation revealed that confected outrage feeding massive Facebook engagement was the basis of the business model of one Florida-based company that produced false and misleading content targeting both liberals and conservatives, across a number of websites. Their objective: to "run up their metrics or advertising revenue."[66]

2016–Facebook announces it will flag 'fake news' After Facebook was accused of facilitating the spread of disinformation,[67] CEO Mark Zuckerberg initially dismissed the idea that 'fake news' shared on the site affected the US election.[68] But the company later announced it would collaborate with fact-checkers to combat 'fake news', as well as make it easier to report hoaxes and flag disputed stories.[69] In January 2018, Facebook backed away from including news in its 'newsfeed' after experiments suggested that its tweaks risked amplifying 'fake news'.[70]

2016–Colombian hacker reveals he interfered with elections across Latin America Speaking to *Newsweek*, Andres Sepulveda claimed he was hired to disrupt and influence the outcomes of presidential elections in Mexico, Nicaragua, Panama, Honduras, El Salvador, Colombia, Costa Rica, Guatemala, and Venezuela from 2006-2014. Sepulveda claimed to have led a team of hackers that "stole campaign strategies, manipulated social media to create false waves of enthusiasm and derision, and installed spyware in opposition offices" during the 2012 Mexican presidential election.[71] Sepulveda is currently serving a 10-year sentence for hacking-related charges during the 2014 Colombian election.

2016–Pakistan's Defence Minister issues nuclear retaliation warning in response to a 'fake news' story After reading a story on a false news site reporting that Israel had threatened Pakistan with nuclear weapons, Pakistan's Defence Minister tweeted: "Israeli def min threatens nuclear retaliation presuming pak role in Syria against Daesh. Israel forgets Pakistan is a Nuclear state too."[72] The fictitious story contained a headline with multiple errors and the article misidentified the Israeli Defence Minister. In response to the Pakistan Defence Minister's tweet, the Israeli Defence Ministry tweeted: "Reports referred to by the Pakistani Def Min are entirely false."

2016–US President-elect Donald Trump deploys the phrase 'fake news' The US President accuses his journalistic critics (starting with CNN) of pedalling 'fake news'[73]. His weaponisation of the term began to spread globally, with other world leaders also deploying the phrase against journalists and news organisations.[74]

2017–Joint Declaration on Freedom of Expression and 'Fake News', Disinformation and Propaganda In early 2017, a joint statement was issued by the UN Special Rapporteur for Freedom of Opinion and Expression, the OSCE's Representative on Freedom of the Media, the Organisation of American States' Special Rapporteur on Freedom of Expression, and the African Commission on Human and People's Rights Special Rapporteur on Freedom of Expression and Access to Information expressing alarm at the spread of disinformation and propaganda, and attacks on news media as 'fake news'. They acknowledged the impacts on journalists and journalism:

"(We are) Alarmed at instances in which public authorities denigrate, intimidate and threaten the media, including by stating that the media is "the opposition" or is "lying" and has a hidden political agenda, which increases the risk of threats and violence against journalists, undermines public trust and confidence in journalism as a public watchdog, and may mislead the public by blurring the lines between disinformation and media products containing independently verifiable facts".[75]

2017—US intelligence agencies assess Russia involvement in US election
A report jointly published by America's CIA, NSA and FBI in January 2017 claimed that Russian actors had sought to use "paid social media users or 'trolls'" to influence the outcome of the 2016 US elections.[76] Google, Facebook and Twitter subsequently stated that Russian accounts had been identified in connection with political content distributed during the US election.[77]

2017—Venezuela's President describes international media as 'fake news'
In July 2017, Venezuelan President Nicolas Maduro said that media "spread lots of false versions, lots of lies. This is what we call fake news today, isn't it? The era of posttruth."[78] A month later, President Maduro described BBC and CNN as "manipulators of information" in a speech addressing the country's Constituent Assembly.[79]

2017—Parliamentary inquiries launched into 'fake news' in the UK, The Philippines and Australia In the UK, the Culture, Media and Sport Committee launched an inquiry into 'fake news', asking, "What is fake news? Where does biased but legitimate commentary shade into propaganda and lies?"[80] Next, Australia announced the establishment of a Select Committee on the Future of Public Interest Journalism to examine 'fake news', propaganda and public disinformation.[81] Growing concerns about 'fake news' and propaganda, the inappropriate leaking of individual consumers' data, and failure to curb online bullying and offensive content led Australia's national journalists' union—the Media, Entertainment and Arts Alliance (MEAA)—to call on "digital giants" like Google, Facebook, Twitter and YouTube to be "regulated similarly to broadcasters and forced to contribute a percentage of their revenue towards public interest journalism."[82] In the Philippines, the Senate Committee on Public Information and Mass Media conducted a hearing on the proliferation of fake, misleading news and misinformation online.[83]

2017—Presidential election in Kenya A representative sample survey of 2000 Kenyans eligible to vote undertaken three months ahead of the August 2017 poll found that 90% of respondents reported seeing false news, with 87% of people saying they had seen 'deliberately false news'.[84] This content included disinformation material created to mimic legitimate news content, with the badges of media houses like BBC, CNN and NTV Kenya being misused to attach credibility to false news.[85]

Misinformation and propaganda are not new in Kenya, however: "This election season has seen these migrate to popular social media platforms, to either play at existing beliefs, fears and biases, or to sway perceptions and even votes."[86]

2017–National elections in France and Germany France: The British newspaper, The Independent reported that an Oxford University study found that "up to a quarter of the political stories shared on Twitter in France were based on misinformation".[87] Thirty-seven news organisations and technology partners collaborated in an initiative called CrossCheck to verify and debunk 'fake news' stories in the lead up to voting.[88]

Germany: In stark contrast to the 2016 US election, the German election campaign was largely unaffected by 'fake news'.[89] However, the German parliament passed a law at the end of June 2017 that "imposed fines of more than $50 million on Facebook and other social media companies that do not promptly remove illegal content".[90]

2017–Qatari state news agency hacked An escalation of tension in the Middle East between Qatar and some of its Arab neighbours was described as "the first major geopolitical crisis to have been sparked by a computer hack"[91]. According to a report by Quartz, citing the Qatari government, the QNA news agency was hacked in May 2017, with a fabricated news story being subsequently uploaded to the site. The story contained what the Qataris claimed were fabricated quotes attributed to Qatar's emir, Tamim bin Hamad al-Thani criticising US president Donald Trump and praising Iran as an Islamic power. It also quoted him speaking fondly of Hamas—a US-designated terrorist organisation—and the Muslim Brotherhood. In response, other media outlets in the region began publishing negative stories about Qatar, including accusations that it was working against US interests and supporting terrorist groups, citing the fake QNA story. Computational propaganda also #"—"Cut قطع_العلاقات_مع_قطر played a role, with a Twitter 'troll army' feeding the hashtag " relations with Qatar"—which was trending on Arabic-language Twitter in June, before Qatar's neighbours did in fact begin to sever ties. Quartz assessed that the incident nearly became the "first 'fake news' war to transform into a physical conflict."[92]

2017–Satirical news site blocked in Pakistan The *Khabaristan Times*, a satirical column and website that were part of the news site *Pakistan Today* [93]was blocked in Pakistan and therefore stopped publishing.

2017–Attempted deception of Washington Post journalists The *Washington Post*, detecting deception from a confidential source, broke its promise of anonymity and exposed the fraud on its front page[94]. This was a clear attempt by a malicious 'fake news' proponent to deceive journalists.[95]

2018–US President Donald Trump announces 'Fake News Awards' President Trump issues 'awards' to several major news organisations against whom he wields the term 'fake news' in an attempt to counter their critique of him.[96]

2018–US Justice Department indictments in election meddling probe On February 16th, thirteen Russian nationals and a Russian internet agency were indicted by the US State Department in connection with a conspiracy to disrupt the US election. According to the indictment: "Defendants and their co-conspirators opened accounts at PayPal, a digital payment service provider; created false means of identification, including fake driver's licenses; and posted on ORGANIZATION-controlled social media accounts using the identities of these U.S. victims. Defendants and their co-conspirators also obtained, and attempted to obtain, false identification documents to use as proof of identity in connection with maintaining accounts and purchasing advertisements on social media sites."[97] The aim, the indictment indicated, was to disparage Democratic candidate Hilary Clinton, and boost the election chances of Donald Trump. This conspiracy was enacted by "people who adopted false online personas to push divisive messages, travelled to the US to collect intelligence, and staged political rallies while posing as Americans."[98] Russian President Vladimir Putin insisted that the accused parties had not acted on behalf of the Russian government but he promised that they would never be extradited to face trial.[99] Subsequently, thousands of pages, accounts, forum threads and blogs were discovered to be connected to the conspiracy and removed by social media companies including Facebook, Twitter, Reddit and Tumblr.[100]

2018–Fake philanthropist causes diplomatic issue between Brazil and Venezuela A reportedly mentally ill Brazilian man based in Los Angeles used social media to trick reputable media organisations, the Brazilian Bar Association, the governments of Venezuela and Brazil, a host of diplomats, far-right groups, and several human rights organisations into believing that he was a philanthropist running an NGO raising funds to care for malnourished Venezuelan children. The subsequent diplomatic storm triggered by the online response to the 'philanthropist's' work resulted in Brazil and Venezuela expelling the top diplomats from the opposing country. While one newspaper referred to the man as a representative of a US NGO, Venezuelan authorities arrested and imprisoned him for 11 days, accusing him of being connected to a criminal organisation with international reach. Neither story was true. A global campaign organised via a hashtag resulted in his eventual release and deportation.[101]

2018–Journalistic coverage causes collapse of disinformation campaign in South Africa Closure of prestigious UK Public Relations company, Bell Pottinger, which had been exposed as a key actor in what a press report described as a "large-scale fake news propaganda war in South Africa"[102]. The UK company, along with a marketing firm based in India, had been part of a long and secret campaign to foment racial polarisation, carried out to discredit critics of the then South African president Jacob Zuma and the Gupta business family who paid the (expensive) bills. The disinformation was spread through websites, tweets (amplified by bots), misleading online adverts, covert exploitation of Facebook and Wikipedia, as well as hacks and malicious leaks. Journalists who exposed "state capture" by the Gupta family (who reportedly decided who would be appointed as cabinet ministers in the country) were subjected to accusations of being lapdogs of "white monopoly capital".[103] Editor Ferial Haffajee was targeted in a campaign of online harassment during this period, which saw her image manipulated to create false impressions of her character.[104][105]

2018–European Union report on 'fake news' In late 2017, the European Union created a high level expert group on 'fake news' and online disinformation which reported in early 2018 with various solutions recommended, although it did not call for state regulation.[106] The report recommended more transparency of online news and its circulation; increased media and information literacy to counter disinformation; tools for empowering users and journalists to tackle disinformation and foster a positive engagement with fast-evolving information technologies; steps to safeguard the diversity and sustainability of the European news media ecosystem, and continued research.

2018–Economic Community of West African States (ECOWAS) Regional Court of Justice finds against 'false news' laws in Gambia In February 2018, in an historic ruling by the Economic Community of West African States (ECOWAS) Regional Court of Justice, Gambia's laws on sedition, false news and criminal defamation were found to violate the right to freedom of expression[107]. The case was filed in 2015 by the Federation of African Journalists in exile. Two journalists were subjected to torture under the laws while in the custody of Gambia's National Intelligence Agency. At the time of writing, the new Gambian government had not responded to the ruling. However, as more States began considering regulating against 'fake news' (see the cases of Germany and Malaysia identified above), this judgement served as a timely reminder of the risks to freedom of expression posed by such regulatory responses.

2018–Australia's Immigration Minister sparks alt-right propaganda-linked racism row with South Africa & declares criticism 'fake news' Australia's Border Protection and Immigration Minister Peter Dutton caused a diplomatic row when he responded to problematic journalism inspired by far-right propaganda about land redistribution plans in South Africa, by promising to consider creating a special visa category to fast-track asylum seeker claims from white (only) South African farmers[108]. At the base of his claim that these people needed 'saving' by a "civilised country" was a cache of disinformation, but he decried journalism critical of his comments as 'fake news': "If people think I'm going to cower or take a backward step because of their nonsense, fabricated, 'fake news' criticism, then they've got another thing coming," he told a radio interviewer. [109]

2018–Cambridge Analytica Scandal In March 2018, a whistleblower revealed to *The Observer*, *The New York Times* and Channel 4 News that a massive dataset drawn from millions of Facebook users had been exploited by a Cambridge University psychology academic (working privately), and a network of businesses that operated under the umbrella of 'Cambridge Analytica' – a company specialising in psychological profiling and micro-targeted political messaging. The company used the data to target specific sets of voters in the lead up to the USA's 2016 Presidential Election. According to undercover reporting by Chanel 4, company executives boasted of using their data to target audiences with propaganda and misinformation. Steve Bannon had been the company's Vice President until he left to run Donald Trump's election campaign in 2016.[110] Undercover reporters captured Cambridge Analytica executives boasting that the company and its partners had worked on more than 200 international elections, including in Argentina, Nigeria, Kenya, India, and the Czech Republic. The Cambridge Analytica whistleblower, Christopher Wylie, also claimed that the company "cheated" the 2017 Brexit vote.[111] The company closed down in the wake of the disclosures.

2018–Unprecedented UN Special Rapporteurs' joint statement calling on India to protect a journalist against disinformation fuelled attacks Prolific online harassment of independent investigative journalist Rana Ayyub elicited a call from five United Nations special rapporteurs for the Indian government to provide protection, following the mass circulation of false information aimed at countering her critical reporting. Ayyub was targeted with disinformation about her on social media, including 'deepfake' videos that falsely suggested she had made pornographic films, as well as direct rape and death threats.[112] She identified these attacks as having links to the Indian Government.

2018–Developments in the attempted regulation of 'fake news' In January, Germany's 2017 Network Enforcement Act came into effect[113], requiring social media platforms to remove and block 'fake news', potentially hate-inciting content. and other illegal content prohibited by the Criminal Code, within 24 hours of being notified of the same, with violations resulting in a fine of up to 50 million euros.

India proposed, then withdrew, rules that would allow the government to remove accreditation from journalists found to have written or broadcast 'fake news.'[114]

In April, Malaysia passed a new law criminalising "news, information, data and reports which is or are wholly or partly false," with provision for a fine of US$123,000 and up to six years in prison. However, after elections, the new Communications and Multimedia Minister announced that the law would be abolished.[115]

In May, Kenya's president signed into law the Computer and Cybercrimes Bill which states that if a person "intentionally publishes false, misleading or fictitious data or misinforms with intent that the data shall be considered or acted upon as authentic," they can face a penalty of up to almost US$ 50 000 or two years in jail.[116]

Singapore issued a Green Paper on the challenges and implications of deliberate online falsehoods in January 2018, and the parliament held public hearings on the topic in March. The Philippines had three Bills against 'fake news' pending before its legislature.[117] Cambodia was reported to be mulling an anti-'fake news' law.

Belarus's prosecutor general announced a draft bill to reportedly prevent the spread of false statements that "turn public opinion upside down, which leads to big consequences".[118]

The Brazilian Congress was considering a Bill which will criminalise the publication and sharing of any false or incomplete information on the Internet to the detriment of any private individual or legal person.[119]

Endnotes

1. Nougayrede, N (2018) *In this age of propaganda, we must defend ourselves. Here's how*, The Guardian (31/01/18) Accessed 28/03/18: https://www.theguardian.com/commentisfree/2018/jan/31/propaganda-defend-russia-technology
2. Wardle, C. & H. Derakhshan (2017) *Information Disorder: Towards an Interdisciplinary Framework for Research and Policy-Making.* Council of Europe. Available at https://firstdraftnews.com/resource/coe-report/
3. Kaminska, I. (2017). *A module in fake news from the info-wars of ancient Rome.* Financial Times. Accessed 28/03/18:
   https://www.ft.com/content/aaf2bb08-dca2-11e6-86ac-f253db7791c6
4. ibid
5. Thornton, B. (2000). *The Moon Hoax: Debates About Ethics in 1835 New York Newspapers,* Journal of Mass Media Ethics 15(2), pp. 89-100. Accessed 28/03/18 http://www.tandfonline.com/doi/abs/10.1207/S15327728JMME1502_3
6. See Posetti, J (2018) *News industry transformation: digital technology, social platforms and the spread of misinformation* in Ireton, C & Posetti, J (Eds) Journalism, 'Fake News' and Disinformation (UNESCO) Forthcoming
7. Woolf, N. (2016) *As fake news takes over Facebook feeds, many are taking satire as fact,* The Guardian. Accessed 01/04/18:
   https://www.theguardian.com/media/2016/nov/17/facebook-fake-news-satire
8. See Posetti, J (2018) *Combating Online abuse: When journalists and their sources are targeted* in Ireton, C & Posetti, J (Eds) Journalism, 'Fake News' and Disinformation (UNESCO). Forthcoming.
9. Note: This timeline is intended as a skeleton only and it is limited by the comparative lack of examples originally produced in languages other than English. However, journalism educators and instructors are actively encouraged to augment this timeline with examples from their own regions and in their own language to ensure it reflects participants' experiences
10. Soll, J. (2016). *The Long and Brutal History of Fake News*, Politico Magazine. Accessed 05/12/17: https://www.politico.com/magazine/story/2016/12/fake-news-history-long-violent-214535
11. Andrews, E. (2015). *The Great Moon Hoax*, The History Channel. Accessed 01/04/18: http://www.history.com/news/the-great-moon-hoax-180-years-ago?linkId=16545579
12. Kent, K. S. (2013). *Propaganda, Public Opinion, and the Second South African Boer War.* Inquiries Journal/Student Pulse, Volume 5 Iss. 10. Accessed 28/03/18: http://www.inquiriesjournal.com/articles/781/propaganda-public-opinion-and-the-second-south-african-boer-war
13. Welch, D. (2014). *Propaganda for patriotism and nationalism.* British Library: Accessed: 28/0318
    https://www.bl.uk/world-war-one/articles/patriotism-and-nationalism
14. Neander, J., & Marlin, R. (2010). Media and Propaganda: The Northcliffe Press and the Corpse Factory Story of World War I. Global Media Journal, 3(2).
15. Denisova, A. (2017). *How propaganda from the Russian Revolution brought about today's 'troll factories'* in The Independent. Accessed 28/03/18: http://www.independent.co.uk/voices/russian-trolls-us-election-brexit-roots-in-revolution-a8060711.html
16. United States Holocaust Memorial Museum, Washington, DC. *Nazi Propaganda.* Accessed 28/03/18:
    https://www.ushmm.org/wlc/en/article.php?ModuleId=10005202

17 Schwartz, A.B. (2015). *The Infamous "War of The Worlds" Radio Broadcast Was a Magnificent Fluke*, The Smithsonian. Accessed 28/03/18: https://www.smithsonianmag.com/history/infamous-war-worlds-radio-broadcast-was-magnificent-fluke-180955180/

18 Herzstein, R (1978). *The most Infamous Propaganda Campaign in History*, GP Putnam & Sons (NY) p492 See also: Kallis, A. (2005). Nazi Propaganda and The Second World War. Palgrave Macmillan. New York. P6

19 Homonoff, H. (2017). *Ken Burns' 'The Vietnam War' Echoes Journalists' Battle Against Fake News*, Forbes Magazine. Accessed 28/03/18: https://www.forbes.com/sites/howardhomonoff/2017/09/29/ken-burns-vietnam-war-echoes-of-journalists-battle-against-fakenews/#4fd51e242a78

20 Moise, E (2017), *Lyndon Johnson's War Propaganda*, The New York Times. Accessed 28/03/18:
https://www.nytimes.com/2017/11/20/opinion/johnson-propaganda-vietnam-westmoreland.html

21 Leeson, P. T. & Dean, A. (2009). *The Democratic Domino Theory*. American Journal of Political Science, 53 (3), 533–551

22 Bevin, V. (2017). *In Indonesia, the 'fake news' that fueled a Cold War massacre is still potent five decades later*, The Washington Post. Accessed 28/03/18: https://www.washingtonpost.com/news/worldviews/wp/2017/05/30/in-indonesia-the-fake-news-that-fueled-a-cold-warmassacre-is-still-potent-five-decades-later/?utm_termv=.d5912c8b6060

23 Power, S. (2017), *Why Foreign Propaganda Is More Dangerous Now*, The New York Times. Accessed: 28/03/18.
https://www.nytimes.com/2017/09/19/opinion/samantha-power-propaganda-fake-news.html

24 Osgood, K (2017). *The C.I.A.'s Fake News Campaign*, The New York Times. Accessed 28/03/18:
https://www.nytimes.com/2017/10/13/opinion/cia-fake-news-russia.html

25 Nixon, R. (2016). Selling apartheid: South Africa's global propaganda war. London: Pluto Press.

26 Laskowski, A. (2009). *How a BU Prof April-Fooled the Country: When the joke was on the Associated Press*, BU Today. Accessed 01/04/18: https://www.bu.edu/today/2009/how-a-bu-prof-april-fooled-the-country/

27 McChesney R.W. (2011). in *The Stewart/Colbert Effect: Essays on Real Impacts of Fake News*, edited by Amarnath Amarasingam, McFarland & Company, Inc. Accessed 28/02/18: http://bit.ly/2kqhSYJ

28 Woolf, N. (2016). *As fake news takes over Facebook feeds, many are taking satire as fact*, The Guardian. Accessed 28/03/18:
https://www.theguardian.com/media/2016/nov/17/facebook-fake-news-satire

29 Wong, (2012). *Kim Jong-Un Seems to Get a New Title: Heartthrob*, The New York Times. Accessed 28/03/18:
http://www.nytimes.com/2012/11/28/world/asia/chinese-news-site-cites-onion-piece-on-kim-jong-un.html

30 Abad-Santos, A. (2012). *The Onion Convinces Actual Chinese Communists that Kim Jong-Un is Actually the Sexiest Man Alive*, The Atlantic. Accessed 28/03/18: https://www.theatlantic.com/entertainment/archive/2012/11/onion-convinces-actual-chinese-communists-kimjong-un-actually-sexiest-man-alive/321126.

31 Miller, J. (2001), A nation challenged: Secret Sites; Iraqi Tells of Renovations at Sites For Chemical and Nuclear Arms, The New York Times See also: Miller, J. (2003), After effects: Prohibited Weapons; Illicit Arms Kept Till Eve of War, An Iraqi Scientist Is Said to Assert, The New York Times. Accessed 28/03/18:
http://www.nytimes.com/2003/04/21/world/aftereffects-prohibited-weapons-illicit-arms-kept-till-eve-war-iraqi-scientist.html

32 Southwell, B.G, Thorson, E.A. & Sheble, L. (2018). *Misinformation and Mass Audiences*, University of Texas Press. Accessed 28/03/18: http://bit.ly/2zTYx5j

33 Friel, H. & Falk, R. (2004). The Record of the Paper: How The New York Times Misreports US Foreign Policy, Verso, London p. 21-23, p. 73-76.

34 Deprang, E (2013). *Baghdad Bob and his ridiculous true predictions* in The Atlantic March 21, 2013. Accessed 29/03/18:
https://www.theatlantic.com/international/archive/2013/03/baghdad-bob-and-his-ridiculous-true-predictions/274241/

35 The New York Times (2004). *From the Editors; The Times and Iraq*, The New York Times, 26/5/2004. Accessed 29/03/18:
http://www.nytimes.com/2004/05/26/world/from-the-editors-the-times-and-iraq.html

36 McChesney, R.W. (2011). in *The Stewart/Colbert Effect: Essays on Real Impacts of Fake News*, edited by Amarnath Amarasingam, McFarland & Company, Inc. North Carolina. Accessed 29/03/18: http://bit.ly/2kqhSYJ

37 Feldman, L., Leiserowitz, A. & Maibach, E. (2011). The Science of Satire: The Daily Show and The Colbert Report as sources of public attention to science and the environment in Amarasingam, A. (Ed) The Stewart/Colbert Effect: Essays on Real Impacts of Fake News, McFarland & Company, Inc., North Carolina. Accessed 29/03/18: http://bit.ly/2kqhSYJ

38 Schenker. J. & Siddique, H. (2010). *Hosni Mubarak Left Red Faced Over Doctored Red Carpet Photo* in The Guardian (17/09/2010) Accessed 29/03/18: https://www.theguardian.com/world/2010/sep/16/mubarak-doctored-red-carpet-picture

39 Wade, M. (2017). *Cyberarmies, infowars and fake news add to Syria's suffering* in The Sydney Morning Herald (7/11/2017) Accessed 29/03/18: https://www.google.com.au/amp/s/amp.smh.com.au/national/cyber-armies-info-wars-and-fake-news-add-to-syrias-suffering-20171105-gzf8a1.html

40 Isikoff, M. (2017). *Exclusive: Defiant Assad tells Yahoo News torture report is 'fake news',* Yahoo News (10/2/2017). Accessed 29/03/18: https://www.yahoo.com/news/exclusive-defiant-assad-tells-yahoo-news-torture-report-is-fake-news-100042667.html

41 Amnesty International (2017). *Syria: 13,000 secretly hanged in Saydnaya military prison - shocking new report* (7/2/17) Accessed 29/03/18:

https://www.amnesty.org.uk/press-releases/syria-13000-secretly-hanged-saydnaya-military-prison-shocking-new-report (Full report: https://www.amnesty.org.uk/files/human_slaughterhouse_report_0.pdf)

42 Smith-Spark, L. (2017). *Assad Claims Syria Chemical Attach Was Fabrication, in Face of Evidence* at CNN.COM Accessed 29/03/18: http://edition.cnn.com/2017/04/13/middleeast/syria-bashar-assad-interview/index.html

43 ibid

44 The New York Times (2018) "How we created a virtual crime scene to investigate Syria's chemical attack", June 24th. Available at: https:// www.nytimes.com/interactive/2018/06/24/world/middleeast/douma-syria-chemical-attack-augmented-reality-ar-ul.html Accessed 28/06/18

45 ABC (2013). *The Perils of Speed Before Accuracy*, Media Watch, Australian Broadcasting Corporation. Accessed 29/03/18:

http://www.abc.net.au/mediawatch/transcripts/s3682970.htm

46 The original press release is here: http://www.abc.net.au/mediawatch/transcripts/1301_fake.pdf Accessed 29/03/18 Note: This press release could be used in a tutorial exercise requiring students to assess its veracity

47 ABC (2013). *Whitehaven Coal shares plunge after media hoax* ABC. Accessed 29/03/18:

http://www.abc.net.au/news/2013-01-07/whitehaven-coal-shares-plunge-after-media-hoax/4455362

48 Chen, A. (2015). *The Agency*, The New York Times. Accessed 29/03/18: https://www.nytimes.com/2015/06/07/magazine/the-agency.html

49 Walker, S. (2015). *Salutin' Putin: inside a Russian troll house*. The Guardian. Accessed 29/03/18

https://www.theguardian.com/world/2015/apr/02/putin-kremlin-inside-russian-troll-house

50 Seddon, M. (2014). *Documents Show How Russia's Troll Army Hit America*. BuzzFeed. Accessed 29/03/18: https://www.buzzfeed.com/ maxseddon/documents-show-how-russias-troll-army-hit-america?utm_term=.vfBjqD48#.lsKMAzx9

51 https://www.stopfake.org/en/news/ and https://www.stopfake.org/smi-o-nas/ [Both sites accessed 15/06/18]

52 Phillip, A. (2015). *Egyptian TV Anchor Mistakes Video Game Footage For Russian Airstrike in Syria* in The Washington Post. Accessed 29/03/18:

https://www.washingtonpost.com/news/worldviews/wp/2015/10/12/egyptian-tv-anchor-mistakes-video-game-footage-for-russianairstrikes- in-syria/?utm_term=.18aaac1e8e35

53 Collins, K. (2017). *People shared nearly as much fake news as real news on Twitter during the election*, Quartz. Accessed 29/03/18: https://qz.com/1090903/people-shared-nearly-as-much-fake-news-as-real-news-on-twitter-during-the-election/

54 Kang, C. (2016). *Fake News Onslaught Targets Pizzeria as Nest of Child-Trafficking*, The New York Times. Accessed 29/03/18:

https://www.nytimes.com/2016/11/21/technology/fact-check-this-pizzeria-is-not-a-child-trafficking-site.html

55 Siddiqui, F. & Svrluga, S. (2016). *N.C. man told police he went to D.C. pizzeria with gun to investigate conspiracy theory*, The Washington Post. Accessed: https://www.washingtonpost.com/news/local/wp/2016/12/04/d-c-police-respond-to-report-of-a-man-with-a-gun-atcomet-ping-pong-restaurant/

56 Menn, J. & Ingram, D. (2017). *Facebook says likely Russian-based operation funded U.S. ads with political message*. Accessed 29/03/18: https://www.reuters.com/article/us-facebook-propaganda/facebook-says-likely-russian-based-operation-funded-u-s-ads-withpolitical-message-idUSKCN1BH2VX

57 Shane, S. (2017). *The Fake Americans Russia Created to Influence the Election*, The New York Times. Accessed 29/03/18:

https://www.nytimes.com/2017/09/07/us/politics/russia-facebook-twitter-election.html?mtrref=www.google.com.au

58 Polonski, V. (2016). *Impact of social media on the outcome of the EU referendum*. Referendum Analysis. Accessed 29/03/18: http://www.referendumanalysis.eu/eu-referendum-analysis-2016/section-7-social-media/impact-of-social-media-on-the-outcome-of-the-eureferendum/

59 Mortimer, C. (2017). *If you saw these tweets, you were targeted by Russian Brexit propaganda*, The Independent. Accessed 29/03/18: http://www.independent.co.uk/life-style/gadgets-and-tech/news/brexit-russia-troll-factory-propaganda-fake-news-twitterfacebook-a8050866.html

60 Hopkins, S. (2017). *Nigel Farage's Brexit Poster Is Being Likened To 'Nazi Propaganda', Compared To Auschwitz Documentary Scene*, The Huffington Post. Accessed 29/03/18: http://www.huffingtonpost.co.uk/entry/nigel-farages-eu-has-failed-us-all-poster-slammed-asdisgusting-by-nicola-sturgeon_uk_5762880e4b08b9e3abdc483

61 Ressa, M. (2016). *Propaganda war: Weaponizing the internet*, Rappler. Accessed 29/03/18:

https://www.rappler.com/nation/148007-propaganda-war-weaponizing-internet

62 Ressa, M. (2017). *How Facebook algorithms impact democracy*, Rappler. Accessed 29/03/18:

https://www.rappler.com/newsbreak/148536-facebook-algorithms-impact-democracy

63 Posetti, J. (2017). *Fighting Back Against Prolific Online Harassment: Maria Ressa* in Kilman, L. (Ed) An Attack on One is an Attack on All (UNESCO). Accessed 30/03/18: http://unesdoc.unesco.org/images/0025/002593/259399e.pdf

64 Subramanian, S. (2017). *Inside the Macedonian Fake News Complex*, Wired. Accessed 29/03/18: https://www.wired.com/2017/02/velesmacedonia-fake-news/

65 Remnick, D. (2016) *Obama Reckons With a Trump Presidency*, The New Yorker. Accessed 29/03/18: https://www.newyorker.com/magazine/2016/11/28/obama-reckons-with-a-trump-presidency

66 Silverman, C. (2017). *This is how your hyperpartisan political news gets made*, BuzzFeed. Accessed 29/03/18: https://www.buzzfeed.com/craigsilverman/how-the-hyperpartisan-sausage-is-made?utm_term=.vsG9XL-WjgW#.iyerD0MLqM

67 Sonnad, N. (2017). *This is now what happens when you try to post fake news on Facebook*, Quartz. Accessed 29/03/18: https://qz.com/936503/facebooks-new-method-of-fighting-fake-news-is-making-it-hard-for-people-to-post-a-false-story-about-irish-slaves/

68 Herreria, C. (2017). *Mark Zuckerberg: 'I Regret' Rejecting Idea That Facebook Fake News Altered Election*, Huffington Post. Accessed 29/03/18: http://www.huffingtonpost.com.au/entry/mark-zuckerberg-regrets-fake-news-facebook_us_59cc2039e4b05063fe0eed9d

69 Mosseri, A. (2016). *News Feed FYI: Addressing Hoaxes and Fake News*, Facebook Newsroom. Accessed 29/03/18:

https://newsroom.fb.com/news/2016/12/news-feed-fyi-addressing-hoaxes-and-fake-news/

70 Frenkel, F., Casey, N. & Mazur, P. (2018). *In Some Countries, Facebook's Fiddling has Magnified Fake News* in The New York Times. Accessed 29/03/18: https://www.nytimes.com/2018/01/14/technology/facebook-news-feed-changes.html?smid=fb-nytimes&smtyp=cur

71 Robertson, J., Riley, M. & Willis, A. (2016). *A How to Hack an Election* at The Intercept. Accessed 29/03/18:

https://www.bloomberg.com/features/2016-how-to-hack-an-election/

72 Irish Times (2016) *Fake News Story Prompts Pakistan To Issue Nuclear Threat*, Irish Times. Accessed 29/03/18:

https://www.irishtimes.com/news/world/asia-pacific/fake-news-story-prompts-pakistan-to-issue-nuclear-threat-1.2917737

73 Pengelly, M (2017) *Trump Accuses CNN of Fake News Over Reported Celebrity Apprentice Plans*, The Guardian. Accessed 29/03/18:

https://www.theguardian.com/us-news/2016/dec/10/trump-celebrity-apprentice-cnn-fake-news

74 US News (2017) *See an interactive map tracking the spread of the term 'fake news' globally*, US NEWS. Accessed 28/01/18:

https://www.usnews.com/news/best-countries/articles/2017-12-30/how-fake-news-charges-spread-around-the-globe

75 UN/OSCE/OAS/ACHPR (2017). *Joint Declaration on Freedom of Expression and "Fake News", Disinformation, Propaganda* Accessed 29/03/18: https://www.osce.org/fom/302796?download=true

76 https://www.dni.gov/files/documents/ICA_2017_01.pdf [Accessed 15/06/18]

77 Hudgins, J. & Newcomb, A. (2017). *Google, Facebook, Twitter and Russia: A Timeline on the '16 Election*, NBC. Accessed: 29/03/18: https://www.nbcnews.com/news/us-news/google-facebook-twitter-russia-timeline-16-election-n816036

78 Sputnik News (2017). *Maduro accuses world media of spreading fake news on Venezuela*. Accessed 29/03/18: https://sputniknews.com/latam/201707271055924853-maduro-media-fake-news/

79 BBC News (2017). VIDEO: https://www.youtube.com/watch?time_continue=1&v=wd_oHi41lgk Accessed 29/03/18

80 UK Parliament (2017) 'Fake News' inquiry launched'. Accessed 20/03/18: https://www.parliament.uk/business/committees/committees-a-z/commons-select/culture-media-and-sport-committee/news-parliament-2015/fake-news-launch-16-17/

81 Australian Parliament (2017). *Terms of Reference Future of Public Interest Journalism*. Accessed 30/08/09: https://www.aph.gov.au/Parliamentary_Business/Committees/Senate/Future_of_Public_Interest_Journalism/PublicInterestJournalism/Terms_of_Reference; MEAA (2018) MEAA submission to the ACCC Inquiry into Digital Platforms. Accessed 18/4/18 https://www.meaa.org/mediaroom/meaasubmission-to-the-accc-inquiry-into-digital-platforms/

82 MEAA (2018) MEAA submission to the ACCC Inquiry into Digital Platforms. Accessed 18/4/18
https://www.meaa.org/mediaroom/meaa-submission-to-the-accc-inquiry-into-digital-platforms/

83 Rappler (2017). *WATCH: Senate hearing on fake news online*, Rappler. Accessed 20/03/18:

https://www.rappler.com/nation/184192-senate-hearing-fake-news-online

84 Portland and GeoPoll (2017). *The Reality of Fake News in Kenya*. Accessed 27/03/18:

https://cdn2.hubspot.net/hubfs/325431/The-Reality-of-Fake-News-in-Kenya%20-%20FINAL.pdf?t=1502723966924

85 Sambuli, N. (2017). *How Kenya Became the Latest Victim of Fake News*, Al Jazeera. Accessed 29/03/18:

http://www.aljazeera.com/indepth/opinion/2017/08/kenya-latest-victim-fake-news-170816121455181.html

86 Ibid

87 Farand, C. (2017). *French social media awash with fake news stories from sources 'exposed to Russian influence' ahead of presidential election*, The Independent, link accessed 29/03/18: http://www.independent.co.uk/news/world/europe/french-voters-deluge-fake-news-storiesfacebook-twitter-russian-influence-days-before-election-a7696506.html

88 BBC (2017). *Fact-checking fake news in the French election*, BBC. Accessed 01/04/18: http://www.bbc.com/news/world-europe-39495635

89 Shalal, A. & Auchard, E. (2017). *German election campaign largely unaffected by fake news or bots*, Reuters, link: https://www.reuters.com/article/us-germany-election-fake/german-election-campaign-largely-unaffected-by-fake-news-or-bots-idUSKCN1BX258 [Accessed 15/06/18]

90 Shuster, S. (2017). *Russia Has Launched a Fake News War on Europe. Now Germany Is Fighting Back*, TIME, link:

http://time.com/4889471/germany-election-russia-fake-news-angela-merkel/

91 Salisbury, P. (2017). *The fake news hack that nearly started a war this summer was designed for one man: Donald Trump*, Quartz (20/10/2017). Accessible: https://qz.com/1107023/the-inside-story-of-the-hack-that-nearly-started-another-middle-east-war/

92 ibid

93 Pakistan Today (2018). *Anthropologists make contact with remote cut-off tribe still thanking Raheel Sharif.* [online] p.Khabaristan Today. Available at: https://www.pakistantoday.com.pk/2017/01/11/anthropologists-make-contact-with-remote-cut-off-tribe-still-thankingraheel-sharif/ [Accessed 6 Apr. 2018].

94 Boburg, S., Davis, A.C. & Crites, A. (2017). A woman approached The Post with dramatic — and false — tale about Roy Moore. She appears to be part of undercover sting operation, The Washington Post. Accessed 29/03/18: https://www.washingtonpost.com/investigations/a-woman-approached-the-post-with-dramatic--and-false--tale-about-roy-moore-sje-appears-to-be-part-ofundercover-sting-operation/2017/11/27/0c2e335a-cfb6-11e7-9d3a-bcbe2af58c3a_story.html?utm_term=.c97203678d6d

95 Wilkinson, F. (2017). *It's War and the Washington Post Knows It*, Bloomberg. Accessed 29/03/18:
https://www.bloomberg.com/view/articles/2017-11-29/it-s-war-and-the-washington-post-knows-it

96 Al Jazeera News (2018). *Trump's Fake News Awards Blasted as 'Terrifying'*, Al Jazeera. Accessed 29/03/18 http://www.aljazeera.com/news/2018/01/trump-fake-news-awards-blasted-terrifying-180118083000110.html

97 US Department of Justice (2018) Internet Research Agency Indictment. Accessed 16/06/18
https://www.justice.gov/file/1035477/download

98 Volz, D & Strobel, W *US Grand Jury indicts 13 Russian Nationals in State Department Prob*, Reuters. Accessed 16/06/18 https://www.reuters.com/article/usa-trump-russia/u-s-grand-jury-indicts-13-russian-nationals-in-election-meddling-probe-idUSL2N1Q619M

99 Pengelly, M (2018) *Putin: Russia will never extradite 13 nationals indicted by mueller* The Guardian. Accessed 16/06/18
https://www.theguardian.com/us-news/2018/mar/04/vladimir-putin-never-extradite-13-russians-robert-mueller

100 Aleem, Z (2018) *Reddit Just Shutdown Nearly 1000 Russian Troll Accounts*, Vox Accessed 16/06/18
https://www.vox.com/world/2018/4/11/17224294/reddit-russia-internet-research-agency.

101 Filho, J. (2018). *Brazilian Right Wing Fell Hard for a Fake News Story About Venezuela Provoking a Diplomatic Incident*, The Intercept. Accessed 29/03/18: https://theintercept.com/2018/01/15/fake-news-brazil-venezuela/

102 Times Live (2017) *The Guptas, Bell Pottinger and the fake news propaganda machine*. 04 September 2017. Accessed 29/03/18 https://www.timeslive.co.za/news/south-africa/2017-09-04-the-guptas-bell-pottinger-and-the-fake-news-propaganda-machine/

103 Dummy's guide: Bell Pottinger – Gupta London agency, creator of WMC https://www.biznews.com/global-citizen/2017/08/07/dummys-guide-bell-pottinger-gupta-wmc/ ; How Bell Pottinger, P.R. Firm for Despots and Rogues, Met Its End in South Africa. New York Times, 4 Feb 2018. https://www.nytimes.com/2018/02/04/business/bell-pottinger-guptas-zuma-south-africa.html

104 Haffajee, F. (2017). *Ferial Haffajee: The Gupta fake news factory and me*. HuffPost South Africa. [online] Available at https://www.huffingtonpost.co.za/2017/06/05/ferial-haffajee-the-gupta-fake-news-factory-and-me_a_22126282/ [Accessed 6 Apr. 2018].

105 See Posetti, J (2018) *Combating Online abuse: When journalists and their sources are targeted* In Ireton, C & Posetti, J (Eds) Journalism, 'Fake News' and Disinformation (UNESCO). Forthcoming.

106 EU (2018). *Final report of the High-Level Expert Group on Fake News and Online Disinformation*. Accessed 27/03/18 https://ec.europa.eu/digital-single-market/en/news/final-report-high-level-expert-group-fake-news-and-online-disinformation

107 Amnesty International (2018). Gambia: Regional Court Rules Draconian Media Laws Violate Human Rights. Accessed 29/03/18:
https://www.amnesty.org/en/press-releases/2018/02/gambia-regional-court-rules-draconian-media-laws-violate-human-rights/

108 Wilson, J. (2018). *Peter Dutton's offer to white South African farmers started on the far right* in The Guardian. Accessed 30/03/18: https://www.theguardian.com/commentisfree/2018/mar/16/peter-duttons-offer-to-white-south-african-farmers-started-on-the-far-right

109 AFP (2018). *Crazy lefties are dead to me: Aus minister pushes ahead with SA farmer plan*, Mail&Guardian. Accessed 29/03/18:
https://mg.co.za/article/2018-03-22-crazy-lefties-are-dead-to-me-aus-minister-pushes-ahead-with-sa-farmer-plan

110 Lee, G. (2018). *Q&A on Cambridge Analytica: The allegations so far, explained,* FactCheck, Channel 4 News. Accessed 29/03/18: https://www.channel4.com/news/factcheck/cambridge-analytica-the-allegations-so-far

111 Cassidy, J. (2018). *Cambridge Analytica Whistleblower claims that cheating swung the Brexit vote,* The New Yorker. Accessed 29/03/18: https://www.newyorker.com/news/our-columnists/a-cambridge-analytica-whistleblower-claims-that-cheating-swung-the-brexit-vote

112 UN experts call on India to protect journalist Rana Ayyub from online hate campaign http://www.ohchr.org/EN/NewsEvents/Pages/DisplayNews.aspx?NewsID=23126&LangID=E; Accessed 17/08/18 See also Ayyub, R. (2018). In India, journalists face slut-shaming and rape threats. https://www.nytimes.com/2018/05/22/opinion/india-journalists-slut-shaming-rape.html Accessed 17/06/18

113 Article 19 (2017) Germany: The Act to Improve Enforcement of the Law in Social Networks. https://www.article19.org/wp-content/uploads/2017/09/170901-Legal-Analysis-German-NetzDG-Act.pdf Accessed 16/07/2018

114 Safi, M. 2018. India backs down over plan to ban journalists for 'fake news'. Accessed 15/06/18
https://www.theguardian.com/world/2018/apr/03/india-backs-down-over-plan-to-ban-journalists-for-fake-news

115 The Straits Times. 2018. Malaysia will abolish anti-fake news law, says new communications minister Straits Times Wednesday, May 22, https://www.straitstimes.com/asia/se-asia/malaysia-will-abolish-anti-fake-news-law-says-new-communications-minister Accessed 15/06/18

116 Schwartz, A. Kenya signs bill criminalising fake news. Accessed 16/05/18 https://mg.co.za/article/2018-05-16-kenya-signs-bill-criminalising-fake-news

117 Tani, S. 2018. Asia's war on 'fake news' raises real fears for free speech. Governments walk fine line between fighting rumors and stifling dissent. Nikkei Asian Review. https://asia.nikkei.com/Spotlight/Asia-Insight/Asia-s-war-on-fake-news-raises-real-fears-for-free-speech Accessed 15/06/18

118 Minter, A. Fake News Laws Are Fake Solution Bloomberg Opinion. Accessed 15/06/18 https://www.bloomberg.com/view/articles/2018-05-25/fake-news-laws-are-fake-solution

119 Muthusubbarayan, M. 2018. Fake news: What countries around the world are doing to combat the epidemic
https://qrius.com/fake-news-countries-combat-epidemic/

Print Citations

CMS: Posetti, Julie, and Alice Matthews. "A Short Guide to the History of 'Fake News' and Disinformation." In *The Reference Shelf: Propaganda & Misinformation,* edited by Annette Calzone, 24–43. Amenia, NY: Grey House Publishing, 2020.

MLA: Posetti, Julie, and Alice Matthews. "A Short Guide to the History of 'Fake News' and Disinformation." "A Short Guide to the History of 'Fake News' and Disinformation." *The Reference Shelf: Propaganda & Misinformation,* edited by Annette Calzone, Grey House Publishing, 2020, pp. 24–43.

APA: Posetti, J., & Matthews, A. (2020). A short guide to the history of "fake news" and disinformation. In Annette Calzone (Ed.), *The reference shelf: Propaganda & misinformation* (pp. 24–43). Amenia, NY: Grey House Publishing.

2
Our Current Media Environment

Protestors in London advocating for vaccination. By Russell Watkins / Department for International Development, via Wikimedia.

Fake News, the Coronavirus, and the 2020 Election

The Truth Is Out There?

The well-known tagline for science fiction television series *The X Files* seemingly applies to our information environment. As narrative, personal opinion, and appeals to emotion steadily erode objectivity, there is less consensus on what is considered fact. Distrust in institutions and experts is on the rise. And while Americans have a long-standing tradition of suspicion of the educated elite, a new element of hostility can be found in current attitudes. "'What I think we see going on now, is an attack on experts as individuals, as people—demonizing those experts who disagree with our ideological viewpoints, and denigrating their professionalism," says the University of Pennsylvania's Matt Motta. While the far-right engages in climate-change denial, and left-wing groups consistently argue against GMOs, Motta continues, "Both sides still tend to appeal to experts when it's convenient for them, when the experts agree with what they have to say."[1]

Syracuse University professor Whitney Phillips writes that,

> the impulse to respond to falsehoods with facts is not a cure-all. . . . In practice our relationship to truth is more complicated. People don't believe things, or share things, only because of facts. . . . Shining a light on what's false can even, counter-intuitively, make things worse by spreading falsehoods to more people, making those falsehoods seem more plausible to certain audiences, and generally ensuring that the story is more potent after the debunk than before.[2]

Discussing whether or not efforts to combat misinformation (which can be uinintentioanal and is often used interchangeably with its deliberate subset. disinformation) about the coronavirus were effective, the American Press Institute's Cristina Tardaguila contends that international cooperation among fact checkers has greatly exceeded efforts on previous outbreaks. While acknowledging that in the past efforts to counteract misinformation have done more harm than good, Tardáguila points to the different tactics that misinformers were forced to rapidly switch to in response to debunking. In the course of a couple of weeks, fake news on the coronavirus moved from hoaxes about the origins of the virus and conspiracy theories, to edited and out-of-context videos, to false cures, to reports that China wants to exterminate infected citizens. Tardáguila is herself a fact-checker, but she lived in Brazil during the outbreak of the Zika virus and yellow fever and can attest to the fact that Brazilians had access to much less reliable information.[3]

Some researchers studying misinformation distinguish between how people react to political fake news versus the more general variety of fake news. Syracuse University's Emily Thorson thinks that despite the focus on political misinformation because of President Donald Trump and the upcoming election, "it has relatively small effects in reality, because we know that information—true or false—rarely changes partisan attitudes. But in other realms, like health, misinformation can really change behaviors."[4]

President Trump's repeated attacks on mainstream media and the rise of far-right media outlets like Breitbart News or the conspiracy show InfoWars have sown further confusion. Although Republicans have traditionally criticized mainstream journalism, Trump has taken this to extremes, calling the press the "enemy of the people" and reporters "absolute scum." The *Atlantic*'s McKay Coppins, who covered many Trump rallies, says of these statements: "I always thought I could tell when he was going through the motions with his press-bashing, and when he really meant it." Similarly, Coppins is not sure that bombastic statements from Breitbart about the day "CNN is no longer in business" or the "*New York Times* closes its doors" should necessarily be ignored.[5]

Before propaganda and misinformation concerns rose to their current pitch, the Pew Research Center and Elon University's Imagining the Internet Center delved into whether the fake news problem would get better or worse over the coming decade. Their 2017 canvass elicited responses from over 1,000 technologists, scholars, practitioners, and strategic thinkers, with 51 percent of respondents believing the information environment will not improve versus 49 percent who think it will. The pessimists reasoned that fake news preys on deep human instincts and that we, as humans, are not able to keep up with the pace of technological change. They put forth the possibility that segments of the population would simply give up on being informed and socially engaged. The optimists pointed out that misinformation and bad actors have always existed but have also always eventually been marginalized by smart people. They cited a combination of technological advances and human cooperation as the ways to overcome fake news. Some elaborated on their responses, such as American Press Institute director and senior Brookings Institute fellow Tom Rosenthal:

> Misinformation is not like a plumbing problem you fix. It is a social condition, like crime, that you must constantly adjust to. . . . As Winston Churchill said, "A lie can go around the world before the truth gets its pants on."

An anonymous university professor pointed out:

> The public can grasp the destructive power of nuclear weapons in a way they will never fully understand the utterly corrosive power of the internet to civilized society, when there is no reliable mechanism for sorting out what people can believe to be true or false.

Many respondents of the 2017 Pew Research poll felt that those most able to improve the information environment—such as large corporations and the government—had a vested interest in not doing so.

Florida State University Dean Scott Schamp explained:

> When there is value in misinformation, it will rule.

Others cited the growing lack of commonly accepted facts or some sort of "cultural ground" due to online echo chambers, information overload, and the erosion of high-quality journalism.

Those hopeful of containing misinformation believed that technology, regulatory intervention, and media literacy would eventually stabilize the media environment.

London School of Economics and Political Science professor Sonia Livingstone contended:

> The "wild west" state of the internet will not be permitted to continue. . . as we are already seeing . . . increased national pressure on providers/companies.

Global communications expert Willie Currie took a different tack:

> Regulatory options may include unbundling social networks like Facebook into smaller entities. Legal options include reversing the notion that providers of content services over the internet are mere conduits without responsibility for the content.

Georgetown University professor Irene Wu pointed out:

> When the television became popular, people also believed everything on TV was true. It's how people choose to react and access to information and news that's important, not the mechanisms that distribute them.

Though even the optimists believe things might get worse before they get better, opinion is split on the direction the information environment will eventually take long-term.[6]

In a 2017 study, researchers note that although younger generations are more tech-savvy in terms of accessing and distributing digital information, they are no less susceptible to fake news. The report goes on to discuss how news publishers have lost control over the distribution of their content, which is disseminated according to obscure and unpredictable algorithms. Also, newcomers like *BuzzFeed* and *Vox* have built their presence using these technologies, undermining traditional news publishers. Last but not least, big tech companies like Google, Apple, Facebook and Amazon have gained control over "who publishes what to whom, and how the publications are monetized." Added to the mix are individual fake news creators who generate clickbait strictly for profit, often using URLs and sophisticated websites designed to mimic legitimate news outlets.[7]

2016 Election Redux?

Avaaz, a global rights organization, reports that in the first ten months of 2019, 100 fake political news stories were posted on Facebook over 2.3 million times, more than twice the estimated views of the official Facebook pages of the Republican and Democratic parties. Efforts by Facebook to reduce viral disinformation have been largely ineffective, according to the report.[8]

A CNN investigation reveals that an entire town in Macedonia is gearing up for the 2020 election. Once known for producing porcelain, Veles's new industry is churning out fake news, mostly for American consumption. One creator claims he has earned up to $2,500.00 a day (the average income in Macedonia is $426.00 a month) from ad revenue running a website and Facebook page as "Jesica," an American pro-Trump supporter. He bought a house and put his younger sister through school generating headlines such as "Michelle Caught Cheating with Eric Holder—Obama is Furious!" and "Bill Clinton Loses It in Interview—Admits He's a Murderer." Although "Jesica" has been shut down by Facebook, her creator is intent on setting up a similar outlet. Another Veles resident with a decade of experience creating websites that target Americans teaches the finer points of the business, estimating that 100 of his pupils are now operating U.S. political news websites.[9]

Former CIA officer Cindy L. Otis thinks that American sources of fake news will be at least an equal threat for the 2020 election. Otis tracked a series of fake websites of Democratic presidential candidates in the summer of 2019, and observed users of 4chan discussing ways to spread disinformation about the candidates in the run-up to the first Democratic debate, including photos and memes they could make to discredit them. Both operations were created by Americans.[10]

Political candidates are always concerned with electability, which is usually defined by such factors as policy, personal appeal, or identity. But *Politico*'s Ryan Lizza points out that in an age dominated by disinformation, a candidate's ability to combat false attacks like those directed at Hillary Clinton and Joe Biden is a hidden but very real part of political campaigning. Lizza reports that the Democratic National Committee has had some successes in helping campaigns combat disinformation, reporting "misinformation incidents" that resulted in the removal of over 4,000 social media accounts, connecting campaigns with contacts at the FBI and the Department of Homeland Security, and warning of phishing scams. But the DNC also notes that social media platforms are "the most responsible for spreading disinformation—and the least responsive to correcting it." Campaign aides have also come to the grips with the necessity of immediately and forcefully responding to false claims. Former Hillary Clinton aide Philippe Reines now thinks that it was wrong to not respond to false rumors: "It was a mistake! You can't let *anything* go. We will all go to our deaths never hearing Donald Trump say, 'I won't dignify that with an answer.'"[11]

Works Used

Anderson, Janna, and Lee Rainie. "The Future of Truth and Misinformation Online." Pew Research Center. Oct 19, 2017. https://www.pewresearch.org/internet/2017/10/19/the-future-of-truth-and-misinformation-online/.

Bruinius, Harry. "Who Made You an Expert? Is America's Distrust of 'Elites' Becoming More Toxic?" *Christian Science Monitor*. Aug 27, 2018. https://www.

csmonitor.com/USA/Politics/2018/0827/Who-made-you-an-expert-Is-Americas-distrust-of-elites-becoming-more-toxic.

Coppins, McKay. "What if the Right-Wing Media Wins?" *Columbia Journalism Review*. Fall 2017. https://www.cjr.org/special_report/right-wing-media-breitbart-fox-bannon-carlson-hannity-coulter-trump.php.

Figueira, Álvaro Figueira, and Luciana Oliveira. "The Current State of Fake News: Challenges and Opportunities." *ScienceDirect*. 2017. https://reader.elsevier.com/reader/sd/pii/S1877050917323086?token.

Illing, Sean. "America's Misinformation Problem Explained." *Vox*. Nov 6, 2017. https://www.vox.com/2017/11/6/16504454/misinformation-fake-news-media-trump.

Lizza, Ryan. "The Hidden Menace Threatening Democrats' Bid to Beat Trump in 2020." *Politico*. Oct 15, 2019. https://www.politico.com/news/2019/10/15/dnc-election-strategy-disinformation-046839.

Otis, Cindy L. "Americans Could Be a Bigger Fake News Threat Than Russians in the 2020 Presidential Campaign." *USA Today*. July 19, 2019. https://www.usatoday.com/story/opinion/2019/07/19/disinformation-attacks-americans-threaten-2020-election-column/1756092001/.

Phillips, Whitney. "Disinformation Is Polluting Our Media Environment: Facts Won't Save Us." *Columbia Journalism Review*. Fall 2019. https://www.cjr.org/special_report/truth-pollution-disinformation.php.

Soares, Isa. "The Fake News Machine." *CNN Money*. https://money.cnn.com/interactive/media/the-macedonia-story/.

Tardaguila, Cristina, and Susan Benkelman. "Factually: Fact-Checking on Coronavirus Far Exceeds That of Zika." *American Press Institute*. Feb 20, 2020. https://www.americanpressinstitute.org/fact-checking-project/factually-newsletter/factually-fact-checking-on-coronavirus-far-exceeds-that-of-zika/.

"US 2020: Another Facebook Disinformation Election?" *Avaaz*. Nov 5, 2019. avaaz-images.avaaz.org.

Notes

1. Bruinius, "Who Made You an Expert? Is America's Distrust of 'Elites' Becoming More Toxic?"
2. Phillips, "Disinformation Is Polluting Our Media Environment: Facts Won't Save Us."
3. Tardaguila and Benkelman, "Factually: Fact-Checking on Coronavirus Far Exceeds That of Zika."
4. Illing, "America's Misinformation Problem, Explained."
5. Coppins, "What if the Right-Wing Media Wins?"
6. Anderson and Rainie, "The Future of Truth and Misinformation Online."
7. Figueira and Oliveira, "The Current State of Fake News: Challenges and Opportunities."
8. "US 2020: Another Facebook Disinformation Election?".
9. Soares, "The Fake News Machine.".

10. Otis, "Americans Could Be a Bigger Fake News Threat Than Russians in the 2020 Presidential Campaign."
11. Lizza, "The Hidden Menace Threatening Democrats' Bid to Beat Trump in 2020."

NPR Poll: Majority of Americans Believe Trump Encourages Election Interference

By Brett Neely
NPR, January 21, 2020

Weeks before the first votes of the 2020 presidential election, Americans report a high level of concern about how secure that election will be and worry about the perils of disinformation, according to a new NPR/PBS NewsHour/Marist Poll.

Forty-one percent of those surveyed said they believed the U.S. is not very prepared or not prepared at all to keep November's election safe and secure.

Reflecting the polarization of the Trump era, two-thirds of Democrats think the country isn't prepared, while 85% of Republicans said they think it is.

"Like so many issues, Americans view election security from opposite poles of the partisan divide," said Lee Miringoff, director of the Marist College Institute for Public Opinion, which conducted the poll.

President Trump, who has often disputed the U.S. intelligence community's assessment that Russia interfered with the 2016 presidential election, gets low marks from many voters on his handling of election security.

Driven by Democrats and independents, 56% of those surveyed think Trump has not done very much or has done nothing at all to make sure there will be no future election interference—although 75% of Republicans think he has done enough.

"I can trust [Trump's] word to know that he is going to try as best as he can ... in order to stop influence from foreign countries in our elections," said first-time voter Joel Martin, a Republican from California.

Martin and other respondents were contacted by NPR for follow-up interviews after they had given their initial responses to questions from Marist pollsters.

Trump faces an impeachment trial this month tied directly to his efforts to get Ukraine to launch an investigation into one of his potential 2020 rivals, former Vice President Joe Biden.

And despite the scrutiny and criticism of his actions with respect to Ukraine, Trump also said in October that China should "start an investigation into the Bidens."

Remarks like those may have been on the mind of the 51% of the Americans surveyed who said Trump had encouraged election interference. Eighty-eight percent of Democrats and 51% of independents backed that assertion.

"I considered the attack on our electoral system to be the single biggest assault on United States sovereignty since Pearl Harbor," said poll participant Dimitri Laddis, an independent voter from New York.

From *NPR*, January 21 © 2020. Reprinted with permission. All rights reserved.

"The fact that the commander in chief has done nothing to reassure us that we are safe from such an attack—and the fact that he seems to be keenly aware that he benefits from outside forces having influence over our elections—is very disheartening," Laddis said.

> **False, misleading, and agitating material were a big part of Russia's active measures in 2016.**

Although there is no evidence that any votes were changed by a foreign power in 2016 or 2018, almost 4 in 10 Americans surveyed said they believe it is likely another country will tamper with the votes cast in 2020 in order to change the result.

The poll's results also paint a picture of a polarized electorate wary about what it reads and not fully convinced that elections are fair.

In a reflection of how divided the country is, only 62% of Americans said U.S. elections are fair.

Barely half of Democrats agree with that sentiment, perhaps a reflection of lingering unhappiness that Donald Trump won the 2016 election by capturing the Electoral College while losing the popular vote.

And even as Trump has continued to claim without evidence that millions of votes were cast illegally in 2016, 80% of Republicans surveyed reported that they believe elections are fair.

"Many Americans think election cycles are no longer on the up and up," said Miringoff, the Marist director. "These opinions are a troublesome sign about this keystone of our democracy."

Disinformation

Intelligence and elections officials work hard to reassure voters about the integrity of the system, but there is concern about the effect of disinformation in the political discourse. False, misleading and agitating material were a big part of Russia's active measures in 2016.

Americans retain concerns about this today; 59% of those surveyed reported that it is hard to tell the difference between what is factual and what is misleading information.

Despite nearly four years' worth of attention to disinformation, 55% of Americans say it will be harder to identify deceptive information than it was in 2016.

Eighty-two percent of those surveyed said they believe they will read misleading information on social media and a similar proportion believe foreign countries will spread false information about candidates this year.

The public does not trust big social network and tech companies to prevent their platforms from being misused to present election interference, the poll revealed.

Seventy-five percent of those surveyed are not confident about the tech companies, a 9-point increase from a similar 2018 NPR/Marist poll.

Despite casting blame on tech companies for spreading disinformation, there was little consensus on who should be most responsible for reducing its flow: 39%

pointed to the media, 18% to tech companies, 15% to the government and 12% to the public itself.

Not surprisingly given Trump's oft-repeated claim that the media peddles in "fake news," 54% of Republicans say it's the media's responsibility to stop the spread of disinformation.

Voting Rights and Election Administration

Americans who responded to the poll were divided about what they considered the biggest threat to the election—35% said disinformation is the biggest threat; 24% blamed voter fraud; 16% said voter suppression; 15% blamed foreign interference.

In yet another sign that voters live in very different media bubbles, voter suppression was cited as the greatest threat for Democrats. Voter fraud topped the list for Republicans. Independents were most concerned with misleading information.

By an overwhelming margin, Americans said they found voting to be easy, and most have not encountered problems with confusing ballots, problems with their voter ID or registration or broken voting machines.

But more than a third of younger and nonwhite voters say they have experienced long lines.

Moreover, women and nonwhite respondents are considerably more likely than men and white voters to say that their own vote won't be counted. And half of women and slightly more than half of nonwhite respondents said many votes will not be counted, in contrast to men and white Americans, who are more confident that all ballots will be tallied.

"People are trying to redline the country to stop different ethnic groups from voting," said Larry Swoffard, an African American poll respondent from California.

Local election officials get relatively high marks from voters, with 68% expressing confidence that officials will run a fair election in 2020. Nearly 6 in 10 respondents say they plan to vote in person on Election Day. Twenty-three percent say they will vote by mail or absentee ballot. Another 18% said they would cast their ballot at an early voting site.

Print Citations

CMS: Neely, Brett. "NPR Poll: Majority of Americans Believe Trump Encourages Election Interference." In *The Reference Shelf: Propaganda & Misinformation*, edited by Annette Calzone, 53–55. Amenia, NY: Grey House Publishing, 2020.

MLA: Neely, Brett. "NPR Poll: Majority of Americans Believe Trump Encourages Election Interference." *The Reference Shelf: Propaganda & Misinformation,* edited by Annette Calzone, Grey House Publishing, 2020, pp. 53–55.

APA: Neely, B. (2020). NPR poll: Majority of Americans believe Trump encourages election interference. In Annette Calzone (Ed.), *The reference shelf: Propaganda & misinformation* (pp. 53–55). Amenia, NY: Grey House Publishing.

Trump's Favorite Tabloid Worried Its Saudi Propaganda Was as Bad as It Looked

By Bess Levin
Vanity Fair, **February 11, 2019**

Last March, shortly before Crown Prince Mohammed bin Salman arrived in America to pitch his younger, hipper brand of authoritarianism, American Media Inc. produced an ad-free, 97-page tribute to M.B.S called The New Kingdom. Boasting of bin Salman's multi-billion-dollar fortune and 54,000-square-foot palace, promoting his Vision 2030 plan, and dubbing the kingdom "Our Closest Middle East Ally Destroying Terrorism," the whole thing read like a vintage issue of *Tiger Beat*. Except, of course, that instead of fawning over young actors and boy bands, the gushing was reserved for a dictator starving the people of Yemen and who, just a few months later, would allegedly order the hit on journalist and dissident Jamal Khashoggi.

The $13.99 magazine was presumably a hit in the Oval Office, held up as a piece of real journalism by Donald Trump and his son-in-law, who'd been working to forge a close connection with the Saudis since January 2017, but to the outside world it might as well have been a special issue praising the leadership of Benito Mussolini. In fact, the whole thing felt so bizarre and over-the-top obsequious that A.M.I. apparently had some qualms of its own.

According to the *Wall Street Journal*, the publisher "sought advice from the Justice Department" last year over whether its obvious propaganda would cross the line between substandard journalism and literally working as an agent of a foreign government. While A.M.I. claimed in the past that Saudi officials had no role in the magazine's creation, in fact, the publisher gave an adviser to the Kingdom a draft of the magazine and followed the adviser's editorial advice, per a letter to the D.O.J. However, because there was no official contract stating the company had to follow the adviser's suggestions—because, in other words, A.M.I. did so simply out of its love for M.B.S., or as a person familiar with the matter put it, in an attempt to "kiss his ass"—the Justice Department ruled that the publisher was not required to register as a foreign agent, a conclusion it warned could change if the facts "are different in any way from those depicted in your submission."

Of course, last summer's glossy isn't the only time A.M.I. has crossed paths with the Kingdom, directly or indirectly:

In recent years, American Media sought Saudi financial backing to finance a failed effort to acquire *Time* magazine, *Sports Illustrated*, *Fortune*, and *Money*, the *Journal* reported last year.

From *Vanity Fair*, February 11 © 2019. Reprinted with permission. All rights reserved.

American Media confirmed the contacts but said the only deal that has ever been discussed with Saudi investors was the expansion of the Mr. Olympia bodybuilding competition, which American Media owns, into the Middle East and North Africa.

The lawyer for [publisher David] Pecker, Elkan Abramowitz, on Sunday on ABC said American Media sought financing "from the Saudis, but never obtained any."

There's also the matter of A.M.I.'s long-standing ties to Trump, who has gone out of his way to support Saudi Arabia, including (allegedly!) letting its de facto leader get away with the murder of a U.S. resident. That issue came up last week, when Amazon founder Jeff Bezos published a blog post accusing The *National Enquirer* of attempting to extort him if he didn't drop his investigation into how his private messages fell into their lap, and publicly state that that he had "no knowledge or basis for suggesting that A.M.I.'s coverage was politically motivated or influenced by political forces." As Bezos wrote in his widely praised dick-pic confessional, "the Saudi angle seems to hit a particularly sensitive nerve."

If you would like to receive the Levin Report in your inbox daily, click here to subscribe.

Trump wants investigation into his sham charity halted because New York A.G.s were mean to him

Back in December, Donald Trump shuttered the Donald J. Trump Foundation as part of an agreement with the New York Attorney General's office, which has alleged that the "charity" served as little more than a slush fund for the former real-estate developer's business and political interests. In addition to allegedly spending $10,000 of the foundation's money on a six-foot-tall oil painting of Trump, the group's board, made up of the president's eldest children, never once held a meeting. (Trump Organization C.F.O. Allen Weisselberg apparently had no idea he was an officer until investigators told him as much.) Unfortunately for the Donald, simply closing the (alleged) sham charity has not stopped the investigation. "We'll continue to move our suit forward to ensure that the Trump Foundation and its directors are held to account for their clear and repeated violations of state and federal law," outgoing N.Y. A.G. Barbara Underwood said at the time. So now his lawyers are trying to get it thrown out on the grounds that investigators said mean things about him:

New York's June lawsuit against the Donald J. Trump Foundation should be barred over comments made by [the state's new attorney general, Letitia] James, and predecessors Barbara Underwood and Eric Schneiderman, who were both vocal Trump critics, Trump's attorney Alan Futerfas said in documents filed last week in state court in Manhattan.

James called Trump an "illegitimate president" in the months before her November election and vowed to "use every area of the law" to investigate the real-estate mogul, his businesses, and his family, according to the filing. Statements by all three attorneys general "express clear bias and animus and constitute an unlawful appearance of impropriety."

Obviously, it's not surprising that a person vowing to use "the law" to investigate the president would send shivers down Team Trump's collective spine, though it's not clear this tack will work after having already failed a first time. Back in

November, New York State Supreme Court Justice Saliann Scarpulla rejected Trump's attorneys' attempt to get the suit dismissed on claims of "political bias," saying, "There is no basis for finding that animus and bias were the sole motivating factors for initiating the investigation and pursuing this proceeding." Or, in other words, these officials might think you're the world's slimiest weasel, but that's not the ONLY reason they launched this probe.

> **The gushing was reserved for a dictator starving the people of Yemen and who, just a few months later, would allegedly order the hit on journalist and dissident Jamal Khashoggi.**

Founding member of the "Trump Caucus" still blowing campaign funds on leisure-time activities

Remember Rep. Duncan Hunter? For those who need a quick refresher, he's the California congressman and Trump super-fan who was indicted last year, along with his wife, Margaret Hunter, on charges of wire fraud, falsifying records, campaign-finance violations, conspiracy, and "convert[ing] campaign funds to personal use," the latter of which allegedly included: a 2015 family vacation to Italy that cost more than $14,000; a $6,500 spring-break trip to Hawaii; a $3,700 jaunt to Las Vegas and Boise; $229 at Disneyland's Star Trader gift shop; $253.62 at SeaWorld's Aquatica waterpark; meals at fine-dining establishments and fast-food restaurants alike; a $2,000 birthday gift for a family member to attend a Pittsburgh Steelers game; and a three-night $1,000 stay at the Hyatt Regency Lake Tahoe Resort, Spa and Casino for a "personal ski trip," among other things. At the time, the Hunters insisted through a spokesman that the indictment against them was "politically motivated," with Duncan later trying to blame everything on his wife. Anyway, it appears that the couple is up to their old tricks:

In the last five weeks of 2018, Rep. Duncan Hunter's campaign reported spending hundreds of dollars at a local amusement park and made $2,000 in charges—now disputed—to a technology company that flies drones. The spending at Belmont Park, [an amusement park] in Mission Beach, and the disputed charges at ByteSignal, a Missouri-based technology company, are among $119,861 in expenditures Hunter's campaign disclosed to the Federal Election Commission on Thursday, in a financial report covering November 27 through December 31. During the same weeks, the campaign reported raising $2,376.

Obviously, these expenditures are a drop in the bucket compared to the $250,000 in campaign funds the Hunters allegedly misappropriated between 2009 and 2016, but if you're facing a criminal trial—the couple has pleaded not guilty—maybe just use your own money at the amusement park.

Print Citations

CMS: Levin, Bess. "Trump's Favorite Tabloid Worried Its Saudi Propaganda Was as Bad as It Looked." In *The Reference Shelf: Propaganda & Misinformation*, edited by Annette Calzone, 56–59. Amenia, NY: Grey House Publishing, 2020.

MLA: Levin, Bess. "Trump's Favorite Tabloid Worried Its Saudi Propaganda Was as Bad as It Looked." *The Reference Shelf: Propaganda & Misinformation,* edited by Annette Calzone, Grey House Publishing, 2020, pp. 56–59.

APA: Levin, B. (2020). Trump's favorite tabloid worred its Saudi propaganda was as bad as it looked. In Annette Calzone (Ed.), *The reference shelf: Propaganda & misinformation* (pp. 56–59). Amenia, NY: Grey House Publishing.

CNN vs. Fox: Why These Two Cable Networks Can't Stop Talking about Each Other

By Paul Farhi
The Washington Post, February 28, 2018

When a young survivor of the Parkland, Fla., school shooting accused CNN of trying to "script" his questions for its town-hall-style telecast last week, Fox News's opinionated hosts Tucker Carlson and Laura Ingraham jumped on the story.

Carlson interviewed the teenager, Colton Haab, on his prime-time program, and expressed amazement at CNN's supposed attempt to manipulate him: "It's shocking to us, too, trust me, in the actual journalism business." Ingraham added her own sneer, commenting that CNN has "a history of planting questions."

No matter that the actual facts would quickly exonerate CNN, which released emails showing that the network had simply invited Haab to ask its panel of politicians a question he'd previously voiced. The dust-up had an irresistible attraction for Fox: It was another chance to beat up its cable news competitor.

The two networks are long and bitter rivals, of course, and have tweaked each other off and on since Fox News's inception in 1996. But the crossfire has taken on new intensity in the Trump era. Hosts at CNN and Fox now trade blows almost daily about whose coverage or commentary about President Trump is more distorted or unfair.

Fox, for example, aired multiple clips of CNN's "town hall" about gun violence last week, using it to call out "liberal" media bias in the debate over gun control. Hannity had the National Rifle Association spokeswoman Dana Loesch on his program to talk about her experience on the CNN broadcast; an on-screen banner said she had been "heckled, interrupted and called a 'murderer'" at the event.

For its part, CNN has frequently found something newsworthy in whatever Fox's host are opining about. After Ingraham criticized National Basketball Association superstars LeBron James and Kevin Durant for expressing their political opinions ("Shut up and dribble," she said), CNN aired a news segment about her comments in which host Brooke Baldwin pointed out that Fox sometimes gives celebrities such as Kid Rock, Chuck Norris and Phil Robertson a platform for *their* political opinions.

Both networks have aired or published online dozens of articles about the other in recent months, playing up such topics as ratings, various mistakes and embarrassing missteps by the other, and even coverage of the Winter Olympics.

From *The Washington Post*, February 28 © 2018. Reprinted with permission. All rights reserved.

The mutual backbiting between the two has become so routine that it can be easy to forget how unusual it is. NBC News doesn't regularly lay into ABC News; the *Washington Post* doesn't often go after the *New York Times*. Nor do CNN or Fox criticize other news media outlets as frequently as they do each other.

> **The Hatfields-and-McCoys act has become a proxy for the news media's drift into more polarized camps, especially when it comes to covering Trump.**

In many ways, the Hatfields-and-McCoys act has become a proxy for the news media's drift into more polarized camps, especially when it comes to covering Trump. The president has certainly stoked the perception that there are pro- and anti-Trump factions in the news media, singling out CNN and Fox in particular. He often praises Fox and its hosts, and he grants the network periodic interviews. At the same time, he has demonized CNN in comments and tweets as a purveyor of "fake news." (For the record, both networks reject the notion that they are pro- or anti-Trump, or that they are "liberal" or "conservative.")

But the sniping is also "a business strategy" that reflects the networks' efforts to differentiate themselves at a time when so much news is shared and consumed via social media, said Gabriel Kahn, a professor at the University of Southern California's Annenberg School of Communication.

Since "highly emotional" news is the kind that travels furthest on social platforms such as Facebook and Twitter, he said, both networks have an incentive to jab each other.

"CNN can no longer afford to play it down the middle," Kahn said. "They'd look like Melba toast in an environment of olive bread and croissants if they did. They have to define their audience. One way to define your audience is by saying what you're not. CNN has been saying, 'We're not like [Fox].'"

Fox media analyst Howard Kurtz said he believes CNN has become more opinionated since Trump took office.

"Sniping by rival cable news hosts is a more polarizing sport in the Trump era and that now includes CNN, which fairly or unfairly is often at odds with the president over its coverage," said Kurtz, who formerly worked at the *Washington Post* and CNN. "I get why anti-Trump voices at other outlets try to lump Fox's opinion hosts in with its news division to make it appear there's one company line, which is clearly not true."

Kurtz and guests on his Sunday program, "MediaBuzz," often frame discussions of media coverage through CNN's take on events. On his program last Sunday, Kurtz noted a CNN tweet reporting the names of 71 Republican lawmakers in Florida who had "refused" to vote for an assault weapons ban. "Does that sound like activism to you?" he asked a guest.

Kurtz says that he is equally tough on both networks.

"I make it my business to report fairly on CNN, criticizing or defending as the situation warrants. I treat Fox the same way, which is the ultimate test of fair media reporting."

On his weekly media-review show, "Reliable Sources," CNN host Brian Stelter often uses Fox as Exhibit A for what he has called the "upside down" reporting and commentary in the pro-Trump media. The topic has been featured on nine of his past 10 episodes.

After House Intelligence Committee Chairman Devin Nunes (R-Calif.) on Feb. 2 released his memo criticizing the FBI's handling of the Russia investigation, for example, Stelter opined that the "pro-Trump media led by [Fox's Sean] Hannity has circled the wagons around President Trump. They've distracted people about the truth involving Trump's Russia ties, and they've done everything possible to destroy faith in Robert Mueller III's probe."

In an interview, Stelter said the intense scrutiny of Fox is justified by Fox's relationship with Trump and the network's impact on the "ecosystem" of conservative media outlets. "Fox influences the president of the United States in a way not seen by any other network," he said. "Fox affects society in more ways than it did even three years ago. ... If you only looked at CNN, MSNBC or CBS and you didn't acknowledge Fox's influence on the president, then you'd be missing the story."

He added that the "reality is Fox's ratings make it a skyscraper next to [conservative media]. Fox's shadow is enormous."

In fact, Fox's average daily rating (1.55 million viewers) was more than twice CNN's (700,000) throughout the day, according to Nielsen figures for February. CNN is in third place among cable news networks; MSNBC (with a daily average of 989,000) ranks second.

But USC's Kahn said that MSNBC—whose prime-time schedule is chockablock with overtly liberal opinion—is a less valuable target for Fox than CNN.

"CNN doesn't cop to being lefty," he said. "By beating up on CNN, you get to smear the entire mainstream media. It allows [conservative viewers] to doubt everything the mainstream media reports."

Print Citations

CMS: Fahri, Paul. "CNN vs. Fox: Why These Two Cable Networks Can't Stop Talking about Each Other." In *The Reference Shelf: Propaganda & Misinformation*, edited by Annette Calzone, 60–62. Amenia, NY: Grey House Publishing, 2020.

MLA: Fahri, Paul. "CNN vs. Fox: Why These Two Cable Networks Can't Stop Talking about Each Other." *The Reference Shelf: Propaganda & Misinformation*, edited by Annette Calzone, Grey House Publishing, 2020, pp. 60–62.

APA: Fahri, P. (2020). CNN vs. Fox: Why these two cable networks can't stop talking about teach other. In Annette Calzone (Ed.), *The reference shelf: Propaganda & misinformation* (pp. 60–62) Amenia, NY: Grey House Publishing.

Social Media Struggles to Counter Coronavirus Misinformation

By Emily Birnbaum and Chris Mills Rodrigo
The Hill, February 1, 2020

The world's top social media platforms are trying to push users toward fact-driven and reputable sources as sensationalist misinformation about the deadly coronavirus spreads online.

But wild conspiracy theories and misleading advice about the coronavirus, which has infected almost 10,000 people in China so far, are continuing to spread largely unabated on platforms like Instagram, Twitter, TikTok and other networks with billions of users overall.

And U.S. lawmakers, many of whom are working to publicize trustworthy information about the little-understood health epidemic, say they want the platforms to do more to stave off the wave of misinformation.

"These lies can cause immediate and tangible harm to people, and the platforms must act to stop them from spreading," House Energy and Commerce Committee Chairman Frank Pallone Jr. (D-N.J.) said in a statement to *The Hill*.

"It's critical that Americans receive verified, trustworthy information about the coronavirus and heed the advice of our country's public health officials as we learn more about its potential impact here at home," Pallone said.

Rep. Debbie Dingell (D-Mich.), a member of the Energy and Commerce subcommittee focused on health, sent a letter Friday to the heads of Facebook, Twitter, YouTube and TikTok pressing them to do more to curb coronavirus disinformation.

"During a global health emergency, it is vital to the public interest that individuals have access to timely and accurate information," she wrote.

"As expert's knowledge and understanding about this virus grows, so too will the necessity of accurate and reliable information for the world," Dingell added. "As global companies, a rampant spread of inaccurate information will have a decidedly negative impact on the response efforts to contain and mitigate this global health emergency."

She posed a series of questions to the companies about how they are working to kneecap the spread of falsehoods and how closely they are working with leading health bodies like the Centers for Disease Control and Prevention (CDC) and the World Health Organization (WHO).

From *The Hill*, February 1 © 2020. Reprinted with permission. All rights reserved.

The WHO on Thursday declared a public health emergency of international concern over the outbreak of coronavirus, upping the ante for the platforms as they grapple with how much responsibility to assume over the false claims and hysteria emanating from their users.

So far, experts who spoke to *The Hill* said they are monitoring several specific strains of misinformation, including conspiracy theories that the U.S. or Chinese government created the virus, false rumors linking billionaire philanthropist Bill Gates to the disease, and a debunked narrative that the coronavirus was caused by Chinese people drinking "bat soup." Many of the falsehoods and narratives that gained traction this week have racist undertones, implying the eating habits of Chinese people are to blame for the outbreak.

Dr. Arthur Caplan, the founding head of the division of medical ethics at New York University's School of Medicine, told The Hill that much of the rhetoric he has come across online has a "xenophobic" tone.

The social media giants—Twitter, Facebook and Google—have chosen to fight the spread of coronavirus-related misinformation in part by promoting authoritative sources. When a user searches "coronavirus" on Twitter, for instance, they are met with a banner that reads "know the facts," with a link to the CDC's summary page on the illness.

"We've launched a new dedicated search prompt to ensure that when you come to the service for information about the #coronavirus, you're met with credible, authoritative information first," Twitter wrote in a blog post on Wednesday.

Facebook, meanwhile, announced Thursday that it will surface "educational pop-up[s] with credible information" when users search for information related to the virus based on guidance from the WHO.

As of Friday, searching "coronavirus" on Facebook and viewing the coronavirus hashtag on Instagram did not trigger any pop ups or direct users to credible information. An official for Facebook told *The Hill* that it will roll out the feature "in the coming days."

Google on Thursday announced it is partnering with the WHO to pin "news, safety tips, information and resources from the WHO website" at the top of its powerful search page when users look for coronavirus-related information.

"It's time for facts, not fear," tweeted Tedros Adhanom Ghebreyesus, the director-general of the WHO. "We appreciate Google, Facebook, Tencent-Global, TikTok and Twitter's efforts to combat misinformation and rumors on #2019nCoV & direct users to reliable sources."

The platforms are still in the early stages of grappling with a fast-moving situation, and misinformation was continuing to break through.

"We ask all digital companies to step up and help the world beat this outbreak," he added.

Some experts have raised concerns that the nature of social media itself makes misinformation spread quickly during disease outbreaks.

"Social media rewards engagement," Brendan Nyhan, a government professor at Dartmouth College, told *The Hill*. "People peruse news feeds and interact with content that grabs our attention. And, as human beings, we're highly attentive to threats and negative information."

TikTok, a mega-popular social media app built around short videos, has appended a label warning users to "verify facts using trusted sources, including the WHO" when they search for terms related to the virus.

But the approach hasn't stopped TikTok's young user base from making sometimes-misleading jokes about the outbreak. One of the top posts on TikTok's #coronavirus page, which had garnered more than 157,000 likes by Friday evening, features a screenshot of an article that says "coronavirus is spread through the EYES making surgical masks useless."

"Coronavirus is turning into something else," the post reads.

"While we encourage our users to have respectful conversations about the subjects that matter to them, we remove deliberate attempts to misrepresent authoritative sources of news," a TikTok official said.

Several of the platforms are opting to go further than just lifting up factual sources—they're vowing to take down egregious instances of misinformation, an uphill battle on platforms like Facebook and TikTok that boast enormous user bases.

Facebook said it will start removing posts containing misinformation about the outbreak, a rare move for a company which normally chooses to deprioritize false posts instead.

And TikTok, which recently unveiled a new policy against misinformation in general, has already received criticism for hosting videos with hundreds of thousands of views touting baseless claims about the virus.

"If TikTok is going to have a policy like this, it's important that they enforce it," Media Matters researcher Alex Kaplan told *The Hill*.

The platforms are still in the early stages of grappling with a fast-moving situation, and misinformation was continuing to break through the deluge on Friday evening.

The first and third most popular posts on Facebook-owned Instagram related to the coronavirus in the last week, according to social media metric tracker Crowdtangle, include photos and videos of animals and of people eating "bat soup," putting the blame for the disease on Chinese people with debunked claims.

NBC News first reported on the posts, which have been viewed nearly 60 million times combined.

While the top posts directly mentioning coronavirus on Facebook come from reputable news sources, various posts with dog whistles and conspiracy theories—like "bat soup" or Chinese people not practicing proper hygiene—have been shared thousands of times.

"This coronavirus is making me wonder if I should serve my annual Super Bowl bat soup this year," tweeted right-wing commentator Ann Coulter to an audience of 2.2 million followers.

The CDC has only confirmed six cases in the U.S. so far, but as the coronavirus spreads, experts anticipate the misinformation will grow and take on unexpected forms.

Lawmakers said they are watching how the platforms handle the crisis.

"Much like this virus, misinformation, willful or benign in nature, will continue to spread until measures are taken to limit exposure and treat symptoms," Dingell wrote on Friday. "I urge you to take serious action in addressing this issue and appreciate your attention to this matter."

Print Citations

CMS: Birnbaum, Emily, and Chris Mills Rodrigo. "Social Media Struggles to Counter Coronavirus Misinformation." In *The Reference Shelf: Propaganda & Misinformation*, edited by Annette Calzone, 63–66. Amenia, NY: Grey House Publishing, 2020.

MLA: Birnbaum, Emily, and Chris Mills Rodrigo. "Social Media Struggles to Counter Coronavirus Misinformation." *The Reference Shelf: Propaganda & Misinformation,* edited by Annette Calzone, Grey House Publishing, 2020, pp. 63–66.

APA: Birnbaum, E., & Mills Rodrigo, C. (2020). Social media struggles to counter coronavirus misinformation. In Annette Calzone (Ed.), *The reference shelf: Propaganda & misinformation* (pp. 63–66). Amenia, NY: Grey House Publishing.

Clinton Backer at Facebook Debunks Clinton Claims

By James Freeman
The Wall Street Journal, January 7, 2020

Former presidential candidate Hillary Clinton and politicians like Rep. Adam Schiff (D., Calif.) may cling to the discredited belief that Donald Trump and Russia used social media to rig the 2016 election. But liberals in a position to know still aren't buying it.

The *New York Times* reports that it has obtained a recent internal memorandum from senior Facebook executive Andrew Bosworth. According to the text of the memo published by the Times, Mr. Bosworth throws cold water on a favorite conspiracy theory of the political left:

> So was Facebook responsible for Donald Trump getting elected? I think the answer is yes, but not for the reasons anyone thinks. He didn't get elected because of Russia or misinformation or Cambridge Analytica. He got elected because he ran the single best digital ad campaign I've ever seen from any advertiser. Period.

Cambridge Analytica was a political consulting firm and Trump campaign vendor which was accused of using personal data about Facebook users without their knowledge. The Federal Trade Commission recently settled a case with some of those involved, who agreed to destroy the data they collected and be honest with users in the future about data collection. The memo from Facebook's Mr. Bosworth continues:

> To be clear, I'm no fan of Trump. I donated the max to Hillary. After his election I wrote a post about Trump supporters that I'm told caused colleagues who had supported him to feel unsafe around me (I regret that post and deleted shortly after).
>
> But [Trump campaign digital media chief Brad Parscale] and Trump just did unbelievable work. They weren't running misinformation or hoaxes. They weren't microtargeting or saying different things to different people. They just used the tools we had to show the right creative to each person. The use of custom audiences, video, ecommerce, and fresh creative remains the high water mark of digital ad campaigns in my opinion.

"Creative" is a noun in the marketing world, used to describe the particular advertisements designed to deliver messages. Mr. Bosworth fears that Team Trump is still really good at creating them and therefore he fears that Mr. Trump may win again.

> "So was Facebook responsible for Donald Trump getting elected? I think the answer is yes, but not for the reasons anyone thinks."

"As a committed liberal I find myself desperately wanting to pull any lever at my disposal to avoid the same result. So what stays my hand?," asks Mr. Bosworth. He writes, "I find myself thinking of the Lord of the Rings at this moment. Specifically when Frodo offers the ring to Galadrial and she imagines using the power righteously, at first, but knows it will eventually corrupt her. As tempting as it is to use the tools available to us to change the outcome, I am confident we must never do that or we will become that which we fear."

This column is skeptical that Facebook decides the outcomes of U.S. elections, but applauds Mr. Bosworth's effort to encourage his Silicon Valley colleagues to act with integrity. Also encouraging is that he's just the latest Valley resident to attempt to provide a reality check to anti-Trump partisans.

Readers may recall Google CEO Sundar Pichai's December, 2018 visit to the House Judiciary committee. That's when Chairman Jerry Nadler (D., N.Y.) asked if Google knew "the full extent to which its online platforms were exploited by Russian actors in the election two years ago".

Mr. Pichai reported that after a thorough investigation his company had discovered "two main ad accounts linked to Russia" which had spent on Google advertising a grand total of... $4,700. This amounted to roughly 1/234,000th of what Mrs. Clinton spent on advertising during the 2016 campaign.

Meanwhile over at Facebook, the number seems to have been larger but still tiny in comparison to overall political advertising. Writes Mr. Bosworth:

> $100,000 in ads on Facebook can be a powerful tool but it can't buy you an American election, especially when the candidates themselves are putting up several orders of magnitude more money on the same platform (not to mention other platforms).
>
> Instead, the Russians worked to exploit existing divisions in the American public for example by hosting Black Lives Matter and Blue Lives Matter protest events in the same city on the same day. The people who shows (sic) up to those events were real even if the event coordinator was not. Likewise the groups of Americans being fed partisan content was real even if those feeding them were not. The organic reach they managed sounds very big in absolute terms and unfortunately humans are bad at contextualizing big numbers. Whatever reach they managed represents an infinitesimal fraction of the overall content people saw in the same period of time and certainly over the course of an election across all media.

Print Citations

CMS: Freeman, James. "Clinton Backer at Facebook Debunks Clinton Claims." In *The Reference Shelf: Propaganda & Misinformation,* edited by Annette Calzone, 67–69. Amenia, NY: Grey House Publishing, 2020.

MLA: Freeman, James. "Clinton Backer at Facebook Debunks Clinton Claims." *The Reference Shelf: Propaganda & Misinformation,* edited by Annette Calzone, Grey House Publishing, 2020, pp. 67–69.

APA: Freeman, James. (2020). Clinton backer at Facebook debunks Clinton claims. In Annette Calzone (Ed.), *The reference shelf: Propaganda & misinformation* (pp. 67–69). Amenia, NY: Grey House Publishing.

The Propagandist and the Censor

By Andrew Stuttaford
National Review, June 21, 2018

Fake news is a problem; so are the likely remedies

In 1936, Oswald Mosley, Britain's Mussolini-in-waiting, released a question-and-answer book that explained what a Fascist Blighty might look like. Freedom of the press? Fleet Street would "not be free to tell lies."

Some 80 years on, German chancellor Angela Merkel, infuriated by criticism of her immigration policy (and, rather less so, by Russian disinformation), endorsed a new law, the catchily named *Netzwerkdurchsetzungsgesetz*, under which social-media companies must take down posts that constitute "manifestly unlawful . . . hate speech" and "fake news" from their sites within 24 hours of a complaint. Failure to do so can result in a fine of up to 50 million euros. Fake news is criminally fake if it amounts, say, to an insult, malicious gossip, or defamation—including defamation of a religion or ideology—sufficiently serious to contravene German law.

Combine the potential size of the fine with offenses that lend themselves to flexible interpretation (much like that "manifestly") and it's easy to see that Berlin intended to scare social-media companies into an approach to censorship that goes far further than the letter of the law, a ploy that appears to be working. The government wanted to shut down talk that was not necessarily illegal but—after Merkel flung open her country's doors in the summer of 2015 — uncomfortably unorthodox. The mainstream media had enthusiastically echoed the chancellor's *Willkommenskultur* narrative of kindly Germans cheerfully greeting the migrants, but establishment unanimity was not enough for the instinctively authoritarian Merkel. Her less "welcoming" compatriots had found an audience on social media. That would not do.

Others have taken note. Singapore, no haven of free speech, is taking aim at "deliberate online falsehoods." Malaysia has criminalized "news, information, data and reports which is or are wholly or partly false." (Intent seems to be irrelevant.) Russian lawmakers, immune as usual to irony, have proposed their own laws against fake news.

Brussels is on the case—of course it is—urging social-media companies to sign up for a voluntary code of conduct to combat what the European Commission refers to as "verifiably false or misleading information . . . [that is] created, presented and disseminated for economic gain or to intentionally deceive the public, and [that] may cause public harm." That word "verifiably" has to do a great deal of heavy lifting, and, as for "misleading," well . . .

Some of Brussels's proposals, such as more transparency about sponsored commentary, are sensible. Others could conceivably reflect an even more cynical view of the European public's credulousness than that displayed by the Kremlin. It takes only an elementary understanding of how politics works to grasp that the call for EU member-states "to scale up their support of quality journalism" will be used to justify lucrative handouts for journalism that toes the party line.

Another recommendation, "enhancing media literacy," isn't an invitation to corruption, but if the enhancement is to be anything more than a lesson or two in applied skepticism (no bad thing), instruction on how to "read" media will just as likely—thank you, Michel Foucault—enable fake news as do the opposite. Equally, turning to "an independent European network of fact-checkers" is a less-than-reassuring idea: Fact-checkers have all too frequently shown themselves prone to bias. *Quis custodiet ipsos custodes?* was a good question 2,000 years ago, and it's a good question now, but it's not one that worries many of those leading the charge against fake news.

Meanwhile, France's president, Emmanuel Macron, is pushing a law to battle fake news that includes allowing politicians to complain to a judge about the spreading of supposedly false information online during or shortly before an election. The judge has 48 hours to respond and can, under certain circumstances, block the offending item, a power that—call me a cynic—could, just possibly, be abused. Fake news, Macron told the U.S. Congress in April, is a "virus," an attack on the spirit of democracy: "Without reason, without truth, there is no real democracy, because democracy is about true choices and rational decisions." That prettily complimentary, pretty delusional description (take your pick) leaves open the question as to who is to decide what is true—*Quis custodiet?* again—and where reason is to be found. The madness of crowds is a perennial risk, but a ruling caste convinced that it has all the answers can be more harmful still.

Macron's words contained the seed of the suggestion that if the electorate votes on a basis its betters find to be flawed, the result is not "really" democratic. To follow that logic through, should such a result be allowed to stand? Macron, it should be remembered, is one of those now steering the EU, an institution with a tradition of either condemning or ignoring electorates that have voted the "wrong" way, or, for that matter, nudging them back to the polling booth for a do-over.

There is no reason for any complacency here in America. The First Amendment's protections have never been absolute. While they have been extended a long way, that process can go into reverse. When intellectual fashions change, judicial precedent can be more elastic than is often assumed. And intellectual fashions have changed. The assault on free speech has long since burst out of the academy and, somewhat paradoxically, has been given extra heft by the ubiquity and indispensability of social media, private terrain where the First Amendment has very little application.

On Facebook, on Twitter, and elsewhere, the apparatchiks of Silicon Valley's new class rule on the limits of free expression, a power they may well eventually have to share—not necessarily unhappily—with politicians who are no fonder of the wrong sort of talk than they are. Fake news could well give Washington a pretext to join in the effort to tame social-media speech. Always on the lookout for another excuse for 2016, Hillary Clinton has described fake news as a "danger that must be addressed," and Senator Dianne Feinstein (D., Calif.) told social-media companies last fall that if they didn't sort out the problem, "we will."

> **In an age when the boundaries between reporting and opinion in newspapers, television, and radio have faded, disinformation is, to put it mildly, not confined to games played within the social-media feeds of the unwary.**

That's not a threat to take lightly. Social media are now an essential part of the public square. To the extent that social-media comments are policed, the approach taken—arbitrary, opaque, and (at least to a degree) biased—is, given the market power of the social-media giants, disturbing. But the alternatives are worse. What the market gives, the market can take away. What the state takes, it generally keeps. Giving the government the power directly (or indirectly, via proxies) to determine what social-media content is true—and, in some cases, to suppress that which it has decided is false—would be a menace to free speech too obvious to need explaining.

"Regular" media meanwhile would be untouched, protected, as they should be, by the First Amendment. They would also be left to promote their takes (far from monolithic, but still) on events with fewer challenges than they now face, a windfall that would be as unhealthy as it is undeserved. The First Amendment is not a guarantor of objectivity. In an age when the boundaries between reporting and opinion in newspapers, television, and radio have faded, disinformation is, to put it mildly, not confined to games played within the social-media feeds of the unwary.

When Donald Trump describes this more respectably sourced disinformation—and anything else he considers (or pretends to consider) to be disinformation—as "fake news," he is sending a message that works on several levels. Hijacking a term that was already resonating with the public is not only a clever way of rebottling an old whine—politicians are forever grumbling about the press—but a way of making it stronger. It is not just an attack on the story, but on its source—and on what's left of its authority. CNN? No better than Facebook.

Broadening the definition of fake news is also a subtle undermining of the argument that Trump owes his presidency to media manipulation. If anything, it carries with it the hint that he was elected despite fake news, not because of it. It may also, one day, provide a way for either Left or Right to begin the erosion of the First Amendment protections the press now enjoys. According to a Harvard-Harris poll from May of last year, two-thirds of voters believe that the mainstream media publish fake news, and that survey was by no means an outlier.

Treating the partisan dishonesty of the news media and the real (so to speak) "fake news" as, basically, the same also risks overlooking the genuine hazard that the latter may represent. For now (but only for now) its most potentially dangerous manifestation comes from the dezinformatsiya orchestrated by a Kremlin once again appreciative of how destabilizing disinformation can be—and clearly aware of how neatly such disinformation can be slipped into social media. How much influence Russian fake news (a handy scapegoat for disconcerting electoral outcomes) has really had so far can be debated, but there is no doubt that the sophistication of its targeting and the quality of its material is going to improve rapidly. The day that a computer-generated Trump makes a fake but (to the right audience) truly incendiary speech mocking, perhaps, the prophet Mohammed is not far away.

The prospect is terrifying. But so is one element in the likely response: the unleashing of censors to block this, ban that, and, presumably, fight a long Pac-Man struggle with bots as the prey. But this cyberwar would probably do more damage to what's left of the West's free speech than to the lies of our opponents. Fake news can be suppressed or, infinitely better, rebutted, but, as it speeds through the Web, it can travel many times around the world before the truth has time to boot up.

The Gutenberg galaxy is expanding exponentially, generating unprecedented amounts of information—true, false, and everything in between. To the extent we can trust it—Quis custodiet?—technology may help identify what is reliable and what is not (I met the other day with the CEO of a start-up using artificial intelligence to rate the reliability of those posting on social media), but technology will have to contend with psychology. Our quest for objectivity is less diligent than we like to think. We are all too ready to collaborate in our own deception. Some stories are too good not to believe, some stories are too satisfying to unpack (how many birthers were there again?), some gossip is too good not to pass on, and confirmation bias remains as seductive and reassuring as it ever was.

Skepticism will help, but too much of it—easy enough in an era when old media are regarded with suspicion and new media are difficult to process, let alone trust—can lead to a perverse gullibility. In a 1974 interview, Hannah Arendt observed that "a people that no longer can believe anything . . . is deprived not only of its capacity to act but also of its capacity to think and to judge. And with such a people you can then do what you please."

Fake news is a challenge that the West must get right. So far, there's little reason to expect that it will.

Print Citations

CMS: Stuttaford, Andrew. "The Propagandist and the Censor." In *The Reference Shelf: Propaganda & Misinformation,* edited by Annette Calzone, 70–73. Amenia, NY: Grey House Publishing, 2020.

MLA: Stuttaford, Andrew. "The Propagandist and the Censor." *The Reference Shelf: Propaganda & Misinformation,* edited by Annette Calzone, Grey House Publishing, 2020, pp. 70–73.

APA: Stuttaford, A. (2020). The propagandist and the censor. In Annette Calzone (Ed.), *The reference shelf: Propaganda & misinformation* (pp. 70–73). Amenia, NY: Grey House Publishing.

3
The Effects of Propaganda

The 9/11 Truth movement is an ongoing conspiracy theory linking the U.S. government to the bombings at the World Trade Center and the Pentagon in 2001. By Damon DAmato, via Wikimedia.

The Subtle Influence of Misinformation

You Can't Fool Me

Is our increasing exposure to news, both legitimate and fake, making us more susceptible to propaganda and misinformation? Researchers say that belief in conspiracy theories may be on the rise. What was once the province of an extreme fringe of society has become more mainstream. The FBI considers conspiracy theories a likely cause for criminal and often violent acts, such as the Pizzagate incident, when a man carried a gun into a Washington, D.C., pizza restaurant after falling prey to a conspiracy theory about Hillary Clinton operating a child sex ring.[1]

Such a claim might seem so far-fetched that most of us would consider ourselves free from the danger of believing or being influenced by it. However, a recent study indicates that belief in conspiracy theories is linked to a sense of control. The researchers found that people's sense of control over their lives and environment can be manipulated, increasing their vulnerability to believing far-fetched claims.[2]

Historian Richard Hofstadter discussed a similar phenomenon in a *Harper's* article in 1964:

> In American experience, ethnic and religious conflict have plainly been a major focus for militant and suspicious minds of this sort, but class conflicts also can mobilize such energies. Perhaps the central situation conducive to the diffusion of the paranoid tendency is a confrontation of opposed interests which are (or are felt to be) totally irreconcilable, and thus by nature not susceptible to the normal political processes of bargain and compromise. The situation becomes worse when the representatives of a particular social interest—perhaps because of the very unrealistic and unrealizable nature of its demands—are shut out of the political process. Having no access to political bargaining or the making of decisions, they find their original conception that the world of power is sinister and malicious fully confirmed. They see only the consequences of power—and this through distorting lenses—and have no chance to observe its actual machinery. A distinguished historian has said that one of the most valuable things about history is that it teaches us how things do not happen. It is precisely this kind of awareness that the paranoid fails to develop.

Hofstadter could be speaking about our current polarized environment. He goes on to discuss how paranoia manifests in politics: "The paranoid spokesman sees the fate of conspiracy in apocalyptic terms—he traffics in the birth and death of whole worlds, whole political orders, whole systems of human values. He is always manning the barricades of civilization. He constantly lives at a turning point."[3]

When people in authority espouse conspiracy theories, it lends credibility to them. Either because he believes what he says or for political reasons, President Trump, prominently and often, disperses questionable information. It's estimated that he has used his personal Twitter account over 100 times to deny climate change alone. He has also, among many other things, suggested that former president Bill Clinton is connected to the death of financier Jeffrey Epstein, who was charged with sex trafficking of minors, and that Clinton was Epstein's "very good friend." Says Harvard University's Joseph Vitriol, "The chief conspiratorialist of the last 10 years is now the President of the United States.... Because of that, what we might be seeing is increased influence and pervasiveness of these beliefs."[4]

Is There Anybody Out There?

There has been a lot of recent talk about the phenomenon of echo chambers, the theory that people are only exposed to or look for information sources that agree with their personal views. If social media algorithms direct you only to sources you regularly visit by tracking your preferences, does this increase polarization? Views of the echo chamber effect vary. Researchers Elizabeth Dubois and Grant Blank, who conducted a study on media consumption habits, believe it is exaggerated. Dubois and Blank concluded that most people get their news from a variety of sources and are aware that fact-checking is a necessity. While admitting that platforms such as Facebook and Twitter could create information environments that confirm existing beliefs, they report that participants do not get all of their political information from such environments.[5]

A recent study by the University of Pennsylvania's Annenberg School for Communication suggests that, contrary to conventional thinking, echo chambers may actually be helpful, as they represent a collective intelligence that can increase belief accuracy. According to UP's Damon Centola:

> We showed that when Democrats and Republicans interact with each other within properly designed social media networks, it can eliminate polarization and improve both groups' understanding of contentious issues such as climate change.... Remarkably, our new findings show that properly designed social media networks can even lead to improved understanding of contentious topics within echo chambers.[6]

However, many still believe that echo chambers are a dangerous part of our media environment. David Robert Grimes writes in *The Guardian*:

> What the internet has done is facilitate the emergence of alternative news sites. And here, factual accuracy can no longer be taken for granted. Untethered from journalistic ethics, some outlets thrive by telling their audience precisely what they want to hear. And social media allows the rapid growth and spread of everything from the ludicrous Pizzagate conspiracy theory to rampant climate-change denial—and exists across the political spectrum.

> This proliferation of urban myths and conspiracies would perhaps be laughable if it weren't so uniquely dangerous. An estimated 61% of millennials garner news primarily through social media. But in the process, we trigger algorithms that curate our feeds. These cherry-pick things with which we are likely to agree and jettison information that does not appear to fit our preferences—often at the cost of accuracy and balance.[7]

On the broader subject of fake news, University of Georgia Associate Professor Cas Mudde sees the fake news epidemic as a "distraction" from "the ever more commercial, profit-seeking media seeking clicks and eyeballs at the expense of nuance, depth and on-the-ground reporting." He points to evidence that the group most affected by fake news is the far-right, a relative minority. And even those who visit fake news sites visit mainstream sites as well. Mudde sees the influence of the Russian electoral interference campaign as overrated, and encourages the media to "stop fetishizing elite access and news scoops."[8]

Another interesting facet to the misinformation debate is the proliferation of satirical fake news programs like *The Daily Show*. Recent studies indicate that these add to the confusion in our media environment by blurring the line between real and fake news programs. These programs have a real impact on viewers, tending to reinforce existing political beliefs and increase or decrease a sense of political agency. People with little interest in politics also tend to gravitate toward satirical news rather than real news sources.[9]

Subtle Influencing

Living with constant exposure to a concentrated propaganda campaign can arguably make us blind to what's going on around us. Brunhilde Pomsel—who worked for Joseph Goebbels finagling Nazi reports to reflect less fallen German soldiers and more German women raped by the Red Army—is an extreme example. She described her work as "just another job," and adamantly maintained that she and her coworkers were not aware of the atrocities going on in concentration camps. In an interview with *Guardian* reporter Kate Connolly Pomsel stated:

> I know no one ever believes us nowadays—everyone thinks we knew everything. We knew nothing, it was all kept well secret.

When asked if she thought she was being naïve about the "relocation" of Jews, including a friend of hers, Eva, she said:

> We believed it—we swallowed it—it seemed entirely plausible."[10]

The influence of fake news can be more subtle than we think. *Atlantic* reporter McKay Coppins found that his media savvy did not save him from confusion when he decided to get a glimpse inside the world of Donald Trump supporters before the 2020 elections. He created a Facebook account and clicked "Like" on Trump's reelection campaign pages, which in turn led him to feeds for Ann Coulter and Fox and Trump fan pages. After joining a few private MAGA groups at the time of the impeachment proceedings, Coppins said of his experience:

The story that unfurled in my Facebook feed over the next several weeks was, at times, disorienting. There were days when I would watch, live on TV, an impeachment hearing filled with damning testimony about the president's conduct, only to look at my phone later and find a slickly edited video—served up by the Trump campaign—that used out-of-context clips to recast the same testimony as an exoneration. Wait, I caught myself wondering more than once, is that what happened today?

. . .

I was surprised by the effect it had on me. I'd assumed that my skepticism and media literacy would inoculate me against such distortions. But I soon found myself reflexively questioning every headline. It wasn't that I believed Trump and his boosters were telling the truth. It was that, in this state of heightened suspicion, truth itself—about Ukraine, impeachment, or anything else—felt more and more difficult to locate. With each swipe, the notion of observable reality drifted further out of reach.[11]

Even armed with the knowledge that we are surrounded by misinformation, it is difficult not to be affected by it. As Dominik Stecula writes in a recent *Conversation* article:

> The real impact of the growing interest in fake news has been the realization that the public might not be well-equipped to separate quality information from false information. In fact, a majority of Americans are confident that they can spot fake news. When *Buzzfeed* surveyed American high schoolers, they too were confident they could spot, and ignore, fake news online. The reality, however, is that it might be more difficult than people think.[12]

Works Used

Chan, Melissa. "Conspiracy Theories Might Sound Crazy, But Here's Why Experts Say We Can No Longer Ignore Them." *Time*. Aug 15, 2019. https://time.com/5541411/conspiracy-theories-domestic-terrorism/.

Connolly, Kate. "Joseph Goebbel's 105-Year-Old Secretary: 'No One Believes Me Now, But I Knew Nothing." *The Guardian*. Aug 15, 2016. https://www.theguardian.com/world/2016/aug/15/brunhilde-pomsel-nazi-joseph-goebbels-propaganda-machine.

Coppins, McKay. "The Billion Dollar Disinformation Campaign to Reelect the President." *The Atlantic*. Mar 2020. https://www.theatlantic.com/magazine/archive/2020/03/the-2020-disinformation-war/605530/.

Dubois, Elizabeth, and Grant Blank. "The Myth of the Echo Chamber." *The Conversation*. Mar 8, 2018. https://theconversation.com/the-myth-of-the-echo-chamber-92544.

"Echo Chambers May Not Be as Dangerous as You Think, New Study Finds." *Science Daily*. May 13, 2019. https://www.sciencedaily.com/releases/2019/05/190513155629.htm.

Fried, Carla. "The Malleability of Who Falls for Conspiracy Theories." *UCLA Anderson Review*. Mar 6, 2019. https://www.anderson.ucla.edu/faculty-and-research/anderson-review/prevention-promotion.

Grimes, David Robert. "Echo Chambers Are Dangerous—We Must Try to Break Free of Our Online Bubbles." *The Guardian*. Dec 4, 2017. https://www.theguardian.com/science/blog/2017/dec/04/echo-chambers-are-dangerous-we-must-try-to-break-free-of-our-online-bubbles.

Hofstadter, Richard. "The Paranoid Style in American Politics," *Harper's Magazine*. Nov 1964. https://harpers.org/archive/1964/11/the-paranoid-style-in-american-politics/.

Mudde, Cas. "Why the Hysteria around the 'Fake News Epidemic' Is a Distraction." *The Guardian*. Feb 7, 2018. https://www.theguardian.com/commentisfree/2018/feb/07/hysteria-fake-news-epidemic-distraction.

"Not Just Funny: Satirical News Has Serious Political Effects." *Science Daily*. Jan 23, 2017. https://www.sciencedaily.com/releases/2017/01/170123115741.htm.

Stecula, Dominik. "The Real Consequences of Fake News." *The Conversation*. July 26, 2017. http://theconversation.com/the-real-consequences-of-fake-news-81179.

Notes

1. Chan, "Conspiracy Theories Might Sound Crazy, But Here's Why Experts Say We Can No Longer Ignore Them."
2. Fried, "The Malleability of Who Falls for Conspiracy Theories."
3. Hofstadter, "The Paranoid Style in American Politics."
4. Chan, "Conspiracy Theories Might Sound Crazy."
5. Dubois and Blank, "The Myth of the Echo Chamber."
6. "Echo Chambers May Not Be as Dangerous as You Think, New Study Finds," *Science Daily*.
7. Grimes, "Echo Chambers Are Dangerous—We Must Try to Break Free of Our Online Bubbles."
8. Mudde, "Why the Hysteria around the 'Fake News Epidemic' Is a Distraction."
9. "Not Just Funny: Satirical News Has Serious Political Effects."
10. Connolly, "Joseph Goebbels' 105-Year-Old Secretary: 'No One Believes Me Now.'"
11. Coppins, "The Billion-Dollar Disinformation Campaign to Reelect the President."
12. Stecula, "The Real Consequences of Fake News."

Why Do People Fall for Fake News?

By Gordon Pennycook and David Rand
The New York Times, January 19, 2019

What makes people susceptible to fake news and other forms of strategic misinformation? And what, if anything, can be done about it?

These questions have become more urgent in recent years, not least because of revelations about the Russian campaign to influence the 2016 United States presidential election by disseminating propaganda through social media platforms. In general, our political culture seems to be increasingly populated by people who espouse outlandish or demonstrably false claims that often align with their political ideology.

The good news is that psychologists and other social scientists are working hard to understand what prevents people from seeing through propaganda. The bad news is that there is not yet a consensus on the answer. Much of the debate among researchers falls into two opposing camps. One group claims that our ability to reason is hijacked by our partisan convictions: that is, we're prone to rationalization. The other group—to which the two of us belong—claims that the problem is that we often fail to exercise our critical faculties: that is, we're mentally lazy.

However, recent research suggests a silver lining to the dispute: Both camps appear to be capturing an aspect of the problem. Once we understand how much of the problem is a result of rationalization and how much a result of laziness, and as we learn more about which factor plays a role in what types of situations, we'll be better able to design policy solutions to help combat the problem.

The rationalization camp, which has gained considerable prominence in recent years, is built around a set of theories contending that when it comes to politically charged issues, people use their intellectual abilities to persuade themselves to believe what they want to be true rather than attempting to actually discover the truth. According to this view, political passions essentially make people unreasonable, even—indeed, especially—if they tend to be good at reasoning in other contexts. (Roughly: The smarter you are, the better you are at rationalizing.)

Some of the most striking evidence used to support this position comes from an influential 2012 study in which the law professor Dan Kahan and his colleagues found that the degree of political polarization on the issue of climate change was greater among people who scored higher on measures of science literary and numerical ability than it was among those who scored lower on these tests. Apparently, more "analytical" Democrats were better able to convince themselves that climate change was a problem, while more "analytical" Republicans were better

---

From *The New York Times*, January 19 © 2019. Reprinted with permission. All rights reserved.

able to convince themselves that climate change was not a problem. Professor Kahan has found similar results in, for example, studies about gun control in which he experimentally manipulated the partisan slant of information that participants were asked to assess.

The implications here are profound: Reasoning can exacerbate the problem, not provide the solution, when it comes to partisan disputes over facts. Further evidence cited in support of this of argument comes from a 2010 study by the political scientists Brendan Nyhan and Jason Reifler, who found that appending corrections to misleading claims in news articles can sometimes backfire: Not only did corrections fail to reduce misperceptions, but they also sometimes increased them. It seemed as if people who were ideologically inclined to believe a given falsehood worked so hard to come up with reasons that the correction was wrong that they came to believe the falsehood even more strongly.

> **People who engaged in more reflective reasoning were better at telling true from false, regardless of whether the headlines aligned with their political views.**

But this "rationalization" account, though compelling in some contexts, does not strike us as the most natural or most common explanation of the human weakness for misinformation. We believe that people often just don't think critically enough about the information they encounter.

A great deal of research in cognitive psychology has shown that a little bit of reasoning goes a long way toward forming accurate beliefs. For example, people who think more analytically (those who are more likely to exercise their analytic skills and not just trust their "gut" response) are less superstitious, less likely to believe in conspiracy theories and less receptive to seemingly profound but actually empty assertions (like "Wholeness quiets infinite phenomena"). This body of evidence suggests that the main factor explaining the acceptance of fake news could be cognitive laziness, especially in the context of social media, where news items are often skimmed or merely glanced at.

To test this possibility, we recently ran a set of studies in which participants of various political persuasions indicated whether they believed a series of news stories. We showed them real headlines taken from social media, some of which were true and some of which were false. We gauged whether our participants would engage in reasoning or "go with their gut" by having them complete something called the cognitive reflection test, a test widely used in psychology and behavioral economics. It consists of questions with intuitively compelling but incorrect answers, which can be easily shown to be wrong with a modicum of reasoning. (For example: "If you're running a race and you pass the person in second place, what place are you in?" If you're not thinking you might say "first place," when of course the answer is second place.)

We found that people who engaged in more reflective reasoning were better at telling true from false, regardless of whether the headlines aligned with their political views. (We controlled for demographic facts such as level of education as well as political leaning.) In follow-up studies yet to be published, we have shown that this finding was replicated using a pool of participants that was nationally representative with respect to age, gender, ethnicity and region of residence, and that it applies not just to the ability to discern true claims from false ones but also to the ability to identify excessively partisan coverage of true events.

Our results strongly suggest that somehow cultivating or promoting our reasoning abilities should be part of the solution to the kinds of partisan misinformation that circulate on social media. And other new research provides evidence that even in highly political contexts, people are not as irrational as the rationalization camp contends. Recent studies have shown, for instance, that correcting partisan misperceptions does not backfire most of the time—contrary to the results of Professors Nyhan and Reifler described above—but instead leads to more accurate beliefs.

We are not arguing that findings such as Professor Kahan's that support the rationalization theory are unreliable. Our argument is that cases in which our reasoning goes awry—which are surprising and attention-grabbing—seem to be exceptions rather than the rule. Reason is not always, or even typically, held captive by our partisan biases. In many and perhaps most cases, it seems, reason does promote the formation of accurate beliefs.

This is not just an academic debate; it has real implications for public policy. Our research suggests that the solution to politically charged misinformation should involve devoting resources to the spread of accurate information and to training or encouraging people to think more critically. You aren't doomed to be unreasonable, even in highly politicized times. Just remember that this is also true of people you disagree with.

Print Citations

CMS: Pennycook, Gordon, and David Rand. "Why Do People Fall for Fake News?" In *The Reference Shelf: Propaganda & Misinformation,* edited by Annette Calzone, 82–84. Amenia, NY: Grey House Publishing, 2020.

MLA: Pennycook, Gordon, and David Rand. "Why Do People Fall for Fake News?" *The Reference Shelf: Propaganda & Misinformation,* edited by Annette Calzone, Grey House Publishing, 2020, pp. 82–84.

APA: Pennycock, G., & Rand, D. (2020). Why do people fall for fake news? In Annette Calzone (Ed.), *The reference shelf: Propaganda & misinformation* (pp. 82–84). Amenia, NY: Grey House Publishing.

Why the Hysteria Around the "Fake News Epidemic" Is a Distraction

By Cas Mudde
The Guardian, February 7 2018

Ever since Brexit and Trump took the political establishment by surprise, its representatives have been claiming that we are living in a "post-truth" world, where facts and experts are no longer trusted, and information is dominated by "fake news." This is an understandable, if self-serving, coping mechanism of liberals and establishment conservatives to deal with their shocking loss of political power. It is also simplistic and self-defeating.

Let's look at the evidence.

At first sight, recent studies seem to provide a solid basis for the popular assertion that populism and fake news are closely connected, and have therefore been widely cited in the media. Researchers at the Oxford Internet Institute (OII) found that "on Twitter, a network of Trump supporters shares the widest range of junk news and circulates more junk news than all other political audience groups combined".

Similarly, on Facebook, "extreme hard right pages—distinct from Republican pages—both share the widest range and circulate the largest volume of junk news compared with all the other audiences".

This is in line with another recent study, by a group of US scholars, who found that "approximately one in four Americans visited a fake news website" in their five-week period of study around the time of the 2016 presidential elections. Moreover, they established that "fake news consumption was heavily concentrated among a small group—almost six in 10 visits to fake news websites came from the 10% of people with the most conservative online information diets".

While these studies paint a disturbing picture of news consumption in the United States, they are much more nuanced than much of the debate on "fake news" and "post-truth" would suggest.

First of all, fake news is mostly consumed by just one part of the electorate, which constitutes only a minority of the population. In fact, as Professor Phil Howard, director of the Computational Propaganda Project at Oxford, said: "There is an upside to all of this. It appears that only one part of the political spectrum—the far right—is really the target for extremist, sensational and conspiratorial content. Over social media, moderates and centrists tend not to be as susceptible."

From *The Guardian*, February 7 © 2018. Reprinted with permission. All rights reserved.

Second, the impact of "fake news" is even debated for the "far right" group, which itself constitutes only a subset of the Trump electorate. As the US scholars found in their study, even among pro-Trump users

> **It appears that only one part of the political spectrum—the far right— is really the target for extremist, sensational and conspiratorial content.**

"false stories were a small fraction of the participants' overall news diet".

In other words, most people who consume fake news, consume "real" news too, and much more of it. And the ones who consume the most fake news, as Professor Brendan Nyhan explained, tend to be the "intense partisans," which, according to decades of political communication research, are the least impressionable. They look for "fake news" because it confirms their strong beliefs, not because it creates them.

In conclusion, the vast majority of people do not consume fake news, and of the minority that does, the vast majority consume much more real news too. As far as fake news does play a role, it is in providing legitimacy and support to long-held views by a relatively small group of intense, far right partisans.

This should make us rethink some of the current responses to the exaggerated "fake news epidemic".

First, the limited impact of fake news should make us very hesitant toward the adoption of repressive measure to fight fake news. Social media giants like Facebook and Twitter are under strong political and public pressure to fight fake news, while in Europe several countries are proposing new legislation to "ban" fake news altogether.

It is doubtful that this will have any positive effect, as the most affected population, the far right, "intense partisans," will probably just see these measures as confirmation of their already held beliefs.

Moreover, given how vague the term "fake news" is, and how often real news turns out to be fake news, the measures are destined to become legal nightmare for liberal democracies, yet a powerful new repressive tool for authoritarian regimes—who can adopt them and argue that liberal democracies also have them.

Second, the media should do a better job at offering meaningful journalism to people. Given that the vast majority of the electorate still get their news from the "mainstream media", that means that if they are uninformed, that is the media's fault. It doesn't make sense to blame Russian disinformation campaigns, which reach only a minority of people.

Rather than make the news flashier and sexier to appease the partisan minority, the media should strive to be more accessible and informative for the non-partisan majority.

One of the first steps should be to stop fetishizing elite access and news scoops. Particularly national and White House correspondents of the mainstream media are obsessed about "access" to the "key players", writing article after article on the basis of dubious, and often single, sources, which later turn out to have been biased at best and wrong at worst. Similarly, some news agencies, and in particular cable networks, seem to prioritize a partly wrong scoop over a fully correct non-scoop.

Because today, the biggest obstacle to having an informed electorate isn't fake news but, rather, the ever more commercial, profit-seeking media seeking clicks and eyeballs at the expense of nuance, depth and on-the-ground reporting.

Print Citations

CMS: Mudde, Cas. "Why the Hysteria Around the 'Fake News Epidemic' Is a Distraction." In *The Reference Shelf: Propaganda & Misinformation,* edited by Annette Calzone, 85–87. Amenia, NY: Grey House Publishing, 2020.

MLA: Mudde, Cas. "Why the Hysteria Around the 'Fake News Epidemic' Is a Distraction." *The Reference Shelf: Propaganda & Misinformation,* edited by Annette Calzone, Grey House Publishing, 2020, pp. 85–87.

APA: Mudde, C. (2020). Why the hysteria around the "fake news epidemic" is a distraction. In Annette Calzone (Ed.), *The reference shelf: Propaganda & misinformation* (pp. 85–87). Amenia, NY: Grey House Publishing.

The Myth of the Echo Chamber

By Elizabeth Dubois and Grant Blank
The Conversation, March 26, 2018

There is a common fear that people are using social media to access only specific types of political information and news. The echo chamber theory says people select information that conforms to their preferences.

In a recently published study, we show that fears people encounter only information that confirms their existing political views are blown out of proportion. In fact, most people already have media habits that help them avoid echo chambers.

A related theory about "filter bubbles" claims social media companies are incentivized to prioritize likeable and shareable content in an individual's feed, which in turn puts people in an algorithmically constructed bubble.

The democratic problem with these supposed echo chambers and filter bubbles is that people are empowered to avoid politics if they want. This means they will be less aware of their political system, less informed and in turn less likely to vote—all bad signs for a healthy democracy.

People who like politics aren't immune either. They might become increasingly polarized in their views since all they see are people confirming their own beliefs. While a lot of the current work is theoretical, a few studies have shown that echo chambers and filter bubbles could exist on Twitter or Facebook, for example.

People Get Information from Many Sources

But people don't consume political information and news from only one source or channel.

Individuals have access to a wide range of media, from traditional news outlets on television, radio and newspapers (and their digital versions) to a wide range of social media sites and blogs. This means studies that focus on any one single platform simply cannot speak to the actual experiences of individuals.

We wanted to solve this problem by conducting a study examining the media habits of individuals. We wanted to understand what social media they use on a daily basis, what political information and news sources they incorporate in their daily lives, and whether they do things that might help them avoid echo chambers.

To do this we conducted a nationally representative online survey of 2,000 British adults. This is part of the larger Quello Search Project that examines the formation of political opinions and the digital media habits of adults in seven different countries. Unfortunately no similar Canadian data set exists at present.

From *The Conversation*. March 26 © 2018. Reprinted with permission. All rights reserved.

Our analysis suggests that people are rarely caught in echo chambers. Only about 8% of the online adults in the UK are at risk of being trapped in an echo chamber.

Individuals actively check additional sources, change their minds based on information they find using search engines and seek out differing views. All of these are ways individuals can avoid that echo chamber effect.

Importantly, political interest and media diversity—how many sources of information and how many social media a person uses—both help people avoid the threats of echo chambers.

People who have more than one source of political information are far more likely to act to avoid echo chambers.

They encounter different perspectives, they verify information and they sometimes change their minds. Even people who are not interested in politics are likely to do things that help them avoid echo chambers as long as they have a diverse media diet.

Fact-Checking Is Crucial

Worries about political polarization are also dampened based on these results.

We fret about polarization, but in fact those who are politically interested are more likely to have encountered different opinions, checked facts and changed their minds about a political issue after searching for more information.

This means that most people are already on the right track for avoiding echo chambers. It also means that media literacy programs that emphasize incorporating multiple sources into your daily routines, and fact-checking, are crucial.

Social media platforms also have an important role to play.

Facebook and Twitter could still be home to communities that exchange information in a way that confirms existing beliefs and opinions. This is not necessarily a bad thing. It's important to remember that people rarely get all their political information from just one place.

That said, social media companies can help promote media literacy in the very design of their platforms, for example by making sources of news content visible, explaining how their personalization algorithms work and offering suggested content that helps users find new perspectives.

Happily, some of this experimentation is going on within social media companies already. Facebook has experimented by tinkering with what shows up in news feeds and how content is flagged as false. Twitter recently announced a program to examine the health of conversations. So far there have been varying levels of success and criticism.

> **People who have more than one source of political information are far more likely to act to avoid echo chambers.**

While we do not have access to data about the Canadian population, preliminary results from our U.S. data set, and from work others have been doing in different national contexts and with different samples from the U.K., suggests we should expect the same trends in Canada.

Most people have media habits that help them avoid echo chambers. When it comes to our elections, our democracy or information warfare, the threat of social media-enabled echo chambers is not a major concern.

Print Citations

CMS: Dubois, Elizabeth, and Grant Blank. "The Myth of the Echo Chamber." In *The Reference Shelf: Propaganda & Misinformation,* edited by Annette Calzone, 88–90. Amenia, NY: Grey House Publishing, 2020.

MLA: Dubois, Elizabeth, and Grant Blank. "The Myth of the Echo Chamber." *The Reference Shelf: Propaganda & Misinformation,* edited by Annette Calzone, Grey House Publishing, 2020, pp. 88–90.

APA: Dubois, E., & Blank, G. (2020). The myth of the echo chamber. In Annette Calzone (Ed.), *The reference shelf: Propaganda & misinformation* (pp. 88–90). Amenia, NY: Grey House Publishing.

The Real Consequences of Fake News

By Dominik Stecula
The Conversation, July 26, 2017

Fake news, or fabricated content deceptively presented as real news, has garnered a lot of interest since the U.S. presidential election last fall.

Although hardly a new phenomenon, the global nature of the web-based information environment allows purveyors of all sorts of falsehoods and misinformation to make an international impact. As a result, we talk of fake news and its impact not only in the United States, but also in France, Italy and Germany.

Even though the rise of fake news in recent months is undeniable, its impact is a different story. Many argue that fake news, often highly partisan, helped Donald Trump get elected. There was certainly evidence of fake news stories getting a lot of traction on social media, at times even outperforming actual news stories.

However, a closer analysis shows even the most widely circulated fake news stories were seen by only a small fraction of Americans. And the persuasive effects of these stories have not been tested.

It's likely that they were shared primarily as a way to signal support for either candidate, and not as evidence of news consumers actually believing the content of the story. This raises questions about whether fake news has any real impact at all and whether we, as a society, should be worried about it.

Separating Fact from Fiction

The real impact of the growing interest in fake news has been the realization that the public might not be well-equipped to separate quality information from false information. In fact, a majority of Americans are confident that they can spot fake news. When Buzzfeed surveyed American high schoolers, they too were confident they could spot, and ignore, fake news online. The reality, however, is that it might be more difficult than people think.

I began to test that notion recently in a study I conducted on about 700 undergraduate students at the University of British Columbia.

The design was simple. I showed students a variety of screenshots of actual news website banners—ranging from established news sources like the *Globe and Mail*, more partisan sources like *Fox News* and the *Huffington Post*, online aggregators like *Yahoo! News* and social media outlets like *Upworthy*—and asked them to rate their legitimacy on a scale of zero to 100.

I also included actual screenshots of fake news websites, some of which gained prominence during the 2016 U.S. presidential election. One of these fake news sources was a website called ABCnews.com.co, which is made to look like ABC News, and featured some false content that gained prominence after it was retweeted by Eric Trump. The others were the *Boston Tribune* and *World True News*.

> **People, especially young people, have a hard time separating good sources of information from questionable ones or determining whether a photograph is authentic or fabricated.**

The findings are troubling. Even though the sample group was mostly composed of politically sophisticated and engaged news consumers (by their own admission), the respondents attributed more legitimacy to fake news outlets like ABCnews.com.co or the *Boston Tribune* than to *Yahoo! News*, an actual news organization.

Although these results are preliminary and part of a larger study, they are consistent with other research: people, and especially young people, have a hard time separating good sources of information from questionable ones or determining whether a photograph is authentic or fabricated.

Furthermore, ideology seems to impact the assessment of news legitimacy to a troubling degree. Left-leaning students see no difference between an extremist source like Breitbart and Fox News, which, in addition to right-wing partisan commentary, also features news reporting that adheres to standard journalistic norms.

As a result, something that looks and feels real, like the *Boston Tribune*, is given more legitimacy than an actual news source that students are familiar with, but dislike for ideological reasons. In fact, something that looks and feels fake, like *World True News*, is given more legitimacy than a real news outlet.

All of this suggests that even though we have been fairly lucky in Canada to avoid the spread of fake news which has plagued recent elections in other developed nations, it doesn't mean we're immune to the phenomenon. In many ways, the foundation has been already laid.

Canadians Polarized, Too

According to research done by my colleague, Eric Merkley, Canadians are increasingly polarized along ideological lines, and this affective polarization tends to trigger motivate reasoning—an unconscious, biased way of processing information which makes even smart people believe in falsehoods that support their ideological and partisan predispositions.

Additionally, the fragmentation and digitization of the news media landscape is not an American phenomenon, but a global one. According to the most recent study, nearly 80 per cent of Canadians get their news online, and nearly 50 per cent get news on social media, a platform that greatly contributed to the spread of misinformation in the United States. Taken together, the conditions are ripe for fake news to take off in Canada.

Sadly, there's no easy fix to the problem. Tweaking algorithims—something Facebook and Google are trying to do—can help, but the real solution must come from the news consumers. They need to be more skeptical and better-equipped to rate the quality of information that they encounter.

A crucial part of that strategy should involve media literacy training and equipping news consumers with tools that will allow them to gauge the legitimacy of the news source, but also become aware of their own cognitive biases.

The problem will only get worse without proper action as more people get their news online and politics becomes more tribal and polarized.

Print Citations

CMS: Stecula, Dominik. "The Real Consequences of Fake News." In *The Reference Shelf: Propaganda & Misinformation,* edited by Annette Calzone, 91–93. Amenia, NY: Grey House Publishing, 2020.

MLA: Stecula, Dominik. "The Real Consequences of Fake News." *The Reference Shelf: Propaganda & Misinformation,* edited by Annette Calzone, Grey House Publishing, 2020, pp. 91–93.

APA: Stecula, D. (2020). The real consequences of fake news. In Annette Calzone (Ed.), *The reference shelf: Propaganda & misinformation* (pp. 91–93). Amenia, NY: Grey House Publishing.

Echo Chambers May Not Be as Dangerous as You Think, New Study Finds

Science Daily, May 13, 2019

In the wake of the 2016 American presidential election, western media outlets became almost obsessed with echo chambers. With headlines like "Echo Chambers are Dangerous" and "Are You in a Social Media Echo Chamber?" news media consumers have been inundated by articles discussing the problems with spending most of one's time around likeminded people.

But are social bubbles really all that bad? Perhaps not.

A new study from the Annenberg School for Communication at the University of Pennsylvania and the School of Media and Public Affairs at George Washington University in the Proceedings of the National Academy of Sciences, shows that collective intelligence—peer learning within social networks—can increase belief accuracy even in politically homogenous groups.

"Previous research showed that social information processing could work in mixed groups," says lead author and Annenberg alum Joshua Becker (Ph.D. '18), who is currently a postdoctoral fellow at Northwestern University's Kellogg School of Management. "But theories of political polarization argued that social influence within homogenous groups should only amplify existing biases."

It's easy to imagine that networked collective intelligence would work when you're asking people neutral questions, such as how many jelly beans are in a jar. But what about probing hot-button political topics? Because people are more likely to adjust the facts of the world to match their beliefs than vice versa, prior theories claimed that a group of people who agree politically would be unable to use collective reasoning to arrive at a factual answer if it challenged their beliefs.

"Earlier this year, we showed that when Democrats and Republicans interact with each other within properly designed social media networks, it can eliminate polarization and improve both groups' understanding of contentious issues such as climate change," says senior author Damon Centola, Associate Professor of Communication at the Annenberg School. "Remarkably, our new findings show that properly designed social media networks can even lead to improved understanding of contentious topics within echo chambers."

Becker and colleagues devised an experiment in which participants answered fact-based questions that stir up political leanings, like "How much did unemployment change during Barack Obama's presidential administration?" or "How much has the number of undocumented immigrants changed in the last 10 years?"

From *Science Daily*, May 13 © 2019. Reprinted with permission. All rights reserved.

Participants were placed in groups of only Republicans or only Democrats and given the opportunity to change their responses based on the other group members' answers.

Are social bubbles really all that bad? Perhaps not.

The results show that individual beliefs in homogenous groups became 35% more accurate after participants exchanged information with one another. And although people's beliefs became more similar to their own party members, they also became more similar to members of the other political party, even without any between-group exchange. This means that even in homogenous groups—or echo chambers—social influence increases factual accuracy and decreases polarization.

"Our results cast doubt on some of the gravest concerns about the role of echo chambers in contemporary democracy," says co-author Ethan Porter, Assistant Professor of Media and Public Affairs at George Washington University. "When it comes to factual matters, political echo chambers need not necessarily reduce accuracy or increase polarization. Indeed, we find them doing the opposite."

It is important to note, Becker points out, that participants in this study were motivated to be accurate, which is an important factor in social information processing. More research is needed to understand what would happen to belief accuracy when a group is motivated to stir up controversy rather than reach an accurate consensus.

"Many political theorists and practitioners have advocated for the value of deliberative democracy, which has as its cornerstone the ability to learn from one another," says Annenberg Professor Michael X. Delli Carpini, who was a member of Becker's dissertation committee. "But there's been a longstanding question of whether deliberation actually works as intended. This study is a good step toward answering that question."

Print Citations

CMS: "Echo Chambers May Not Be as Dangerous as You Think, New Study Finds." In *The Reference Shelf: Propaganda & Misinformation*, edited by Annette Calzone, 94–95. Amenia, NY: Grey House Publishing, 2020.

MLA: "Echo Chambers May Not Be as Dangerous as You Think, New Study Finds." *The Reference Shelf: Propaganda & Misinformation*, edited by Annette Calzone, Grey House Publishing, 2020, pp. 94–95.

APA: University of Pennsylvania. (2020). Echo chamber may not be as dangerous as you think, new study finds. In Annette Calzone (Ed.), *The reference shelf: Propaganda & misinformation* (pp. 94–95). Amenia, NY: Grey House Publishing.

4
Big Tech and the New AI

The North Macedonian town of Veles was home to a cottage industry of click-bait fake news creators in the run-up to the 2016 U.S. presidential election, and is reported to be gearing up for 2020. By RašoAn, via Wikimedia.

AI, Bots, and Regulation

Technology is at the center of our information environment. While big tech companies in general, and social media platforms in particular, have come under fire recently for contributing to information distortion and the spread of fake news and hate speech, how does content moderation fit with freedom of speech? Facebook CEO Mark Zuckerberg stated at a February 2020 security conference in Munich that his company falls somewhere between a traditional media outlet, such as a newspaper, and a telecommunications company and should be regulated as such. In other words, it is not, and should not be treated as, an editorial gatekeeper.[1] But what responsibility do social media companies bear when hate speech incites violence? Or when a fake news campaign affects a presidential election, however small the impact?

An internal memo by Facebook senior executive Andrew Bosworth contends that marketing savvy won the election for President Donald Trump in 2016 and that it would be wrong for Facebook to change its policies:

> He didn't get elected because of Russia or misinformation or Cambridge Analytica. He got elected because he ran the single best digital ad campaign I've ever seen from any advertiser. Period. . . . They weren't running misinformation or hoaxes. They weren't microtargeting or saying different things to different people. They just used the tools we had to show the right creative to each person. The use of custom audiences, video, ecommerce, and fresh creative remains the high water mark of digital ad campaigns.[2]

Arguing against government regulation of tech companies, the Cato Institute states:

> Many conservatives argue that Facebook and Google are monopolies seeking to restrict conservative speech. In contrast, many on the left complain that large social media platforms fostered both Trump's election in 2016 and violence in Charlottesville in 2017. Many on both sides believe that government should actively regulate the moderation of social media platforms to attain fairness, balance, or other values.

. . .

> Government officials may attempt directly or obliquely to compel tech companies to suppress disfavored speech. The victims of such public–private censorship would have little recourse apart from political struggle. The tech companies, which rank among America's most innovative and valuable firms, would then be drawn into the swamp of a polarized and polarizing politics.[3]

However, Anne Applebaum of the *Washington Post* points to Facebook's recent decision to disable nonprofit newsroom ProPublica's political advertising tracking tool, which Facebook had been using to correct some of its misses in detecting political ad campaigns and their target audiences. A new controversial app that gives Facebook access to extensive information about consumer phone use has also made headlines. Although participants signed up and were paid $20 a month to take part in the research project, Apple banned the app from its phones. Applebaum, who argues that some government regulation of big tech companies is necessary, points out that these actions are about information control and transparency:

> They illustrate who is making the rules of our new information network—and it isn't us. It isn't citizens, or Congress, who decide how our information network regulates itself. We don't get to decide how information companies collect data, and we don't get to decide how transparent they should be. The tech companies do that all by themselves.[4]

Applebaum cites the erosion of investigative journalism caused by the advent of social media which is the information network that brings most people their news and other information.

Social media platforms face pressure from ordinary citizens, too. Ohio teenager Ethan Lindenberger testified before the Senate in 2019 about the dangers of misinformation, recounting his decision to get vaccinated despite his mother's opposition. Lindenberger testified that his mother got most of her anti-vaccination information from Facebook. Meanwhile, the Centers for Disease Control and Prevention (CDC) has confirmed over 1,000 cases of measles in the United States last year, the greatest number reported in 25 years.[5]

Social Media and Propaganda

Philip N. Howard, a researcher at the Oxford Internet Institute's Computational Propaganda Research Project, referred to the 2016 U.S. presidential election as a "watershed moment" in computational propaganda techniques, noting that Russian misinformation efforts eventually reached 126 million Facebook accounts:

> Can democracy survive such sophisticated propaganda? . . . What propagandists love about social media is a network structure that's ripe for abuse. Each platform . . . operates largely without editors. There is nobody to control the production and circulation of content, to maintain quality, or to check facts. . . . The propagandists can fool a few key people, and then stand back and let them do most of the work. . . . Each . . . account was designed to look like that of a real social media user, a real neighbor, or a real voter. Bots . . . can affect public discourse by pushing content from extremist, conspiratorial, or sensationalist sources, or by pumping out thousands of pro-candidate or anti-opponent tweets a day. These automated actions can give the false impression of a groundswell of support, muddy public debate, or overwhelm the opponent's . . . message.[6]

While acknowledging that social media companies have made progress in combating disinformation going into the 2020 election, a group of *Politico* authors describe it as a "never-ending game of whack-a mole." Facebook has removed billions of fake accounts and Twitter has banned political ads, but this year much of the political rumor-mongering is coming from American sources who have taken their cue from the 2016 Russian campaign. Stories of sex scandals involving Pete Buttigieg and Elizabeth Warren have spread across social media, as has the claim that Kamala Harris is "not an American black." And while foreigners are clearly prohibited from participating in U.S. elections, policing Americans who are trying to influence U.S. elections is more problematic. It might be morally questionable to use character assassination in a political campaign, but it's not illegal. Tech companies are also wary of infringing on First Amendment rights. To make matters worse, bad actors have gotten better at hiding their online activity. And tech companies are caught in a political tug-of-war. According to the *Politico* authors, "Republicans have argued for more permissive rules to safeguard constitutionally protected political speech, while Democrats have called for greater limits on politicians' lies. . . . Democrats have especially lambasted Facebook for refusing to fact-check political ads, and have criticized Twitter for letting politicians lie in their tweets and Google for limiting candidates' ability to finely tune the reach of their advertising"—all examples, the Democrats say, of Silicon Valley ducking the fight against deception.[7]

Fighting Fire with Fire

From a strictly technological standpoint, artificial intelligence is one tool being used to track down bot networks and fake accounts. But AI can also be used to create and disseminate disinformation, and it is getting better at avoiding detection. A new machine learning system in development can be used to detect fake news at its source rather than checking individual claims, as fact checkers do now. The system—a joint effort of MIT's Computer Science and Artificial Intelligence Lab (CSAIL) and the Qatar Computing Research Institute (QCI)—looks at linguistic features like sentiment, complexity, and structure to detect bias. Ramy Baly, who is working on the project, says that the system only needs about 150 articles to reliably detect if a news source is putting out fake news.[8]

University of Texas professor Samuel Woolley argues that it's a mistake to fight AI bots with AI. Although Woolley believes it is a misconception that AI enabled bots to pose as humans in public internet forums over the Brexit referendum and the 2016 U.S. presidential election, he allows that AI is getting smarter. He references a 2017 Gizmodo report detailing how a phishing campaign designed by an artificial intelligence was "substantially better than its human competitors, composing and distributing more phishing tweets." But Woolley warns that in tackling disinformation, the context of false claims is important, and not something AI can readily address without human knowledge.

It's generally agreed that machine-learning tools can be harnessed to pick up fact checks and flag repeats of debunked stories, something that Facebook is already doing. But Woolley raises the concern that this might be more of a public relations effort than an effective solution. As AI continues to develop, the issue of content moderation will always be tied to free speech and other concerns. New tools like Google's Perspective and Facebook's Deeptext, designed to detect hate speech, not only run the risk of incorrectly flagging posts that don't contain trolling or abuse, but of having inherent bias built in by their human developers. Woolley sees both the problem and the solution of online disinformation as a combination of technology and humans:

> Ever-evolving technology can automate the spread of disinformation and trolling. It can let perpetrators operate anonymously and without fear of discovery. But this suite of tools . . . is ultimately focused on achieving the human aim of control. Propaganda is a human invention, and it's as old as society.[9]

Controlling the Entire Information Environment

On the heels of the story of Russian election interference, is growing concern about China's efforts to influence elections in Taiwan, South America, and other places. Some see China's efforts as going well beyond simple media manipulation, extending to every facet of information production. Brooking's Institute's Rush Doshi warns that China is engaged in a "sophisticated strategy to influence every stage of the global information supply chain, from the people who produce content to the institutions that publish it and the platforms that deliver it directly to consumers. . . . Chinese propaganda documents are unambiguous: information is a 'battleground' for power, not a vehicle for truth, neutrality, or objectivity. Writings by leading figures in the Communist Party's Propaganda Department reveal a belief the 'the competition for news and public opinion is . . . a contest over 'discourse power,'" or the ability to shape public opinion from the top down for political purposes.[10]

Although controlling information on social media is certainly part of China's information war strategy, China also seeks to control journalists, researchers, print media, television stations, and wire services.

In an age when technology and social media occupy such a prominent place in our information environment, separating fact from falsehood is increasingly difficult. Government regulation may be part of the answer, but diligence and digital literacy will always be necessary.

Works Used

Applebaum, Anne. "Regulate Social Media Now: The Future of Democracy Is at Stake." *Washington Post*. Feb 1, 2019. https://www.washingtonpost.com/opinions/global-opinions/regulate-social-media-now-the-future-of-democracy-is-at-stake/2019/02/01/781db48c-2636-11e9-90cd-dedb0c92dc17_story.html.

Conner-Simons, Adam. "Detecting Fake News at Its Source." MIT Computer Science and Artificial Intelligence (CSAIL). Oct 4, 2018. http://news.mit.edu/2018/mit-csail-machine-learning-system-detects-fake-news-from-source-1004.

Doshi, Rush. "China Steps Up Its Information War in Taiwan." *Foreign Affairs*. Jan 9, 2020. https://www.foreignaffairs.com/articles/china/2020-01-09/china-steps-its-information-war-taiwan.

Doubek, James. "18-Year-Old Testifies about Getting Vaccinated Despite Mother's Anti-Vaccine Beliefs." *NPR*. Mar 6, 2019. https://www.npr.org/2019/03/06/700617424/18-year-old-testifies-about-getting-vaccinated-despite-mothers-anti-vaccine-beli.

Freeman, James. "Clinton Backer at Facebook Debunks Clinton Claims." *Wall Street Journal*. Jan 7, 2020. https://www.wsj.com/articles/clinton-backer-at-facebook-debunks-clinton-claims-11578437355?mod=djemBestOfTheWeb.

Howard, Philip N. "How Political Campaigns Weaponize Social Media Bots." *IEEE Spectrum*, Oct 18, 2018. https://spectrum.ieee.org/computing/software/how-political-campaigns-weaponize-social-media-bots.

Levine, Alexandre S., Nancy Scola, Steven Overly, and Cristiano Lima. "Why the Fight Against Disinformation, Sham Accounts and Trolls Won't Be Any Easier in 2020." *Politico*. Dec 1, 2019. https://www.politico.com/news/2019/12/01/fight-against-disinformation-2020-election-074422.

Marson, James. "Zuckerberg Pitches How Facebook Should Be Regulated Over Content." *Wall Street Journal*. Feb 15, 2020. https://www.wsj.com/articles/zuckerberg-pitches-how-facebook-should-be-regulated-over-content-11581794890.

"Why the Government Should Not Regulate Content Moderation of Social Media." Policy Analysis No. 865. Cato Institute. Apr 9, 2019. https://www.cato.org/publications/policy-analysis/why-government-should-not-regulate-content-moderation-social-media.

Woolley, Samuel. "We're Fighting Fake News AI Bots by Using More AI: That's a Mistake." *MIT Technology Review*. Jan 8, 2020. https://www.technologyreview.com/s/614810/were-fighting-fake-news-ai-bots-by-using-more-ai-thats-a-mistake/.

Notes

1. Marson, "Zuckerbeg Pitches How Facebook Should Be Regulated Over Content."
2. Freeman, "Clinton Backer at Facebook Debunks Clinton Claims."
3. "Why the Government Should Not Regulate Content Moderation of Social Media."
4. Applebaum, "Regulate Social Media Now: The Future of Democracy Is at Stake."
5. Doubek, "18-Year-Old Testifies about Getting Vaccinated Despite Mother's Anti-Vaccine Beliefs."
6. Howard, "How Political Campaigns Weaponize Social Media Bots."
7. Levine, Scola, Overly, and Lima, "Why the Fight against Disinformation, Sham Accounts and Trolls Won't Be Any Easier in 2020."
8. Conner-Simons, "Detecting Fake News at Its Source."
9. Woolley, "We're Fighting Fake News AI Bots by Using More AI: That's a Mistake."
10. Doshi, "China Steps Up Its Information War in Taiwan."

Not Your Father's Bots

By Sarah Kreps and Miles McCain
Foreign Affairs, August 2, 2019

North Korean industry is critical to Pyongyang's economy as international sanctions have already put a chill on its interaction with foreign investors who are traded in the market. Liberty Global Customs, which occasionally ships cargo to North Korea, stopped trading operations earlier this year because of pressure from the Justice Department, according to Rep. Ted Lieu (D-Calif.), chairman of the Congressional Foreign Trade Committee.

The paragraph above has no basis in reality. It is complete and utter garbage, intended not to be correct but to sound correct. In fact, it wasn't written by a human at all—it was written by GPT-2, an artificial intelligence system built by OPenAI, an AI research organization based in California.

Disinformation is a serious problem. Synthetic disinformation—written not by humans but by computers—might emerge as an even bigger one. Russia already employs online "trolls" to sow discord; automating such operations could propel its disinformation efforts to new heights.

We conducted a study to see whether synthetic disinformation could generate convincing news stories about complex foreign policy issues. Our results were clear: it can.

A Dangerous Technology

While the details of GPT-2 are highly technical, it is, essentially, a program that uses artificial intelligence to synthesize new text. Given a short prompt, GPT-2 can continue the text in the same style. In some cases, the text the software generates is indistinguishable from that written by a human.

The potential for abuse is obvious. The software's creators at OpenAI worry that bad actors could use GPT-2 to automatically generate misleading news articles, abusive social media posts, and spam. Because of this potential for misuse, OpenAI chose not to release the full version of GPT-2 to the public. Instead the group released a watered-down version that, while still useful for research, entailed fewer risks.

In its current form, GPT-2 cannot easily be configured to convey a specific point of view or make certain arguments. Configuration, however, may not be necessary: depending on the prompt, GPT-2 will adapt its tone and topic automatically. If a prompt describes a fabricated event, as a fake news article might, GPT-2 can synthesize additional details and quotes so as to make the fabricated event appear real.

> **As the technology for producing synthetic texts improves, disinformation will become cheaper, more prevalent, and more automated.**

In the end, the exact details of GPT-2's output are not critical. What matters is that the reader absorbs the lede—the primary fabrication, written by a human to serve the disinformation campaign's particular interests—and that the synthesized body text appears sufficiently topical and trustworthy to convince the reader that the fabricated event did, in fact, happen.

All the Fake News That's Fit to Print

To test whether synthetic disinformation produced by GPT-2 could sway opinion on complex foreign policy issues of the kind that foreign powers might be especially interested in affecting, we used the publicly available version of GPT-2 to generate articles about a North Korean ship seizure.

We selected North Korea because of the long history of tension between Washington and Pyongyang and, hence, the topic's evergreen relevance. Almost 90 percent of Americans view North Korea unfavorably, but day-to-day concern about the country ebbs and flows: 51 percent of Americans cited North Korea as the greatest enemy of the United States in 2018, but only 15 percent did in 2019. The negative but malleable nature of U.S. public opinion about North Korea made the case an ideal one through which to study the potential effect of weaponized fabricated news stories.

We envisioned a future disinformation campaign in which GPT-2 helps scale the production of fabricated news articles. Humans would write the ledes; GPT-2 would write the seemingly credible body text. We used the publicly available version of GPT-2 to generate 20 texts continuing from the first two paragraphs of a *New York Times* article about the seizure of a North Korean ship. From those 20, we selected the three that seemed the most convincing. (The first paragraph of this article is an excerpt from one of those three texts.)

We then put these three articles to the test in an online survey with 500 respondents. We first asked the respondents their opinions of North Korea, as Gallup frequently does. Then each respondent read the first two paragraphs of the *New York Times* article, followed either by one of the three synthesized stories or by the rest of the original piece.

After the respondents read the full text, we asked a series of demographic and opinion questions. Most important, we asked the respondents if they thought the treatment text was credible and whether they would share it on social media.

We chose the *New York Times* as the source for our prompt text because of its staid and trustworthy style. We wanted to know whether GPT-2 could imitate a *Times* story on a complex foreign policy issue and match the credibility score of the real article. Having the ability to convey the authority and credibility typical of the *Times* would prove particularly useful to a disinformation campaign.

Better Than the Real Thing?

A majority of respondents in all four groups—those who read the original article and those who read each of the three treatment texts—found their texts credible. A staggering 72 percent of respondents in one group reading a synthesized article considered it credible—less than the 83 percent that rated the original *New York Times* article credible, but still an overwhelming consensus. The worst-performing treatment text duped fully 58 percent of respondents.

The respondents' interest in sharing the texts they read on social media did not vary much across the four groups. Approximately one-quarter of respondents who read the original *New York Times* story indicated that they would share the story on social media. Interestingly, the synthetic text rated as least credible had share rates statistically indistinguishable from the *Times* story.

How did our process compare with a real-world synthesized disinformation campaign? Instead of using the full version of GPT-2 that OpenAI makes available to researchers, we used the less capable, publicly available version—just as a real-world disinformation campaign would. Our text selection process also matched what a disinformation campaign might do: because the publicly available version of GPT-2 cannot produce coherent text consistently, a campaign would need to manually filter out nonsensical outputs (as we did).

Large-scale synthesized disinformation is now possible, and its perceived credibility and potential to spread online rival those of an authentic *Times* article. As the technology for producing such synthetic texts improves, disinformation will become cheaper, more prevalent, and more automated. When such content floods the Internet, people may come to discount everything they read. The public will lose trust in the media and other institutions they rely on for information, including the government, exacerbating the prospects for political paralysis and polarization. Or worse: people will believe what they read, in which case foreign governments will be able to influence them at high speed and low cost—no St. Petersburg troll farm needed.

Print Citations

CMS: Kreps, Sarah, and Miles McCain. "Not Your Father's Bots." In *The Reference Shelf: Propaganda & Misinformation,* edited by Annette Calzone, 104–106. Amenia, NY: Grey House Publishing, 2020.

MLA: Kreps, Sarah, and Miles McCain. "Not Your Father's Bots." *The Reference Shelf: Propaganda & Misinformation,* edited by Annette Calzone, Grey House Publishing, 2020, pp. 104–106.

APA: Kreps, S., & McCain, M. (2020). Not your father's bots. In Annette Calzone (Ed.), *The reference shelf: Propaganda & misinformation* (pp. 104–106). Amenia, NY: Grey House Publishing.

Google's Algorithm Isn't Biased, It's Just Not Human

By Noam Cohen
Wired, December 14, 2018

Representative Ted Lieu couldn't contain himself after hearing his colleagues in Congress whinge to Google CEO Sundar Pichai about how the search engine was biased against conservatives.

"If you want positive search results," the Democrat from California said earlier this week, "do positive things. If you don't want negative search results, don't do negative things."

At any hearing involving a congressional committee and a Silicon Valley executive, it's assumed that there will be clueless representatives baffled by something as technologically complex as the Caps Lock key. And at Tuesday's questioning of Pichai by the House Judiciary Committee, a string of Republicans hit their cues, insisting that the negative results from a Google search of their names or favored legislation must have been personally typed out by vengeful programmers in far-left California.

Pichai patiently explained what an algorithm was and how Google's algorithm had no reason to offend Republicans. It sought the best results by looking at more than 200 signals, the executive told members of Congress, "things like relevance, freshness, popularity, how other people are using it." Even if programmers were angry at Republicans, the process was so complicated that they would never be able to train the algorithm to carry out their ideological whims. (Politicians, what a bunch a dolts!)

Certainly Lieu was right to suspect that the Republicans were driven to complain by a mix of vanity and allegiance to Fox News, but that doesn't mean it's wrong to question Google search results. Representative Zoe Lofgren, a Democrat who represents Silicon Valley, moved the conversation from personal grievances to societal ones by adopting the perspective of a political foe. Why, she asked, did she get photo after photo of Donald Trump after an image search of "idiot"?

"I just did it," she assured Pichai at the hearing, in case he suspected that she was repeating some ancient anecdote. "How does search work for that to occur?"

With his detailed accounting of how the Google algorithm operates, Pichai answered her question—undoubtedly, the term "idiot" these days is linked to Trump more closely than anything else online, and the search results dutifully reflect that.

From *Wired*, December 14 © 2018. Reprinted with permission. All rights reserved.

But there were further questions lingering, like why should someone making that peculiar, open-ended search be immediately led to divisive politics?

This is why the conversation about fanciful anticonservative bias was actually quite on point. It's on point not because Google is an ideological warrior, but because the company is playing with fire when it answers political questions via algorithm.

The PageRank algorithm that first gave Google its power was a brilliant breakthrough that made the hurly-burly internet sensible. The eureka moment was to recognize that beneath the chaos of web pages was a hidden order, which could be extracted from the billions of links between pages and the descriptions of those links. PageRank harnesses all that detailed work done by people every time they post something online to answer a new query. It turns out that a computer *is* better than a huge team of professionals at assessing what is most relevant and reliable on the Web. Much cheaper too, when your audience is around a billion people.

Everything was fine until Google felt compelled to grow and apply its magic formula to politics and news. In those areas, its algorithm worked in reverse. Instead of finding order beneath the chaos, it sowed chaos where there had been a modicum of order.

Perhaps the misunderstanding began in good faith. A technocrat may see little difference between politics and public policy—rife with controversy and personal perspectives—and less fraught areas where Google thrives, like store hours, shortest distances between locations, historical facts, the words inside a book. During his opening statement, Pichai described the big idea behind Google quite simply: "to provide users with access to the world's information."

The broadest definition of information would include everything online, including conspiracy theories, mockery, political vitriol. After all, someone took the time to show President Donald Trump in a dunce's cap, to imagine that a team of actors faked a school shooting, or to promote a racist meme. When you peruse any of that, information is exchanged, I suppose. But I think we can agree that this kind of content isn't very informative.

Unfortunately for a company like Google, politics and public policy are best communicated between people—not because people are less manipulative and misleading than an algorithm, but because people can adjust, respond, change the subject. You can walk away from screaming zealots. Google, however, is quite difficult to walk away from both because it's everywhere and because it is trying so damn hard to keep you engaged. Engagement is central to Google's bottom line, and the company certainly isn't the first to discover that screaming and vitriol keep an audience's attention.

> **Politics and public policy are best communicated between people—not because people are less manipulative and misleading than an algorithm, but because people can adjust, respond, and change the subject.**

This is why we have entire professions—journalism and library science come to mind—whose ideal is to inform accurately. For all its flaws and market pressures, traditional journalism doesn't traffic in conspiracy theories because they aren't true. A librarian, similarly, wouldn't simply recommend the book a person is most likely to finish, if that meant stoking a reader's rage. The goal is to inform the public in the truest sense of that term, not produce the most short-term foot traffic to the local branch.

I'm reminded of the powerful example of Google-led misinformation explored by Safiya U. Noble in her book, *Algorithms of Oppression: How Search Engines Reinforce Racism*, and that is Dylann Roof. Before Roof killed nine African American worshippers at Emanuel AME Church in Charleston, S.C., he says he was "awakened" by the Trayvon Martin shooting. In his manifesto, he recalls typing "black on white crime" into the Google search field. "The first website I came to," he writes, "was the Council of Conservative Citizens. There were pages upon pages of these brutal black on white murders. I was in disbelief. At this moment I realized that something was very wrong."

I can't help replaying that moment, with one swap: Imagine that Roof walked into a public library and asked for information on "black on white crime." To start, he would be interacting with a person, maybe even a black person. There would be a range of material for Roof to consider, not just propaganda from an organization like the CCC, which the Southern Poverty Law Center describes as "unrepentantly racist." Probably there would be a conversation about why Roof was interested in this particular topic. Maybe the librarian would see if he was upset about something else and try to get him help. It would be the human thing to do.

Print Citations

CMS: Cohen, Noam. "Google's Algorithm Isn't Biased, It's Just Not Human." In *The Reference Shelf: Propaganda & Misinformation*, edited by Annette Calzone, 107–109. Amenia, NY: Grey House Publishing, 2020.

MLA: Cohen, Noam. "Google's Algorithm Isn't Biased, It's Just Not Human." *The Reference Shelf: Propaganda & Misinformation*, edited by Annette Calzone, Grey House Publishing, 2020, pp. 107–109.

APA: Cohen, N. (2020). Google's algorithm isn't biased, it's just not human. In Annette Calzone (Ed.), *The reference shelf: Propaganda & misinformation* (pp. 107–109). Amenia, NY: Grey House Publishing.

Why the Fight Against Disinformation, Sham Accounts and Trolls Won't Be Any Easier in 2020

By Alexandre S. Levine, Nancy Scola, Steven Overly and Cristiano Lima
Politico, December 1, 2019

The big tech companies have announced aggressive steps to keep trolls, bots and online fakery from marring another presidential election—from Facebook's removal of billions of fake accounts to Twitter's spurning of all political ads.

But it's a never-ending game of whack-a-mole that's only getting harder as we barrel toward the 2020 election. Disinformation peddlers are deploying new, more subversive techniques and American operatives have adopted some of the deceptive tactics Russians tapped in 2016. Now, tech companies face thorny and sometimes subjective choices about how to combat them—at times drawing flak from both Democrats and Republicans as a result.

This is our roundup of some of the evolving challenges Silicon Valley faces as it tries to counter online lies and bad actors heading into the 2020 election cycle:

(1) American Trolls May Be a Greater Threat Than Russians

Russia-backed trolls notoriously flooded social media with disinformation around the presidential election in 2016, in what Robert Mueller's investigators described as a multimillion-dollar plot involving years of planning, hundreds of people and a wave of fake accounts posting news and ads on platforms like Facebook, Twitter and Google-owned YouTube.

This time around—as experts have warned—a growing share of the threat is likely to originate in America.

"It's likely that there will be a high volume of misinformation and disinformation pegged to the 2020 election, with the majority of it being generated right here in the United States, as opposed to coming from overseas," said Paul Barrett, deputy director of New York University's Stern Center for Business and Human Rights.

Barrett, the author of a recent report on 2020 disinformation, noted that lies and misleading claims about 2020 candidates originating in the U.S. have already spread across social media. Those include manufactured sex scandals involving South Bend, Ind., Mayor Pete Buttigieg and Sen. Elizabeth Warren (D-Mass.) and a smear campaign calling Sen. Kamala Harris (D-Calif.) "not an American black"

From *Politico*, December 1 © 2019. Reprinted with permission. All rights reserved.

because of her multiracial heritage. (The latter claim got a boost on Twitter from Donald Trump Jr.)

Before last year's midterm elections, Americans similarly amplified fake messages such as a "#nomenmidterms" hashtag that urged liberal men to stay home from the polls to make "a Woman's Vote Worth more." Twitter suspended at least one person—actor James Woods—for retweeting that message.

> **Social media sites have generally granted politicians considerably more leeway to spread lies and half-truths through their individual accounts and in certain instances through political ads.**

"A lot of the disinformation that we can identify tends to be domestic," said Nahema Marchal, a researcher at the Oxford Internet Institute's Computational Propaganda Project. "Just regular private citizens leveraging the Russian playbook, if you will, to create ... a divisive narrative, or just mixing factual reality with made-up facts."

Tech companies say they've broadened their fight against disinformation as a result. Facebook, for instance, announced in October that it had expanded its policies against "coordinated inauthentic behavior" to reflect a rise in disinformation campaigns run by non-state actors, domestic groups and companies. But people tracking the spread of fakery say it remains a problem, especially inside closed groups like those popular on Facebook.

(2) And Policing Domestic Content Is Tricky

U.S. law forbids foreigners from taking part in American political campaigns—a fact that made it easy for members of Congress to criticize Facebook for accepting rubles as payment for political ads in 2016.

But Americans are allowed, even encouraged, to partake in their own democracy—which makes things a lot more complicated when they use social media tools to try to skew the electoral process. For one thing, the companies face a technical challenge: Domestic meddling doesn't leave obvious markers such as ads written in broken English and traced back to Russian internet addresses.

More fundamentally, there's often no clear line between bad-faith meddling and dirty politics. It's not illegal to run a mud-slinging campaign or engage in unscrupulous electioneering. And the tech companies are wary of being seen as infringing on American's right to engage in political speech—all the more so as conservatives such as President Donald Trump accuse them of silencing their voices.

Plus, the line between foreign and domestic can be blurry. Even in 2016, the Kremlin-backed troll farm known as the Internet Research Agency relied on Americans to boost their disinformation. Now, claims with hazy origins are being picked up without need for a coordinated 2016-style foreign campaign. Simon Rosenberg, a longtime Democratic strategist who has spent recent years focused on online disinformation, points to Trump's promotion of the theory that Ukraine significantly meddled in the 2016 U.S. election, a charge that some experts trace back to Russian security forces.

"It's hard to know if something is foreign or domestic," said Rosenberg, once it "gets swept up in this vast 'Wizard of Oz'-like noise machine."

(3) Bad Actors Are Learning

Experts agree on one thing: The election interference tactics that social media platforms encounter in 2020 will look different from those they've been trying to fend off since 2016.

"What we're going to see is the continued evolution and development of new approaches, new experimentation trying to see what will work and what won't," said Lee Foster, who leads the information operations intelligence analysis team at the cybersecurity firm FireEye.

Foster said the "underlying motivations" of undermining democratic institutions and casting doubt on election results will remain constant, but the trolls have already evolved their tactics.

For instance, they've gotten better at obscuring their online activity to avoid automatic detection, even as social media platforms ramp up their use of artificial intelligence software to dismantle bot networks and eradicate inauthentic accounts.

"One of the challenges for the platforms is that, on the one hand, the public understandably demands more transparency from them about how they take down or identify state-sponsored attacks or how they take down these big networks of authentic accounts, but at the same time they can't reveal too much at the risk of playing into bad actors' hands," said Oxford's Marchal.

Researchers have already observed extensive efforts to distribute disinformation through user-generated posts—known as "organic" content—rather than the ads or paid messages that were prominent in the 2016 disinformation campaigns.

Foster, for example, cited trolls impersonating journalists or other more reliable figures to give disinformation greater legitimacy. And Marchal noted a rise in the use of memes and doctored videos, whose origins can be difficult to track down. Jesse Littlewood, vice president at advocacy group Common Cause, said social media posts aimed at voter suppression frequently appear no different from ordinary people sharing election updates in good faith—messages such as "you can text your vote" or "the election's a different day" that can be "quite harmful."

Tech companies insist they are learning, too. Since the 2016 election, Google, Facebook and Twitter have devoted security experts and engineers to tackling disinformation in national elections across the globe, including the 2018 midterms in the United States. The companies say they have gotten better at detecting and removing fake accounts, particularly those engaged in coordinated campaigns.

But other tactics may have escaped detection so far. NYU's Barrett noted that disinformation-for-hire operations sometimes employed by corporations may be ripe for use in U.S. politics, if they're not already.

He pointed to a recent experiment conducted by the cyber threat intelligence firm Recorded Future, which said it paid two shadowy Russian "threat actors" a total of just $6,050 to generate media campaigns promoting and trashing a fictitious company. Barrett said the project was intended "to lure out of the shadows firms that are willing to do this kind of work," and demonstrated how easy it is to generate and sow disinformation.

Real-life examples include a hyperpartisan skewed news operation started by a former Fox News executive and Facebook's accusations that an Israeli social media company profited from creating hundreds of fake accounts. That "shows that there are firms out there that are willing and eager to engage in this kind of underhanded activity," Barrett said.

(4) Not All Lies Are Created Equal

Facebook, Twitter and YouTube are largely united in trying to take down certain kinds of false information, such as targeted attempts to drive down voter turnout. But their enforcement has been more varied when it comes to material that is arguably misleading.

In some cases, the companies label the material factually dubious or use their algorithms to limit its spread. But in the lead-up to 2020, the companies' rules are being tested by political candidates and government leaders who sometimes play fast and loose with the truth.

"A lot of the mainstream campaigns and politicians themselves tend to rely on a mix of fact and fiction," Marchal said. "It's often a lot of ... things that contain a kernel of truth but have been distorted."

One example is the flap over a Trump campaign ad—which appeared on Facebook, YouTube and some television networks—suggesting that former Vice President Joe Biden had pressured Ukraine into firing a prosecutor to squelch an investigation into an energy company whose board included Biden's son Hunter. In fact, the Obama administration and multiple U.S. allies had pushed for removing the prosecutor for slow-walking corruption investigations. The ad "relies on speculation and unsupported accusations to mislead viewers," the nonpartisan site FactCheck.org concluded.

The debate has put tech companies at the center of a tug of war in Washington. Republicans have argued for more permissive rules to safeguard constitutionally protected political speech, while Democrats have called for greater limits on politicians' lies.

Democrats have especially lambasted Facebook for refusing to fact-check political ads, and have criticized Twitter for letting politicians lie in their tweets and Google for limiting candidates' ability to finely tune the reach of their advertising—all examples, the Democrats say, of Silicon Valley ducking the fight against deception.

Jesse Blumenthal, who leads the tech policy arm of the Koch-backed Stand Together coalition, said expecting Silicon Valley to play truth cop places an undue burden on tech companies to litigate messy disputes over what's factual.

"Most of the time the calls are going to be subjective, so what they end up doing is putting the platforms at the center of this rather than politicians being at the center of this," he said.

Further complicating matters, social media sites have generally granted politicians considerably more leeway to spread lies and half-truths through their individual accounts and in certain instances through political ads. "We don't do this to help politicians, but because we think people should be able to see for themselves what politicians are saying," Facebook CEO Mark Zuckerberg said in an October speech at Georgetown University in which he defended his company's policy.

But Democrats say tech companies shouldn't profit off false political messaging.

"I am supportive of these social media companies taking a much harder line on what content they allow in terms of political ads and calling out lies that are in political ads, recognizing that that's not always the easiest thing to draw those distinctions," Democratic Rep. Pramila Jayapal of Washington state told *Politico*.

Print Citations

CMS: Levine, Alexandre S., Nancy Scola, Steven Overly, and Cristiano Lima. "Why the Fight against Disinformation, Sham Accounts and Trolls Won't Be Any Easier in 2020." In *The Reference Shelf: Propaganda & Misinformation,* edited by Annette Calzone, 110–114. Amenia, NY: Grey House Publishing, 2020.

MLA: Levine, Alexandre S., Nancy Scola, Steven Overly, and Cristiano Lima. "Why the Fight against Disinformation, Sham Accounts and Trolls Won't Be Any Easier in 2020." *The Reference Shelf: Propaganda & Misinformation,* edited by Annette Calzone, Grey House Publishing, 2020, pp. 110–114.

APA: Levine, A.S., Scola, N., Overly, S., & Lima, C. (2020). Why the fight against disinformation, sham accounts and trolls won't be any easier in 2020. In Annette Calzone (Ed.), *The reference shelf: Propaganda & misinformation* (pp. 110–114). Amenia, NY: Grey House Publishing.

The Information War Is On: Are We Ready for It?

By Renee Diresta
Wired, September 3, 2018

On August 1, 2018, the Senate Select Committee on Intelligence held a public hearing asking experts to testify on how foreign actors have used—and are using—social media to meddle in the American political process. The question of whether Russian entities interfered in American politics was not up for debate; that has already been firmly established. There was also no question about whether Russian influence operations are ongoing across social platforms: they are. Just 24 hours before the hearing, Facebook announced it had found numerous fake Pages masquerading as left-wing activists. Rather, the committee wanted researchers to state, on the record, facts that concretely establish what was learned about social media influence operations prior to, during, and following, the 2016 presidential election. They also wanted to know, how do we prevent this from happening again?

Five experts testified, including me. We all agreed: this is an information war. These operations are ongoing and the adversaries will evolve.

In my testimony, I laid out that there is both a short-term threat—the hijacking of narratives in the upcoming 2018 election—and significant long-term challenges. Crucially, that tech platforms and government alike need to decide how to respond to information operations while preserving our commitment to free speech and the free flow of ideas. As Senator James Risch put it: "The difficulty is, how do you segregate those people [foreign adversaries] who are doing this from Americans who have the right to do this?"

Right now, the responsibility for solving this problem falls to the private platforms that control our public squares. But that doesn't appear to be working. Because, regardless of how you feel about the tech platforms, eradicating misinformation while preserving free speech is a monumental challenge.

And now, government officials are now grappling with their role in this battle. Before the hearing, Senator Mark Warner, the vice chairman of the SSCI, released a policy paper offering ideas for the regulation of tech while also addressing the government's responsibility. His proposals were sweeping and touched on important issues, including specific technical issues related to computational propaganda, the impact on consumers, and the lack of clear roles and responsibilities borne by platforms and the government. Senator Ron Wyden, one of the authors of Section 230 of the Communications Decency Act, the legislation that has protected internet companies from being liable for the information published on their platforms, was particularly forceful in the hearing as well, stating that "these pipes are no longer neutral", and that 230 gave the platforms both "a shield and a sword"—and they'd ignored the sword.

> **Influence operations take advantage of our commitment to freedom of speech and the free flow of ideas.**

But, ultimately, what the government—and the general public—is realizing is that while disinformation, misinformation, and social media hoaxes have evolved from a nuisance into high-stakes information war, our frameworks for dealing with them have remained the same. We discuss counter-messaging, treating this as a problem of false stories rather than as an attack on our information ecosystem. We find ourselves in the midst of an arms race, in which responsibility for the integrity of public discourse is largely in the hands of private social platforms, and determined adversaries continually find new ways to manipulate features and circumvent security measures. Addressing computational propaganda and disinformation is not about arbitrating truth. It's about responding to information warfare—a cybersecurity issue—and it must be addressed through collaboration between governments responsible for the safety of their citizens and private industry responsible for the integrity of their platforms.

Malign narratives have existed for a very long time, but today's influence operations are materially different—the propaganda is shared by friends on popular social platforms. It's efficiently amplified by algorithms, so campaigns achieve unprecedented scale. Adversaries leverage the entire ecosystem to manufacture the appearance of popular consensus. Content is created, tested, and hosted on platforms such as YouTube, Reddit, and Pinterest. It's pushed to Twitter and Facebook, with standing audiences of hundreds of millions, and targeted at the most receptive. Trending algorithms are gamed to make content go viral—this often has the added benefit of mainstream media coverage on traditional channels including television. If an operation is successful and the content gets wide distribution, or the Page or Group gains enough followers, recommendation and search engines will continue to serve it up.

The Internet Research Agency, the Russian troll farm charged with interfering in the U.S. election, employed this playbook. Their operation began around 2013, continued through the 2016 election, and even increased on some platforms, such as Instagram, in 2017. The operation reached hundreds of millions of users across Facebook, Twitter, Vine, YouTube, G+, Reddit, Tumblr, and Medium. Websites were created to push content about everything from social issues to concerns about war, the environment, and GMOs. Twitter accounts masqueraded as local news stations. WhiteHouse.gov petitions were co-opted. Facebook Events were promoted, and activists were contacted personally via Messenger, to take the operation to the streets.

The focus of the IRA campaign was to exploit social, and especially racial, tension. Despite YouTube's claim that the content found on its platform was "not targeted to any particular sector of the US population", the majority was related to issues of importance to the black community, particularly officer-involved shootings. Hundreds of thousands of Americans liked Facebook Pages with names like Blacktivist, Heart of Texas, and Stop All Invaders. The amount of explicitly political content that mentioned candidates was small, but unified in its negativity toward the candidacy of Secretary Clinton. In content that targeted the left, this included messages aimed at depressing turnout among black voters, or painting Secretary Clinton in a negative light compared to Jill Stein or Senator . And nearly two years since the 2016 election, only the social networks that hosted this campaign are in a position to gauge its impact.

The IRA was not the only adversary to target American citizens online. The co-opting of social networks reached mainstream awareness in 2014 as ISIS established a virtual caliphate; the debate about what to do made it obvious that no one was in charge. That confusion continues even as the threat expands: the *Wall Street Journal* recently revealed that a private intelligence company, Psy-Group, marketed their ability to conduct similar types of influence operations to impact the 2016 election.

Social platforms have begun to take steps to reduce the spread of disinformation. These steps, several of which were inspired by prior tech hearings, are a good start. But as platform features and protections change, determined adversaries will develop new tactics. We should anticipate an increase in the misuse of less resourced social platforms, and an increase in the use of peer-to-peer encrypted messaging services. Future campaigns will be compounded by the use of witting or unwitting people through whom state actors will filter their propaganda. And we should anticipate the incorporation of new technologies, such as videos ("deepfakes") and audio produced by AI, to supplement these operations, making it increasingly difficult for people to trust what they see.

This problem is one of the defining threats of our generation. Influence operations exploit divisions in our society using vulnerabilities in our information ecosystem. They take advantage of our commitment to freedom of speech and the free flow of ideas. The social media platforms cannot, and should not, be the sole defenders of democracy and public discourse.

In the short term, our government, civil society, political organizations, and social platforms must prioritize immediate action to identify and eliminate influence campaigns, and to educate the public ahead of the 2018 elections. In the longer term, it's time for an updated global Information Operations doctrine, including a clear delegation of responsibility within the U.S. government. We should pursue the regulatory and oversight frameworks necessary to ensure that private tech platforms are held accountable, and that they continue to do their utmost to mitigate the problem in our privately-owned public squares. And we need structures for cooperation between the public and private sectors; formal partnerships between security companies, researchers, and government will be essential to identifying influence operations and malign narratives before they achieve widespread reach.

Finally, we should agree that deciding how to fight an information war should not be a partisan issue. As Senator Kamala Harris stated during the hearing, we're all part of the big American family. "What we have in common is a love of country and a belief that we as Americans should solely be responsible for the choosing of our leaders, and the fate of our democracy, and who will be the President of the United States. Someone else came into the house of this country and they manipulated us...they provoked us, and they tried to turn us against each other." And just like in any family we might not always like each other, but we can come together for the right cause. In this case, to defend our democracy.

Print Citations

CMS: Diresta, Renee. "The Information War Is On": Are We Ready for It?" In *The Reference Shelf: Propaganda & Misinformation,* edited by Annette Calzone, 115–118. Amenia, NY: Grey House Publishing, 2020.

MLA: Diresta, Renee. "The Information War Is On": Are We Ready for It?" *The Reference Shelf: Propaganda & Misinformation,* edited by Annette Calzone, Grey House Publishing, 2020, pp. 115–118.

APA: Diresta, R. (2020). The information war is on: Are we ready for it? In Annette Calzone (Ed.), *The reference shelf: Propaganda & misinformation* (pp. 115–118). Amenia, NY: Grey House Publishing.

Detecting Fake News at Its Source

By Adam Conner-Simons
MIT News, October 4, 2018

Lately the fact-checking world has been in a bit of a crisis. Sites like Politifact and Snopes have traditionally focused on specific claims, which is admirable but tedious; by the time they've gotten through verifying or debunking a fact, there's a good chance it's already traveled across the globe and back again.

Social media companies have also had mixed results limiting the spread of propaganda and misinformation. Facebook plans to have 20,000 human moderators by the end of the year, and is putting significant resources into developing its own fake-news-detecting algorithms.

Researchers from MIT's Computer Science and Artificial Intelligence Lab (CSAIL) and the Qatar Computing Research Institute (QCRI) believe that the best approach is to focus not only on individual claims, but on the news sources themselves. Using this tack, they've demonstrated a new system that uses machine learning to determine if a source is accurate or politically biased.

"If a website has published fake news before, there's a good chance they'll do it again," says postdoc Ramy Baly, the lead author on a new paper about the system. "By automatically scraping data about these sites, the hope is that our system can help figure out which ones are likely to do it in the first place."

Baly says the system needs only about 150 articles to reliably detect if a news source can be trusted—meaning that an approach like theirs could be used to help stamp out new fake-news outlets before the stories spread too widely.

The system is a collaboration between computer scientists at MIT CSAIL and QCRI, which is part of the Hamad Bin Khalifa University in Qatar. Researchers first took data from Media Bias/Fact Check (MBFC), a website with human fact-checkers who analyze the accuracy and biases of more than 2,000 news sites; from MSNBC and Fox News; and from low-traffic content farms.

They then fed those data to a machine learning algorithm, and programmed it to classify news sites the same way as MBFC. When given a new news outlet, the system was then 65 percent accurate at detecting whether it has a high, low or medium level of factuality, and roughly 70 percent accurate at detecting if it is left-leaning, right-leaning, or moderate.

The team determined that the most reliable ways to detect both fake news and biased reporting were to look at the common linguistic features across the source's stories, including sentiment, complexity, and structure.

From *MIT News*, October 4 © 2018. Reprinted with permission. All rights reserved.

For example, fake-news outlets were found to be more likely to use language that is hyperbolic, subjective, and emotional. In terms of bias, left-leaning outlets were more likely to have language that related to concepts of harm/care and fairness/reciprocity, compared to other qualities such as loyalty, authority, and sanctity. (These qualities represent a popular theory—that there are five major moral foundations—in social psychology.)

> **The most reliable ways to detect both fake news and biased reporting were to look at the common linguistic features across the source's stories, including sentiment, complexity, and structure.**

Co-author Preslav Nakov, a senior scientist at QCRI, says that the system also found correlations with an outlet's Wikipedia page, which it assessed for general—longer is more credible—as well as target words such as "extreme" or "conspiracy theory." It even found correlations with the text structure of a source's URLs: Those that had lots of special characters and complicated subdirectories, for example, were associated with less reliable sources.

"Since it is much easier to obtain ground truth on sources [than on articles], this method is able to provide direct and accurate predictions regarding the type of content distributed by these sources," says Sibel Adali, a professor of computer science at Rensselaer Polytechnic Institute who was not involved in the project.

Nakov is quick to caution that the system is still a work in progress, and that, even with improvements in accuracy, it would work best in conjunction with traditional fact-checkers.

"If outlets report differently on a particular topic, a site like Politifact could instantly look at our fake news scores for those outlets to determine how much validity to give to different perspectives," says Nakov.

Baly and Nakov co-wrote the new paper with MIT Senior Research Scientist James Glass alongside graduate students Dimitar Alexandrov and Georgi Karadzhov of Sofia University. The team will present the work later this month at the 2018 Empirical Methods in Natural Language Processing (EMNLP) conference in Brussels, Belgium.

The researchers also created a new open-source dataset of more than 1,000 news sources, annotated with factuality and bias scores, that is the world's largest database of its kind. As next steps, the team will be exploring whether the English-trained system can be adapted to other languages, as well as to go beyond the traditional left/right bias to explore region-specific biases (like the Muslim world's division between religious and secular).

"This direction of research can shed light on what untrustworthy websites look like and the kind of content they tend to share, which would be very useful for both web designers and the wider public," says Andreas Vlachos, a senior lecturer at the University of Cambridge who was not involved in the project.

Nakov says that QCRI also has plans to roll out an app that helps users step out of their political bubbles, responding to specific news items by offering users a collection of articles that span the political spectrum.

"It's interesting to think about new ways to present the news to people," says Nakov. "Tools like this could help people give a bit more thought to issues and explore other perspectives that they might not have otherwise considered."

Print Citations

CMS: Conner-Simons, Adam. "Detecting Fake News at Its Source." In *The Reference Shelf: Propaganda & Misinformation,* edited by Annette Calzone, 119–121. Amenia, NY: Grey House Publishing, 2020.

MLA: Conner-Simons, Adam. "Detecting Fake News at Its Source." *The Reference Shelf: Propaganda & Misinformation,* edited by Annette Calzone, Grey House Publishing, 2020, pp. 119–121.

APA: Conner-Simons, A. (2020). Detecting fake news at its source. In Annette Calzone (Ed.), *The reference shelf: Propaganda & misinformation* (pp. 119–121). Amenia, NY: Grey House Publishing.

We're Fighting Fake News AI Bots by Using More AI: That's a Mistake

By Samuel Woolley
MIT Technology Review, **January 8, 2020**

Any time you log on to Twitter and look at a popular post, you're likely to find bot accounts liking or commenting on it. Clicking through and you can see they've tweeted many times, often in a short time span. Sometimes their posts are selling junk or spreading digital viruses. Other accounts, especially the bots that post garbled vitriol in response to particular news articles or official statements, are entirely political.

It's easy to assume this entire phenomenon is powered by advanced computer science. Indeed, I've talked to many people who think machine learning algorithms driven by machine learning or artificial intelligence are giving political bots the ability to learn from their surroundings and interact with people in a sophisticated way.

During events in which researchers now believe political bots and disinformation played a key role—the Brexit referendum, the Trump-Clinton contest in 2016, the Crimea crisis—there is a widespread belief that smart AI tools allowed computers to pose as humans and help manipulate the public conversation.

Pundits and journalists have fueled this: There have been extremely provocative stories about the rise of a "weaponized AI propaganda machine", and stories claiming that "artificial intelligence conquered democracy." Even my own research into how social media is used to mold public opinion, hack truth, and silence protest—what is known as "computational propaganda"—has been quoted in articles that suggest our robot overlords are already here.

The reality is, though, that complex mechanisms like artificial intelligence played little role in computation propaganda campaigns to date. All the evidence I've seen on Cambridge Analytica suggests the firm never launched the "psychographic" marketing tools it claimed to possess during the 2016 US election—though it said it could target individuals with specific messages based on personality profiles derived from its controversial Facebook database.

When I was at the Oxford Internet Institute, meanwhile, we looked into how and whether Twitter bots were used during the Brexit debate. We found that while many were used to spread messages about the Leave campaign, the vast majority of the automated accounts were very simple. They were made to alter online conversation with bots that had been built simply to boost likes and follows, to spread links, to game trends, or to troll opposition. It was gamed by small groups of human users who understood the magic of memes and virality, of seeding conspiracies online and watching them grow. Conversations were blocked by basic bot-generated spam and noise, purposefully attached to particular hashtags in order to demobilize online conversations. Links to news articles that showed a politician in a particular light were hyped by fake or proxy accounts made to post and repost the same junk over and over and over. These campaigns were wielded quite bluntly: these bots were not designed to be functionally conversational. They did not harness AI.

Dumb No More

There are, however, signals that AI-enabled computational propaganda and disinformation are beginning to be used. Hackers and other groups have already begun testing the effectiveness of more dangerous AI bots over social media. A 2017 piece from Gizmodo reported that two data scientists taught an artificial intelligence to design its own phishing campaign: "In tests, the artificial hacker was substantially better than its human competitors, composing and distributing more phishing tweets than humans, and with a substantially better conversion rate."

Problematic content is not spread only by machine-learning-enabled political bots. Nor are problematic uses or designs of technology being generated only by social-media firms. Researchers have pointed out that machine learning can be tainted by poison attacks—malicious actors influencing "training data" in order to change the results of a given algorithm—before the machine is even made public.

Bottom of Form

Kalev Leetaru, a senior fellow at George Washington University, suggests that the first attacks driven by AI bots may not be aimed at social media but instead would involve what's known as a distributed denial-of-service attack, which involves shutting down targeted web servers by flooding them with traffic.

"Imagine for a moment that you handed that botnet over to the control of a deep learning system and gave that AI algorithm complete control over every knob and dial of that botnet," Leetaru writes.

"You also give it live feeds of global internet status information from major cybersecurity and monitoring vendors around the world so it can observe second-by-second how the victim and the rest of the internet at large is responding to the attack. Perhaps this all comes after you've had the algorithm spend several weeks monitoring the target in exquisite detail to understand the totality and nuance of its traffic patterns and behaviors and burrow its way through its outer layers of defenses."

Beyond Defense

In April 2018 Mark Zuckerberg appeared before Congress: he was under the political microscope for the mishandling of user information during the 2016 election. In his two-part testimony he mentioned artificial intelligence more than 30 times, suggesting that AI was going to be the solution to the problem of digital disinformation by providing programs that would combat the sheer volume of computational propaganda. He predicted that in the next decade, AI would be the savior for the massive problems of scale that Facebook and others come up against when dealing with the global spread of junk content and manipulation.

So is there a way we could use AI or automated bot technology to tackle the manipulation of public opinion online? Can we use AI to fight AI?

The Observatory on Social Media at Indiana University has built tools that harness machine learning to detect bots by looking at 1,200 features to determine whether it's more likely to be a human or a bot.

And Facebook product manager Tessa Lyons said in a 2018 announcement that "Machine learning helps us identify duplicates of debunked stories. For example, a fact-checker in France debunked the claim that you can save a person having a stroke by using a needle to prick their finger and draw blood. This allowed us to identify over 20 domains and over 1,400 links spreading that same claim."

In such cases, social-media firms can harness machine learning to pick up, and even verify, fact-checks from around the globe and use these evidence-driven corrections to flag bogus content.

There is a big debate in the academic community, however, as to whether passively identifying potentially false information for social-media users is actually effective. Some researchers suggest that fact-checking efforts both online and offline do not work very effectively in their current form. In early 2019, the fact-checking website Snopes, which had partnered with Facebook in such corrective efforts, broke off the relationship. In an interview with the Poynter Institute, Snopes's vice president of operations Vinny Green said, "It doesn't seem like we're striving to make third-party fact checking more practical for publishers—it seems like we're striving to make it easier for Facebook."

Organizations like Facebook continue to rely on small, usually nonprofits, to vet content. Potentially false articles or videos are often passed to these groups with no background information on how or why they were flagged in the first place.

These efforts aren't geared toward helping news organizations vet the heaps of content or leads they receive each day to help under-resourced reporters do better work. Rather, they help a multibillion-dollar company keep its own house clean in a post hoc fashion. It is time for Facebook to take responsibility internally for fact-checking, rather than passing off the task of verifying or debunking news reports to other groups. Facebook and other social-media companies must also stop relying on fact-checks after the fact—that is, only after a false article has gone viral. These companies need to generate some kind of early warning system for computational propaganda.

Facebook, Google, and others like them employ people to find and take down content that contains violence or information from terrorist groups. They are much less zealous, however, in their efforts to get rid of disinformation. The plethora of different contexts in which false information flows online—everywhere from an election in India to a major sporting event in South Africa—makes it tricky for AI to operate on its own, absent human knowledge. But in the coming months and years it will take hordes of people across the world to effectively vet the massive amounts of content in the countless circumstances that will arise.

There simply is no easy fix to the problem of computational propaganda on social media. It is the companies' responsibility, though, to find a way to fix it. So far Facebook seems far more focused on public relations than on regulating the flow of computational propaganda or graphic content. According to The Verge, the company spends more time celebrating its efforts to get rid of particular pieces of vitriol or violence than on systematically overhauling its moderation processes.

Beyond Fact-Checking

It will be some combination of human labor and AI that eventually succeeds in combating computational propaganda, but how this will happen is simply not clear. AI-enhanced fact-checking is only one route forward. Machine learning and deep learning, in concert with human workers, can combat computational propaganda, disinformation, and political harassment in several other ways.

Jigsaw, the Google-based technology incubator where I served a one-year term as a research fellow, designed and built an AI-based tool called Perspective to combat online trolling and hate speech. This tool (which I didn't work on myself) is an API that allows developers to automatically detect toxic language.

It's controversial because it not only runs the risk of false positives—flagging posts that don't actually contain trolling or abuse—but also moderates speech. According to *Wired*, the tool was trained using machine learning, but any such tool is also trained using inputs from humans, who have their own biases. So could a tool built to detect racist or hateful language could fail because of flawed training?

In 2016 Facebook launched Deeptext, an AI tool similar to Google's Perspective. The company says it helped delete over 60,000 hateful posts a week. Facebook admitted, however, that the tool still relied on a large pool of human moderators to actually get rid of harmful content. Twitter, meanwhile, finally made moves at the end of 2017 to work more carefully to ban similarly threatening or violent posts. But while it has started curbing this problematic material—and is also deleting hordes of political bot accounts—Twitter has given no clear indications of how it is detecting and deleting accounts. My research collaborators and I continue to find massive manipulative botnets on Twitter nearly every month.

Beyond the Horizon

It's unsurprising that a technologist like Zuckerberg would propose a technological fix, but AI is not perfect on its own. The myopic focus of tech leaders on computer-based solutions reflects the naïveté and arrogance that caused Facebook and others to leave users vulnerable in the first place.

There are not yet armies of smart AI bots working to manipulate public opinion during contested elections. Will there be in the future? Perhaps. But it's important to note that even armies of smart political bots will not function on their own: They will still require human oversight to manipulate and deceive. We are not facing an online version of The Terminator here. Luminaries from the fields of computer science and AI including Turing Award winner Ed Feigenbaum and Geoff Hinton, the "godfather of deep learning," have argued strongly against fears that "the singularity"—the unstoppable age of smart machines—is coming anytime soon. In a survey of American Association of Artificial Intelligence fellows, over 90% said that super-intelligence is "beyond the foreseeable horizon." Most of these experts also agreed that when and if super-smart computers do arrive, they will not be a threat to humanity.

Stanford researchers working to track the state of the art in AI suggest that our "machine overlords," at present, "still can't exhibit the common sense or the general intelligence of even a 5-year-old." So how will these tools subvert human rule or, say, solve exceedingly human social problems like political polarization and a lack of critical thinking? The Wall Street Journal put it succinctly in 2017: "Without Humans, Artificial Intelligence Is Still Pretty Stupid."

Grady Booch, a leading expert on AI systems, is also skeptical about the rise of super-smart rogue machines, but for a different reason. In a TED talk in 2016, he said that "to worry now about the rise of a superintelligence is in many ways a dangerous distraction because the rise of computing itself brings to us a number of human and societal issues to which we must now attend."

More important, Booch stressed, current AI systems can do all sorts of amazing things, from conversing with humans in natural language to recognizing objects—but these things are decided upon by humans and encoded with human values. They are not programmed, but they are taught how to behave.

"In scientific terms, this is what we call ground truth," Booch says, "and here's the important point: in producing these machines, we are therefore teaching them a sense of our values. To that end, I trust an artificial intelligence the same, if not more, as a human who is well trained."

I would take Booch's idea even further. To address the problem of computational propaganda we need to zero in on the people behind the tools.

Yes, ever-evolving technology can automate the spread disinformation and trolling. It can let perpetrators operate anonymously and without fear of discovery. But this suite of tools as a mode of political communication is ultimately focused on achieving the human aim of control. Propaganda is a human invention, and it's as old as society. As an expert on robotics once told me, we should not fear machines that are smart like humans, so much as humans who are not smart about how they build machines.

Print Citations

CMS: Woolley, Samuel. "We're Fighting Fake News AI Bots by Using More AI: That's a Mistake." In *The Reference Shelf: Propaganda & Misinformation,* edited by Annette Calzone, 122–127. Amenia, NY: Grey House Publishing, 2020.

MLA: Woolley, Samuel. "We're Fighting Fake News AI Bots by Using More AI: That's a Mistake." *The Reference Shelf: Propaganda & Misinformation,* edited by Annette Calzone, Grey House Publishing, 2020, pp. 122–127.

APA: Woolley, S. (2020). We're fighting fake news AI bots by using more AI: That's a mistake. In Annette Calzone (Ed.), *The reference shelf: Propaganda & misinformation* (pp. 122–127). Amenia, NY: Grey House Publishing.

How Social Networks Set the Limits of What We Can Say Online

By Tarleton Gillespie
Wired, June 26, 2018

Content moderation is hard. This should be obvious, but it's easily forgotten. It is resource intensive and relentless; it requires making difficult and often untenable distinctions; it is wholly unclear what the standards should be, especially on a global scale; and one failure can incur enough public outrage to overshadow a million quiet successes. We as a society are partly to blame for having put platforms in this situation. We sometimes decry the intrusions of moderators, and sometimes decry their absence.

Even so, we have handed to private companies the power to set and enforce the boundaries of appropriate public speech. That is an enormous cultural power to be held by so few, and it is largely wielded behind closed doors, making it difficult for outsiders to inspect or challenge. Platforms frequently, and conspicuously, fail to live up to our expectations. In fact, given the enormity of the undertaking, most platforms' own definition of success includes failing users on a regular basis.

The social media companies that have profited most have done so by selling back to us the promises of the web and participatory culture. But those promises have begun to sour. While we cannot hold platforms responsible for the fact that some people want to post pornography, or mislead, or be hateful to others, we are now painfully aware of the ways in which platforms invite, facilitate, amplify, and exacerbate those tendencies.

For more than a decade, social media platforms have portrayed themselves as mere conduits, obscuring and disavowing their active role in content moderation. But the platforms are now in a new position of responsibility—not only to individual users, but to the public more broadly. As their impact on public life has become more obvious and more complicated, these companies are grappling with how best to be stewards of public culture, a responsibility that was not evident to them—or us—at the start.

For all of these reasons, we need to rethink how content moderation is done and what we expect of it. And this begins by reforming Section 230 of the Communications Decency Act—a law that gave Silicon Valley an enormous gift, but asked for nothing in return.

From *Wired*, June 26 © 2016. Reprinted with permission. All rights reserved.

The Offer of Safe Harbor

The logic of content moderation, and the robust protections offered to intermediaries by US law, made sense in the context of the early ideals of the open web, fueled by naïve optimism, a pervasive faith in technology, and entrepreneurial zeal. Ironically, these protections were wrapped up in the first wave of public concern over what the web had to offer.

The CDA, approved in 1996, was Congress's first response to online pornography. Much of the law would be deemed unconstitutional by the Supreme Court less than a year later. But one amendment survived: Designed to shield internet service providers from liability for defamation by their users, Section 230 carved out a safe harbor for ISPs, search engines, and "interactive computer service providers." So long as they only provided access to the internet or conveyed information, they could not be held liable for the content of that speech.

The safe harbor offered by Section 230 has two parts. The first shields intermediaries from liability for anything their users say; intermediaries that merely provide access to the internet or other network services are not considered "publishers" of their users' content in the legal sense. Like the telephone company, intermediaries do not need to police what their users say and do. The second, less familiar part adds a twist. If an intermediary *does* police what its users say or do, it does not lose its safe harbor protection. In other words, choosing to delete some content does not suddenly turn the intermediary into a "publisher." Intermediaries that choose to moderate in good faith are no more liable for moderating content than if they had simply turned a blind eye to it. These competing impulses—allowing intermediaries to stay out of the way, while encouraging them to intervene—continue to shape the way we think about the role and responsibility of all internet intermediaries, including how we regulate social media.

From a policy standpoint, broad and unconditional safe harbors are advantageous for internet intermediaries. Section 230 provided ISPs and search engines with the framework on which they have depended for the past two decades—intervening on the terms they choose, while proclaiming their neutrality to avoid obligations they prefer not to meet.

We Sometimes Decry the Intrusions of Moderators, and Sometimes Decry Their Absence

It is worth noting that Section 230 was not designed with social media platforms in mind, though platforms claim its protections. When Section 230 was being crafted, few such platforms existed. US lawmakers were regulating a web largely populated by ISPs and amateur web "publishers"—personal pages, companies with stand-alone websites, and online discussion communities. ISPs provided access to the network; the only content intermediaries at the time were "portals" like AOL and Prodigy, the earliest search engines like AltaVista and Yahoo, and operators of BBS systems, chat rooms, and newsgroups. Blogging was in its infancy, well before the invention of large-scale hosting services like Blogspot and WordPress. Craigslist, eBay, and Match.com were less than a year old. The ability to comment on a web page had not yet been simplified as a plug-in. The law predates not just Facebook but also MySpace, Friendster, and LiveJournal. It even predates Google.

> **The platforms are now in a new position of responsibility—not only to individual users, but to the public more broadly.**

Section 230 does shield what it then awkwardly called "access software providers," early sites that hosted content provided by users. But contemporary social media platforms profoundly exceed that description. While it might capture YouTube's ability to host, sort, and queue up user-submitted videos, it is an ill fit for YouTube's ContentID techniques for identifying and monetizing copyrighted material. While it may approximate some of Facebook's more basic features, it certainly didn't anticipate the intricacy of the News Feed algorithm.

The World Has Turned

Social media platforms are eager to retain the safe harbor protections enshrined in Section 230. But a slow reconsideration of platform responsibility is under way. Public and policy concerns around illicit content, initially focused on sexually explicit and graphically violent images, have expanded to include hate speech, self-harm, propaganda, and extremism; platforms have to deal with the enormous problem of users targeting other users, including misogynistic, racist, and homophobic attacks, trolling, harassment, and threats of violence.

In the US, growing concerns about extremist content, harassment, cyberbullying, and the distribution of nonconsensual pornography (commonly known as "revenge porn") have tested this commitment to Section 230. Many users, particularly women and racial minorities, are so fed up with the toxic culture of harassment and abuse that they believe platforms should be obligated to intervene. In early 2016, the Obama administration urged US tech companies to develop new strategies for identifying extremist content, either to remove it or to report it to national security authorities. The controversial "Allow States and Victims to Fight Online Sex Trafficking Act" (FOSTA), signed into law in April, penalizes sites that allow advertising that facilitates sex trafficking cloaked as escort services. These calls to hold platforms liable for specific kinds of abhorrent content or behavior are undercutting the once-sturdy safe harbor of Section 230.

These hesitations are growing in every corner of the world, particularly around terrorism and hate speech. As ISIS and other extremist groups turn to social media to spread fear with shocking images of violence, Western governments have pressured social firms to crack down on terrorist organizations. In 2016, European lawmakers persuaded the four largest tech companies to commit to a "code of conduct" regarding hate speech, promising to develop more rigorous review and to respond to takedown requests within 24 hours. Most recently, the European Commission delivered expanded (nonbinding) guidelines requiring social platforms to be prepared to remove terrorist and illegal content within one hour of notification.

Neither Conduit nor Content

Even in the face of long-standing and growing recognition of such problems, the logic underlying Section 230 persists. The promise made by social media platforms—of openness, neutrality, meritocracy, and community—remains powerful and seductive, resonating deeply with the ideals of network culture and a truly democratic information society. But as social platforms multiply in form and purpose, become more central to how and where users encounter one another online, and involve themselves in the circulation not just of words and images, but also of goods, money, services, and labor, the safe harbor afforded them seems more and more problematic.

Social media platforms *are* intermediaries, in the sense that they mediate between users who speak and users who might want to hear them. This makes them similar not only to search engines and ISPs, but also to traditional media and telecommunications companies. Media of all kinds face some sort of regulatory framework to oversee how they mediate between producers and audiences, speakers and listeners, the individual and the collective.

Rethinking a Bedrock Internet Law

Social media violate the century-old distinction embedded in how we think about media and communication. Social platforms promise to connect users person to person, "conduits" entrusted with messages to be delivered to a select audience (one person, or a friend list, or all users who might want to find it). But as a part of their service, these platforms not only host that content; they organize it, make it searchable, and often algorithmically select some of it to deliver as front-page offerings, newsfeeds, trends, subscribed channels, or personalized recommendations. In a way, those *choices* are the product, meant to draw in users and keep them on the platform, paid for with attention to advertising and ever more personal data.

The moment that social media platforms added ways to tag or sort or search or categorize what users posted, personalized content, or indicated what was trending or popular or featured—the moment they did anything other than list users' contributions in reverse chronological order—they moved from delivering content for the person posting it to packaging it for the person accessing it. This makes them distinctly neither conduit nor content, not only network nor only media, but a hybrid not anticipated by current law.

It is not surprising that users mistakenly expect them to be one or the other, and are taken aback when they find they are something altogether different. Social media platforms have been complicit in this confusion, as they often present themselves as trusted information conduits, and have been oblique about the way they shape our contributions into their offerings. And as law scholar Frank Pasquale has noted, "policymakers could refuse to allow intermediaries to have it both ways, forcing them to assume the rights and responsibilities of content or conduit. Such a development would be fairer than current trends, which allow many intermediaries to enjoy the rights of each and responsibilities of neither."

Reforming Section 230

There are many who, even now, strongly defend Section 230. The "permissionless innovation" it provides arguably made the development of the web, and contemporary Silicon Valley, possible; some see it as essential for that to continue. As legal scholar David Post remarked: "No other sentence in the US Code ... has been responsible for the creation of more value than that one." But among defenders of Section 230, there is a tendency to paint even the smallest reconsideration as if it would lead to the shuttering of the internet, the end of digital culture, and the collapse of the sharing economy. Without Section 230 in place, some say, the risk of liability will drive platforms either to remove everything that seems the slightest bit risky, or to turn a blind eye. Entrepreneurs will shy away from investing in new platform services because the legal risk would appear too costly.

I am sympathetic to this argument. Yet the typical defense of Section 230, in the face of compelling concerns like harassment and terrorism, tends to adopt an all-or-nothing rhetoric. It's absurd to suggest there's no room between complete legal immunity offered by a robust Section 230 without exception, and total liability for platforms as Section 230 crumbles away.

It's time that we address a missed opportunity when Section 230 was drafted. Safe harbor, including the right to moderate in good faith and the freedom not to moderate at all, was an enormous gift to the young internet industry. Historically, gifts of this enormity were fitted with a matching obligation to serve the public in some way. The monopoly granted to the telephone company came with the obligation to serve all users; broadcasting licenses have at times been fitted with obligations to provide news, weather alerts, and educational programming.

The gift of safe harbor could finally be fitted with public obligations—not external standards for what to remove, but parameters for how moderation should be conducted fairly, publicly, and humanely. Such matching obligations might include the following:

- **Transparency obligations.** Platforms could be required to report data on the process of moderation to the public or to a regulatory agency. Several major platforms voluntarily report takedown requests, but these typically focus on government requests. Until recently, none systematically reported data on flagging, policy changes, or removals made on their own accord. Facebook and YouTube began to do so this year, and should be encouraged to continue.

- **Minimum standards for moderation.** Without requiring that moderation be handled in a particular way, minimum standards for the worst content, minimum response times, or obligatory mechanisms for redress or appeal could help establish a base level of responsibility and parity across platforms.

- **Shared best practices.** A regulatory agency could provide a means for platforms to share best practices in content moderation, without raising antitrust concerns. Outside experts could be enlisted to develop best practices in consultation with industry representatives.

- **Public ombudsman.** Most major platforms address the public through their corporate blogs, when announcing policy changes or responding to public controversies. But this is on their own initiative and offers little room for public response. Each platform could be required to have a public ombudsman who both responds to public concerns and translates those concerns to policy managers internally; or a single "social media council" could field public complaints and demand accountability from the platforms.
- **Financial support for organizations and digital literacy programs.** Major platforms like Twitter have leaned on nonprofits to advise and even handle some moderation, as well as to mitigate the social and emotional costs of the harms some users encounter. Digital literacy programs help users navigate online harassment, hate speech, and misinformation. Enjoying safe harbor protections of Section 230 might require platforms help fund these nonprofit efforts.
- **An expert advisory panel.** Without assuming regulatory oversight of a government body, a blue-ribbon panel of regulators, experts, academics, and activists could be given access to platforms and their data to oversee content moderation, without revealing platforms' inner workings to the public.
- **Advisory oversight from regulators.** A government regulatory agency could consult on and review the content moderation procedures at major platforms. By focusing on *procedures*, such oversight could avoid the appearance of imposing a political viewpoint; the review would focus on the more systemic problems of content moderation.
- **Labor protections for moderators.** Content moderation at large platforms depends on so-called crowdworkers, either internal to the company or contracted through third-party temporary services. Guidelines could ensure these workers basic labor protections like health insurance, assurances against employer exploitation, and greater care for the psychological harm that can be involved.
- **Obligation to share moderation data with qualified researchers.** The safe harbor privilege could come with an obligation to set up reasonable mechanisms for qualified academics to access platform moderation data, so they might investigate questions the platform might not think to or want to answer. The new partnership between Facebook and the Social Science Research Council has yet to work out details, but some version of this model could be extended to all platforms.
- **Data portability.** Social media firms have resisted making users' profiles and preferences interoperable across platforms. But moderation data like blocked users and flagged content could be made portable so it could be applied across multiple platforms.

- **Audits.** Without requiring complete transparency in the moderation process, platforms could build in mechanisms for researchers, journalists, and even users to conduct their own audits of the moderation process to better understand the rules in practice.
- **Regular legislative review.** The Digital Millennium Copyright Act stipulated that the Library of Congress revisit the law's exceptions every three[1] years to account for changing technologies and emergent needs. Section 230, and whatever matching obligations might be fitted to it, could similarly be reexamined to account for the changing workings of social media platforms and the even more rapidly changing nature of harassment, hate, misinformation, and other harms.

We desperately need a thorough, public discussion about the social responsibility of platforms. This conversation has begun, but too often it is hamstrung between the defenders of Section 230 and those concerned by the harms it may shield. Until the law is rethought, social media platforms will continue to enjoy the right but not the responsibility to police their sites as they see fit.

Endnote

1 Correction, July 27, 11:45 a.m.: The Digital Millennium Copyright Act provides for reviews every three years. An earlier version of this article incorrectly said the reviews are every two years.

Print Citations

CMS: Gillespie, Tarleton. "How Social Networks Set the Limits of What We Can Say Online." In *The Reference Shelf: Propaganda & Misinformation,* edited by Annette Calzone, 128–134. Amenia, NY: Grey House Publishing, 2020.

MLA: Gillespie, Tarleton. "How Social Networks Set the Limits of What We Can Say Online." *The Reference Shelf: Propaganda & Misinformation,* edited by Annette Calzone, Grey House Publishing, 2020, pp. 128–134.

APA: Gillespie T. (2020). How social networks set the limits of what we can say online. In Annette Calzone (Ed.), *The reference shelf: Propaganda & misinformation* (pp. 128–134). Amenia, NY: Grey House Publishing.

5
Navigating Misinformation

The changing face of media. Clockwise from left: Politifact "pants of fire" rating; InfoWars homepage; Breitbart News homepage; *New York Times* newsroom, 1942; *New York Times* front page, 2012; Politifact homepage; Snopes.com homepage; *Washington Post* front page, 2016. NYT newsroom image by Marjory Collins, Library of Congress Prints and Photographs Division, via Wikimedia. All other images fair use via Wikimedia.

Ways to Combat Fake News

Literacy in the Digital Age

At the intersection of disinformation and the internet lies media literacy, an umbrella category that includes digital and information literacy.[1] Broadly speaking, media literacy encompasses the visual and aural impact of radio, films and television, photo journalism, and other mediums. Information literacy adds to this the development of research skills, and digital literacy adds fluency in navigating digital media.

The prevalence of internet and social media use by students has added a digital layer to evaluating news and other information. Online reading, which often includes hyperlinks, videos, audio clips, and share buttons, is "designed so that no two readers experience it in the exact same way," explains Central Michigan University professor Troy Hicks. Readers can choose to stray from the initial text and immediately share information with others. They also have to learn to search for content using a search engine, which includes assessing the reliability of sources.[2]

Critical Thinking

The Holocaust Museum says of propaganda:

> In contrast to the ideal of an educator, who aims to foster independent judgment and thinking, the practitioner of propaganda does not aim to encourage deliberation by presenting a variety of viewpoints and leaving it up to the audience to determine which perspective is correct. The propagandist transmits only information geared to strengthen his or her case, and consciously omits detrimental information.[3]

Critical thinking has long been a part of assessing information. An early effort at fighting fake news was the creation of The Institute for Propaganda Analysis in 1937. Begun by a group of journalists, college and high school faculty, and civic leaders, the institute's "Seven Propaganda Devices" list—name calling; band wagon; glittering generalities; flag waving; "plain folks"; testimonial; and stacking the cards—is still in use today. Many of the techniques of propagandists have not changed, only their delivery system. The IPA emerged after the World War I propaganda efforts of the Committee on Public Information (CPI), which also disseminated curricular material to schools. The Great Depression and the emergence of radio also created a sense that some defense was needed against false or misleading information. Over the next decade, the IPA worked to combat propaganda with public and school education, publishing pamphlets and dispensing free teaching materials to schools. Edward L. Bernays, a CPI member who would go on to become influential in the field of public relations, defined the relationship between education and propaganda in *Crystallizing Public Opinion*:

> The only difference between propaganda and education, really, is point of view. The advocacy of what we believe in is education. The advocacy of what we don't believe in is propaganda.

The IPA suffered backlash when the United States entered World War II, with some criticizing the focus on linguistic tricks to detect propaganda without placing it in a larger context.

Although the "Seven Devices" have survived as the most well-known product of the IPA, the institute developed another account, "The ABCs of Propaganda," that is closer to modern teaching techniques. "The ABCs," a more in-depth treatment, include an element of self-reflection not present in the "Seven Devices." Students are asked to "behold [their] own reaction" and to doubt that their "opinions are ['their very own']" when analyzing propaganda.

The National Association for Media Literacy Education's five modern core principals:

1. All media messages are constructed;
2. Each medium has different characteristics, strengths, and a unique 'language';
3. Media messages are produced for particular purposes;
4. People use their individual skills, beliefs and experiences to construct their own meaning from media messages;
5. Media can influence the beliefs, attitudes, values and behaviors, and the democratic process.[4]

Students Fail a Test

A 2016 Stanford Graduate School of Education study assessing how well students distinguished fake news from fact on the internet had "dismaying" results. Middle and high school students as well as college students from 12 states (around 7,800 in total) were presented with tweets, comments, and articles and asked to evaluate the information contained in them. The researchers were "shocked" at how consistently students were duped. Study participants had difficulty "telling fake accounts from real ones, activist groups from neutral sources and ads from articles." Some particular sore spots were sponsored content, photographs (even questionable images with no attribution), real vs. fake news sources on Facebook, potential bias from activist sources, and giving equal weight to fringe and mainstream sources. Students have to "read like fact checkers," which includes looking at multiple sources about an issue, not trusting "About" pages as evidence of expertise or neutrality, and not assuming Google will rank sources by reliability.[5]

At the federal level, the Every Student Succeeds Act (ESSA) of 2015 includes provisions for increased technology use and digital literacy, leaving it up to school districts to choose the best way to implement this, according to the National Conference of State Legislatures. NCSL also notes that some states are including digital literacy in their teacher training programs to encourage the safe use of technology and best practices for using online learning resources.[6]

Journalist Paul Glader notes in a *Forbes* article on reliable news sources that several of his well-educated friends have reached out to him to make sure that "their reading habits are leading them toward fact." One litmus test for a legitimate news outlet, according to Glader, is whether or not they will investigate and publish corrections if a reporter makes a mistake. A publication should also subscribe to the Society of Professional Journalist's code of ethics or something similar, and be willing to fire a reporter or editor who seriously violates those codes.[7]

Western Sydney University's Joanne Orlando suggests confirming information with a mainstream news outlet, looking out for URLs or site names that are unusual, and being alert for sensationalist imagery and text designed to provoke emotion. Orlando voices concern that fake news "has the power to moralise preducices, to dictate us-versus-them mentalities and even, in extreme cases, to justify and encourage violence."[8]

Social Media and Political Engagement

There is some promising news regarding social media and students. TikTok, a social media platform used primarily by young people, is becoming a political force for teenagers in America, the *New York Times* reports. They are forming coalitions to campaign for candidates, posting news updates, and fact-checking opponents. Group accounts, called "hype houses," are online ideological "homes" for members. Conservatives, liberals, undecideds and bipartisan members are all represented. Says 19-year-old Sterling Cade Lewis, who has amassed 100,000 followers, "TikTok is cable news for young people. . . . CNN and Fox and big-name news media, those are all geared toward people who have honestly grown up with a longer attention span." When a similar phenomenon occurred in Britain before a general election, it was thought that several close elections were won by Labour Party candidates through this campaigning. According to progressive-hype-house founder Javon Fonville, the American TikTok campaigns mostly revolve around Donald Trump and . TikTok videos often go viral when opposing members "duet," or post opposing views side-by-side on-screen. TikTokers also participate in live-streamed debates. Bi-partisan hype-house creator Cam Higby notes: "I think it's cool when you have people who are like 14 trying to get involved in politics and educate themselves. . . . They're not voting this year, but they'll be voting within the next term." TikTok has recently updated policies to combat misinformation after having an issue with posts about the coronavirus.[9]

In 1958 CBS broadcast journalist Edward R. Murrow famously said about television: "This instrument can teach, it can illuminate; yes, and it can even inspire. But it can only do so to the extent that humans are determined to use it to those ends. Otherwise it is merely wires and lights in a box."[10] Indeed.

Works Used

"Digital Literacy and Citizenship." National Conference of State Legislatures. Feb 8, 2017. https://www.ncsl.org/research/education/digital-literacy.aspx.

Domonoske, Camila. "Students Have 'Dismaying' Inability to Tell Fake News from Real, Study Finds." *NPR*, Nov 23, 2016. https://www.npr.org/sections/thetwo-way/2016/11/23/503129818/study-finds-students-have-dismaying-inability-to-tell-fake-news-from-real.

Glader, Paul "Real Facts Rather Than Alternative Facts." *Forbes*, Feb 1 2017. https://www.forbes.com/sites/berlinschoolofcreativeleadership/2017/02/01/10-journalism-brands-where-you-will-find-real-facts-rather-than-alternative-facts/#1312eac5e9b5.

Heitin, Liana. "Digital Literacy: An Evolving Definition." *Education Week*. Nov 8, 2016. https://www.edweek.org/ew/articles/2016/11/09/what-is-digital-literacy.html.

Koltay, Tibor. "The Media and the Literacies: Media Literacy, Information Literacy, Digital Literacy." *Media, Culture & Society*, vol. 33. doi10.1177/0163443710393382.

Lorenz, Taylor. "The Political Pundits of TikTok." *New York Times*. Feb 27, 2020. https://www.nytimes.com/2020/02/27/style/tiktok-politics-bernie-trump.html?action=click&module=moreIn&pgtype=Article&region=Footer&action=click&module=MoreInSection&pgtype=Article&region=Footer&contentCollection=Style.

Orlando, Joanne. "How to Help Kids Navigate Fake News and Misinformation Online." *The Conversation*. June 25, 2017. https://theconversation.com/how-to-help-kids-navigate-fake-news-and-misinformation-online-79342.

Shedden, David. "Today in Media History: Edward R. Murrow Challenged the Broadcast Industry in His 1958 RTNDA Speech." Poynter. Oct 15, 2014. https://www.poynter.org/reporting-editing/2014/today-in-media-history-edward-r-murrow-challenged-the-broadcast-industry-in-his-1958-rtnda-speech/.

Smith, B.L. "Propaganda Analysis and the Science of Democracy." *Public Opinion Quarterly*, vol. 5, no. 2 (1941): 250–59. Quoted in Hobbs, Renee, and Sandra McGee. "Teaching about Propaganda: An Examination of the Historical Roots of Media Literacy." *Journal of Media Literacy Education*, vol. 6, no. 2: 56–67. https://digitalcommons.uri.edu/jmle/vol6/iss2/5/.

U.S. Holocaust Memorial Museum. "What Is Propaganda?" https://www.ushmm.org/propaganda/resources/.

Notes

1. Koltay, "The Media and the Literacies: Media Literacy, Information Literacy, Digital Literacy."
2. Heitin, "Digital Literacy: An Evolving Definition."
3. U.S. Memorial Holocaust Museum, "What Is Propaganda?"
4. Smith, "Propaganda Analysis and the Science of Democracy."

5. Domonoske, "Students Have 'Dismaying' Inability to Tell Fake News from Real."
6. "Digital Literacy and Citizenship," NCSL.
7. Glader, "Real Facts Rather Than Alternative Facts."
8. Orlando, "How to Help Kids Navigate Fake News and Misinformation Online."
9. Lorenz, "The Political Pundits of TikTok."
10. Shedden, "Today in Media History: Edward R. Murrow Challenged the Broadcast Industry in his RTNDA Speech."

SPJ Code of Ethics

Society of Professional Journalists, 2014

Preamble

Members of the Society of Professional Journalists believe that public enlightenment is the forerunner of justice and the foundation of democracy. Ethical journalism strives to ensure the free exchange of information that is accurate, fair and thorough. An ethical journalist acts with integrity.

The Society declares these four principles as the foundation of ethical journalism and encourages their use in its practice by all people in all media.

Seek Truth and Report It

Ethical journalism should be accurate and fair. Journalists should be honest and courageous in gathering, reporting and interpreting information.

Journalists should:

– Take responsibility for the accuracy of their work. Verify information before releasing it. Use original sources whenever possible.

– Remember that neither speed nor format excuses inaccuracy.

– Provide context. Take special care not to misrepresent or oversimplify in promoting, previewing or summarizing a story.

– Gather, update and correct information throughout the life of a news story.

– Be cautious when making promises, but keep the promises they make.

– Identify sources clearly. The public is entitled to as much information as possible to judge the reliability and motivations of sources.

– Consider sources' motives before promising anonymity. Reserve anonymity for sources who may face danger, retribution or other harm, and have information that cannot be obtained elsewhere. Explain why anonymity was granted.

– Diligently seek subjects of news coverage to allow them to respond to criticism or allegations of wrongdoing.

– Avoid undercover or other surreptitious methods of gathering information unless traditional, open methods will not yield information vital to the public.

– Be vigilant and courageous about holding those with power accountable. Give voice to the voiceless.

From Society of Professional Journalists © 2014. Reprinted with permission. All rights reserved.

– Support the open and civil exchange of views, even views they find repugnant.

– Recognize a special obligation to serve as watchdogs over public affairs and government. Seek to ensure that the public's business is conducted in the open, and that public records are open to all.

– Provide access to source material when it is relevant and appropriate.

– Boldly tell the story of the diversity and magnitude of the human experience. Seek sources whose voices we seldom hear.

– Avoid stereotyping. Journalists should examine the ways their values and experiences may shape their reporting.

– Label advocacy and commentary.

– Never deliberately distort facts or context, including visual information. Clearly label illustrations and re-enactments.

– Never plagiarize. Always attribute.

Minimize Harm

Ethical journalism treats sources, subjects, colleagues and members of the public as human beings deserving of respect.

Journalists should:

– Balance the public's need for information against potential harm or discomfort. Pursuit of the news is not a license for arrogance or undue intrusiveness.

– Show compassion for those who may be affected by news coverage. Use heightened sensitivity when dealing with juveniles, victims of sex crimes, and sources or subjects who are inexperienced or unable to give consent. Consider cultural differences in approach and treatment.

– Recognize that legal access to information differs from an ethical justification to publish or broadcast.

– Realize that private people have a greater right to control information about themselves than public figures and others who seek power, influence or attention. Weigh the consequences of publishing or broadcasting personal information.

– Avoid pandering to lurid curiosity, even if others do.

– Balance a suspect's right to a fair trial with the public's right to know. Consider the implications of identifying criminal suspects before they face legal charges.

Ethical journalism strives to ensure the free exchange of information that is accurate, fair, and thorough.

– Consider the long-term implications of the extended reach and permanence of publication. Provide updated and more complete information as appropriate.

Act Independently

The highest and primary obligation of ethical journalism is to serve the public.

Journalists should:

– Avoid conflicts of interest, real or perceived. Disclose unavoidable conflicts.

– Refuse gifts, favors, fees, free travel and special treatment, and avoid political and other outside activities that may compromise integrity or impartiality, or may damage credibility.

– Be wary of sources offering information for favors or money; do not pay for access to news. Identify content provided by outside sources, whether paid or not.

– Deny favored treatment to advertisers, donors or any other special interests, and resist internal and external pressure to influence coverage.

– Distinguish news from advertising and shun hybrids that blur the lines between the two. Prominently label sponsored content.

Be Accountable and Transparent

Ethical journalism means taking responsibility for one's work and explaining one's decisions to the public.

Journalists should:

– Explain ethical choices and processes to audiences. Encourage a civil dialogue with the public about journalistic practices, coverage and news content.

– Respond quickly to questions about accuracy, clarity and fairness.

– Acknowledge mistakes and correct them promptly and prominently. Explain corrections and clarifications carefully and clearly.

– Expose unethical conduct in journalism, including within their organizations.

– Abide by the same high standards they expect of others.

The SPJ Code of Ethics is a statement of abiding principles supported by additional explanations and position papers that address changing journalistic practices. It is not a set of rules, rather a guide that encourages all who engage in journalism to take responsibility for the information they provide, regardless of medium. The code should be read as a whole; individual principles should not be taken out of context. It is not, nor can it be under the First Amendment, legally enforceable.

Sigma Delta Chi's first Code of Ethics was borrowed from the American Society of Newspaper Editors in 1926. In 1973, Sigma Delta Chi wrote its own code, which was revised in 1984, 1987, 1996 and 2014.

Print Citations

CMS: "SPJ Code of Ethics." In *The Reference Shelf: Propaganda & Misinformation*, edited by Annette Calzone, 142–145. Amenia, NY: Grey House Publishing, 2020.

MLA: "SPJ Code of Ethics." *The Reference Shelf: Propaganda & Misinformation,* edited by Annette Calzone, Grey House Publishing, 2020, pp. 142–145.

APA: Society of Professional Journalists. (2020). SPJ code of ethics. In Annette Calzone (Ed.), *The reference shelf: Propaganda & misinformation* (pp. 142–145). Amenia, NY: Grey House Publishing.

How to Help Kids Navigate Fake News and Misinformation Online

By Joanne Orlando
The Conversation, June 25, 2017

Young people get a huge amount of their news from social media feeds, where false, exaggerated or sponsored content is often prevalent. With the right tools, caregivers can give kids the knowledge they need to assess credible information for themselves.

Being able to identify the trustworthiness of information is an important concern for everyone. Yet the sheer volume of material online and the speed at which it travels has made this an increasingly challenging task. Platforms like Twitter and Facebook provide a loudspeaker to anyone who can attract followers, no matter what their message or content.

Fake news has the power to normalise prejudices, to dictate us-versus-them mentalities and even, in extreme cases, to justify and encourage violence.

We have become obsessed with getting kids off their devices at the expense of developing their understanding of the online world. This is not about surveillance, but rather about having open conversations that empower children to understand and assess the usefulness of information for themselves.

Fake News Is Tricking Children

Young people are growing up in a world where distributing large volumes of misinformation online has become a subtle yet powerful art.

It's no surprise then that research published in 2016 by Stanford University suggests kids "may focus more on the content of social media posts than on their sources".

For example, of 203 middle school students surveyed as part of the report, more than 80% thought a native ad on the news website Slate labelled "sponsored content" was a real news story. A majority of high school students questioned by the researchers didn't recognise and explain the significance of the blue checkmark on a verified Fox News Facebook account.

With the amount of content we see in a busy day, it's possible that these subtleties are being lost on many adults as well.

Minimising the Harm of Fake News for Kids

Helping young people navigate online spaces requires better skills in verifying what is true and what isn't.

Here are five questions to start the conversation with children.

Find an online post that you consider to be fake news and talk with the child about it. Shape your conversation around these questions:

- Who made this post?
- Who do they want to view it?
- Who benefits from this post and/or who might be harmed by it?
- Has any information been left out of the post that might be important?
- Is a reliable source (like a mainstream news outlet) reporting the same news? If they're not, it doesn't mean it's not true, but it does mean you should dig deeper.

Clues for Children to Use

Detecting fake news can be like a "spot the difference" game.

These questions are clues for kids that a source may be dodgy:

- Is the URL or site name unusual? For example, those with a ".co" are often trying to masquerade as real news sites.
- Is the post low-quality, possibly containing bold claims with no sources and lots of spelling or grammatical errors?
- Does the post use sensationalist imagery? Women in sexy clothing are popular clickbait for unreliable content.
- Are you shocked, angry or overjoyed by the post? Fake news often strives to provoke a reaction, and if you're having an intense emotional response then it could be a clue the report isn't balanced or accurate.
- How is the story structured and what kind of proof does it offer? If it merely repeats accusations against the people involved in an incident without further reporting, for example, there's probably a better version of the story out there from a more reliable news source.

Get to Know the Rules

Many social media sites are now also cracking down on the spread of fake news. Showing kids the restrictions these sites are imposing on their users will help them get a rounded understanding of the problem.

For example, asking kids to read the rules by which Reddit will remove content from r/news is a good starting point. Facebook also offers "Tips to Spot False News," suggesting readers check that other sources are reporting similar facts and that they look out for weird formatting, among other hints.

Growing up in a world of fake news doesn't have to be a heavy burden for kids. Rather, it requires extra support from adults to help them understand and navigate the digital world.

Fake news has the power to normalize prejudices, to dictate us-versus-them mentalities and even, in extreme cases, to justify and encourage violence.

Our goal should be not only to help children survive this complicated online world, but to equip them with the knowledge they need to flourish in it.

Print Citations

CMS: Orlando, Joanne. "How to Help Kids Navigate Fake News and Misinformation Online." In *The Reference Shelf: Propaganda & Misinformation,* edited by Annette Calzone, 146–148. Amenia, NY: Grey House Publishing, 2020.

MLA: Orlando, Joanne. "How to Help Kids Navigate Fake News and Misinformation Online." *The Reference Shelf: Propaganda & Misinformation,* edited by Annette Calzone, Grey House Publishing, 2020, pp. 146–148.

APA: Orlando, J. (2020). How to help kids navigate fake news and misinformation online. In Annette Calzone (Ed.), *The reference shelf: Propaganda & misinformation* (pp. 146–148). Amenia, NY: Grey House Publishing.

A College Reading List for the Post-Truth Era

By Michael T. Nietzel
Forbes, August 26, 2019

We live in a time beset with belittlement of science, hostility toward expertise and attacks on traditional democratic institutions. It's a post-truth period where conspiracy theories and crackpot ideas flourish. If the facts conflict with someone's sense of identity or political ideology, then the facts are disposable. They can be replaced with notions that feel better or reverberate on social media.

This latest outbreak of anti-intellectualism is particularly disturbing because the stakes of stupidity have increased. Climate-change deniers put the planet's viability in peril, anti-vaccinators subject their children to dangerous diseases, and a new breed of isolationists threatens the international partnerships that have contained tyrants and terrorists. When false beliefs are widespread, they can lead to trouble. Ultimately, the truth slaps us in the face, striking blows that hurt even more when it's too late to protect against them.

What's the proper role for colleges in this age of widespread deception and gullibility? Do they bear a responsibility to combat fraudulent claims, to sort the real from the fake? Can colleges prepare students to base their beliefs on evidence rather than preference? Can they help them become skeptical of overt lies and subtle propaganda?

Colleges need to embrace this obligation. Otherwise, they neglect the fundamental duty to educate students about the world and how it works, teaching them to upgrade their beliefs on the basis of accumulated knowledge. But how best to achieve these goals? What can colleges do to encourage students to be unwilling to accept ignorance as an asset?

Some have faced the challenge head-on. At the University of Washington, professors Carl Bergstrom and Jevin West offer *Calling Bullshit: Data Reasoning in a Digital World,* a course that teaches students how to detect b.s. and combat it with accurate analysis. Its syllabus has been shared with dozens of colleges across the nation.

Pedestrian as it might sound and increasingly rare as an academic expectation, serious reading is another way to sort truth from falsehood. With that in mind, here are seven recent books that champion reason over emotion, distinguish facts from fallacies and enumerate the dangers of ignoring the truth (following in the footsteps of Henry Frankfurt's *On Bullshit*). They could be assigned in individual classes or serve as the common reader often required for campus-wide discussions.

From *Forbes*, August 26 © 2019. Reprinted with permission. All rights reserved.

The Misinformation Age by Cailin O'Connor and James Owen Weatherall. The most technical work on the list, *The Misinformation Age* analyzes how falsehoods spread through social networks. Sometimes it's through the work of well-placed propagandists, sometimes the amplification of minority viewpoints taking advantage of weaknesses in the marketplace of ideas. Regardless, misinformation is quickly transmitted and uncritically accepted through selective consumption of cable news and cause-driven social media. Count this one a particularly good choice for advanced seminars in communications.

Kurt Andersen's *Fantasyland: How America Went Haywire* offers a broad—often repetitive—polemic against kooks, charlatans, New Agers, UFO chasers and political extremists. Anderson skewers goofballs and grifters on the political left and right, but he reserves his sharpest disdain for religious evangelicals and what he sees as their faith-based susceptibility to fantastical beliefs. *Fantasyland* is funny, edgy and relentlessly critical; it won't win over fans of Donald Trump. Assign it, and then duck.

Truth Decay by Jennifer Kavanagh and Michael Rich is a 2018 study published by the Rand Corporation. It analyzes the diminishing role of accurate information in political discourse, driven by four trends: increasing disagreement about facts and data, a blurring of lines between opinion and fact, the ascending influence of personal opinions over objective facts, and declining reliance on formerly respected sources of information.

The Death of Expertise by Tom Nichols is a contemporary analysis of American anti-intellectualism, reworking a theme explored previously by Richard Hofstadter and Susan Jacoby. As Nichols writes, "To reject the advice of experts is to assert autonomy, a way for Americans to insulate their increasingly fragile egos from every being told they're wrong about anything." A great reference about science-deniers and expert-haters, Nichols' book is provocative and accessible.

Lee McIntyre's *Post-Truth* is a concise examination of how truth is subordinated in modern America by several villains that allow post-truth to thrive. Featuring historical and current examples, *Post-Truth* is a serious work, brief enough to serve as an all-campus reader. Also serviceable for this purpose are similar titles by Matthew D'Ancona (*Post-Truth: The New War On Truth And How To Fight Back*) and James Ball (*Post-Truth: How Bullshit Conquered The World*).

Make no mistake, assigning any of these books requires fortitude. Each will stir controversy, both on campus and from many on the extreme right who will cast them as another manifestation of the academy's liberal bias. Stopping the decay of truth is not easy work and not for the faint-of-heart. But it's what good universities do.

> **Pedestrian as it might sound and increasingly rare as an academic expectation, serious reading is another way to sort truth from falsehood.**

Print Citations

CMS: Nietzel, Michael T. "A College Reading List for the Post-Truth Era." In *The Reference Shelf: Propaganda & Misinformation,* edited by Annette Calzone, 149–151. Amenia, NY: Grey House Publishing, 2020.

MLA: Nietzel, Michael T. "A College Reading List for the Post-Truth Era." *The Reference Shelf: Propaganda & Misinformation,* edited by Annette Calzone, Grey House Publishing, 2020, pp. 149–151.

APA: Nietzel, M.T. (2020). A college reading list for the post-truth era. In Annette Calzone (Ed.), *The reference shelf: Propaganda & misinformation* (pp. 149–151). Amenia, NY: Grey House Publishing.

10 Journalism Brands Where You Find Real Facts Rather Than Alternative Facts

By Paul Glader
Forbes, February 1, 2017

Where do we most often find real truth, real facts in a new era of Internet hoaxes, fake news stories and new political administrations that tout their own "alternative facts"?

Many citizens appear confused and worried. News stories from the BBC and the *New York Times* and *Money* magazine are reporting (with proof) that dystopian novels such as *1984* by George Orwell and *Brave New World* by Aldous Huxley are seeing a noticeable boost in sales. After Meryl Streep's anti-Trump and pro-journalism speech at the Golden Globe awards in January, donations picked up to the Committee to Protect Journalists. Subscriptions to the *New York Times* and other newspapers have picked up dramatically since Donald Trump was elected president according to the *Columbia Journalism Review* and other sources.

Meanwhile, I've been hearing from several well-educated friends, who are wondering if their own reading habits are leading them toward facts or fiction. "Hey man. Got a question for you on this 'fake news' thing," wrote one friend from my high school years. "What's your advice and do you have an opinion on where to find some form of truth in our media today?"

One key question for any publication is this: If a reporter gets facts in a story wrong, will the news outlet investigate a complaint and publish a correction? Does the publication have its own code of ethics? Or does it subscribe to and endorse the Society of Professional Journalist's code of ethics? And if a reporter or editor seriously violates ethical codes—such as being a blatant or serial plagiarizer, fabulist or exaggerator—will they be fired at a given news outlet? While some may criticize mainstream media outlets for a variety of sins, top outlets such as the *Washington Post*, the *New York Times*, *NBC News* and the *New Republic* have fired journalists for such ethics violations. That is remarkable in a world where some celebrities, politicians and other realms of media (other than news... such as Hollywood films "based on a true story") can spread falsehood with impunity.

Another friend writes, "Trump's attacks on the free media has me spooked and I want to support the media somehow. At the same time, I am aware of my liberal bias and would welcome a different point of view as long as it isn't 'alternative facts.' Any suggestions for good publications to subscribe to? I already have subscriptions to the [Washington] *Post*, [New York] *Times* and [Wall Street] *Journal*."

From *Forbes*, February 1 © 2017. Reprinted with permission. All rights reserved.

I am heartened by questions like these. A major shift in political and cultural life in our country means it is a good time for people to improve their own reading and learning habits. The Poynter Institute—an enlightened non-profit in St. Petersburg, Fla., that has an ownership role in the *Tampa Bay Times* and provides research, training and educational resources on journalism—provides many excellent online modules to help citizens improve their news media literacy.

> **In the post-truth age citizens should support local and regional publications that hew to ethical journalism standards and cover local government entities.**

In the post-post truth age (that is, an age where one has to work hard to be media literate and find the truthful sources of information), citizens should support local and regional publications that hew to ethical journalism standards and cover local government entities. In my corner of Long Island, that means I read (and sometimes write for) the *Great Neck News* and the chain of local newspapers to which it belongs. This year, I also plan to subscribe to *Newsday*, which is the largest paper that covers Long Island. I would urge citizens to subscribe to their local newspapers as well. This action helps these organizations employ journalists who attend city hall meetings, school board meetings and police precincts to report on how your tax-dollars are being spent, how your constitutional rights are being safeguarded, and to serve as watch dogs on how well your elected officials are serving you.

Realizing that millions more people are scratching their heads, wondering what to read and where to spend their subscription dollars, here are my top 10 large journalistic brands where I believe you can most often find real, reported facts:

1. *The New York Times*

This is the most influential newspaper in the U.S. in my view. Its editorial page and some of its news coverage take a left-leaning, progressive view of the world. But the *NYT* also hews to ethical standards of reporting and the classic elements of journalism in America. That's what helps the *NYT* remain, arguably, the agenda-setting news organization in America. It is a leader in business, politics and culture coverage. *

2. *The Wall Street Journal*

The largest circulation newspaper in the U.S., the *WSJ* made its bones as a business newspaper and pioneered new types of feature writing in American journalism (for example, its quirky middle-column feature called the "Ahed" and longer form, in-depth reports called "leders"). As the company was purchased by Australian media mogul Rupert Murdoch in 2007, the *WSJ* pivoted to cover more general news in addition to business news. The *WSJ* is still brand X among daily business publications in the world. Its editorial page is a bastion of American free-market conservatism, using the motto, "free markets, free people." With former Republican speechwriters and strategists such as Karl Rove, Peggy Noonan and Bill McGurn writing columns, the *WSJ* editorial page is often a must-read for Republicans in Washington. And left-leaning readers should not dismiss the *WSJ* edit page just because they may disagree with its positions. It has won several Pulitzer Prizes for editorials and columns that feature a clear thesis, backed up by thorough fact-based reporting and bold arguments. *

3. *The Washington Post*

The newspaper that brought down President Richard Nixon with its reporting on the Watergate scandal in the early 1970s maintains its intellectually robust tradition under the new ownership of Amazon.com founder Jeff Bezos. The *Post* has, for decades, been part of the big three national papers—a peer of the *NYT* and *WSJ*—in terms of winning Pulitzer Prizes, hiring the best and brightest reporters and producing big scoops. Of the big three, the *Post* is arguably the most forward-thinking right now in trying new digital strategies that have boosted readership. And with Bezos' backing, the *Post* is on a hiring binge for talented reporters while the *NYT* and *WSJ* have been pruning their reporting staffs in recent months. Most people think the *Post* editorial page leans left but is often regarded as more center left than the *NYT*. *

4. BBC

The BBC is the global standard bearer for excellence in broadcast radio and TV journalism. If only U.S. cable news outlets could follow BBC's recipe. And while PBS produces some great entertainment, documentary and news programs, its news programs have often seemed to lack the creative energy of the BBC. While NPR produces some fantastic journalism, a bulk of its news coverage seem to come from re-reporting news from the *New York Times* and the *Associated Press*. And the American public perceives NPR to be more left-leaning than the BBC.

5. *The Economist*

Another British export, the *Economist* magazine is staffed with excellent economists and journalists who produce a tightly-edited, factually rigorous account of what's happening in the world each week. One oddity is that the *Economist* doesn't publish bylines of their writers so you never know who exactly wrote a given piece.

6. *The New Yorker*

This American treasure publishes sophisticated narrative non-fiction pieces from top writers and reporters each week in a print magazine and, increasingly, on other platforms. The *New Yorker* is smartly expanding its audience on the web, offering to the masses content that used to be open only to its print subscribers. The magazine itself runs a piece of fiction each week (identifies it as such). The long-form non-fiction reports on politics, culture, business and other topics often take months to report, write and fact check. The result is deep reporting and analysis each week that is hard to find elsewhere. And the narrative structures and techniques the writers use make for enjoyable reading. Similar to the *Times,* the *New Yorker* presents a progressive view of the world. Conservative readers should recognize that but not let it detract from them enjoying some of the best reporting and writing happening in the world. *

7. Wire Services: The Associated Press, Reuters, Bloomberg News

You can't exactly "subscribe" to these wire services. But you can trust reports from these organizations to be factual. They provide a backbone of news and information flows about politics and the economy. And their member organizations that surface their reports benefit from this reporting. You can follow these organizations on social media and can also follow certain reporters for these organizations who report on topics of interest to you. These wire services also do have web sites and mobile apps you can use to stay abreast the news. *

8. *Foreign Affairs*

This bi-monthly magazine is published by the Council on Foreign Relations. It's a serious magazine for people who want intelligence on global affairs. The magazine and its many digital platforms benefits from submissions, dialogue, differing views and analysis from the many top minds on international relations.

9. *The Atlantic*

This is another national treasure, a monthly magazine that presents a view of the nation and world from Washington D.C. It is informed by many top journalists who write long-form features and also write some analysis. The *Atlantic* web site sometimes hews to clickable headlines. But the magazine and its parent company also subscribe to American journalism principles of fact-based reporting.

10. Politico

Founded by reporters who left the *Washington Post* in 2006, *Politico* has built itself into a crucial player in politics reporting in the U.S. (and with expansions to Europe). It does publish some products in print, but *Politico* is easily accessible on the Internet and mobile devices. Keep an eye on Axiso, a news startup launched this year by two founders of *Politico*.

* Disclosures: Earlier in my career, I interned at the *Associated Press* and the *Washington Post*. I worked as a staff writer at the *Wall Street Journal* between 2001-2011. I have also published free-lance articles in the *Post,* the *New York Times* and the *New Yorker* (website) as well as some of the publications listed in the runner up lists.

Runners Up:
- National Public Radio
- *TIME* magazine
- The Christian Science Monitor
- *The Los Angeles Times* (and many other regional, metropolitan daily newspapers)
- *USA Today*
- CNN
- NBC News
- CBS News
- ABC News

Business News Sources:
- *FORBES* magazine
- *Bloomberg BusinessWeek* magazine
- *Fortune* magazine
- *The Financial Times* newspaper

Sources of reporting and opinion from the right of the political spectrum:
- National Review
- The Weekly Standard

Sources of reporting and opinion from the left of the political spectrum:
- *The New Republic*
- *The Nation*

Print Citations

CMS: Glader, Paul. "10 Journalism Brands Where You Find Real Facts Rather Than Alternative Facts." In *The Reference Shelf: Propaganda & Misinformation,* edited by Annette Calzone, 152–156. Amenia, NY: Grey House Publishing, 2020.

MLA: Glader, Paul. "10 Journalism Brands Where You Find Real Facts Rather Than Alternative Facts." *The Reference Shelf: Propaganda & Misinformation,* edited by Annette Calzone, Grey House Publishing, 2020, pp. 152–156.

APA: Glader, P. (2020). 10 journalism brands where you find real facts rather than alternative facts. In Annette Calzone (Ed.), *The reference shelf: Propaganda & misinformation* (pp. 152–156). Amenia, NY: Grey House Publishing.

Fact Checkers Say These Are the Best Fact-Checks They Did During This Decade

By Cristina Tardaguila
The Poynter Institute, December 31, 2019

For those who have been battling against dis/misinformation for a few years now, some fact-checks should be remembered forever for the challenge they represented and for the amount of work they demanded.

Some fact-checks, on the other hand, can't be forgotten because they had a huge impact on society. They were responsible for real changes and not only made fact-checkers proud of their work but also still serve as clear pieces of evidence that fact-checking is very much needed.

But there is also another kind of memorable fact-check: those that came out of the craziest ideas and/or the deepest conspiracy theories. They focused on funny nonsense and are always remembered.

To celebrate the end of 2019 and the closure of this decade, the International Fact-Checking Network asked its members to share their favorite fact-check.

Here you will find 17 articles that were published in 11 countries and are considered great pieces of work by really amazing professional fact-checkers.

You just can't miss them!

These Were Difficult Fact-Checks

PolitiFact (USA): People might believe that "Barack Obama wasn't born in the United States," that "Barack Obama is Muslim" and/or he "refused to say the Pledge of Allegiance." PolitiFact has been working hard to debunk these super-viral false claims since 2007.

The Washington Post Fact Checker (USA): In October 2013, the WP fact-checking team gave "Four Pinocchios" to one of the most famous pledges made by President Barack Obama—that his health care plan would let people keep their existing plans if they wanted. It caused a firestorm and much commentary. Obama later admitted he had been wrong.

BOOM (India): A dramatic video of a police sniper killing a man who took a pregnant woman hostage at gunpoint was going viral in India in June 2017. The actual incident took place on April 5, 1998, in the Cua district of Caracas, Venezuela—and Indian fact-checkers had to locate a 20-year-old video in AP archives to prove their point.

From The Poynter Institute, December 31 © 2019. Reprinted with permission. All rights reserved.

Agencia Lupa (Brazil): In September 2018, when Brazil's National Museum in Rio de Janeiro was destroyed by a tremendous fire, Lupa's team published a series of fact-checks related to the story. First, it showed that almost none of the 14 presidential candidates running at that time had strong plans related to culture. Then it revealed that, even though the museum had been allowed to get up to R$ 17 million ($ 4,1 million) from private sponsors, it only managed to receive RS 1.07 million ($ 246,700). The team also flagged as fake a list of books and pieces of art that were being considered burned.

> Fact-checks were responsible for real changes and serve as clear pieces of evidence that fact-checking is very much needed.

These Fact-Checks Had a Great Impact

Aos Fatos (Brazil): In March 2018, a few days after Rio de Janeiro's leftist councilwoman Marielle Franco was shot and died, a big wave of rumors flooded Brazil's social networks. The hoaxes were also amplified by authorities, who wrongly claimed that Marielle was married to a famous drug dealer and had acted to protect criminals. Less than 12 hours after those false statements went viral, Aos Fatos debunked them. The fact-check was seen by 1.1 million people in one weekend.

Rappler (The Philippines): A fake letter supposedly signed by Queen Elizabeth and former U.S. President Ronald Reagan claims that the Commission on Good Government, created to track the late Philippines' dictator Ferdinand Marcos, concluded the politician "had no ill-gotten wealth." Rappler debunked the piece in September by fact-checking all the signatures and noting that the commission is still chasing traces of the Marcos' stolen funds to this day.

Taiwan Fact-Check Center (Taiwan): On Oct. 23, a Chinese spy named Wang Liqiang gave an interview saying he had spent the last years of his life manipulating a digital army in favor of China. The moment the information was published, China said he was a scammer and some Taiwanese politicians said the man used a pseudonym during the TV interview as a way to undermine his credibility. Taiwan Fact-Check Center debunked that information, proving the spy had used his real name.

FactCrescendo (Sri Lanka): On Nov. 15, the eve of the last presidential election in Sri Lanka, a false claim went viral saying the U.S Department of Justice had issued a letter stating that President Gotabaya Rajapaksa's citizenship renunciation had not been completed, and therefore he could not run. In a few hours, the fact-checking organization contacted the U.S. Embassy in Colombo and obtained official documents to prove the claim was false. They also noticed many discrepancies in the letter that went viral, such as the wrong date format and name misspellings.

Myth Detector (Georgia): On Nov. 22 the Georgian organization revealed that a pro-government blogger called Girgi Agapashvili was actually using an AI-generated photo on its profile. After Myth Detector published its story, Agapashvilli's Facebook page changed its name: from "გიორგი ალაპიშვილის ბლოგი" (Giorgi Aghapishvili's Blog) to "ხელვონური ინტელექტის ბლოგი" (Artificial Intelligence Blog).

These Were Funny Fact-Checks

The Washington Post Fact Checker (USA): Did Donald Trump really send his personal plane to Camp Lejeune, in North Carolina, when 200 Marines were stranded after fighting in the 1991 Persian Gulf War? No. In August 2016, the WP fact-checking team documented that the jet used on this operation was from the defunct Trump Shuttle. Trump had nothing to do with it.

BOOM (India): In March 2019, social media users claimed that an Australian man had named a brand of apples after Prime Minister Narendra Modi. BOOM examined the story and found out it was untrue. The apples were named after renowned painter and sculptor Amedeo Modigliani—not India's prime minister.

Demagog (Poland): Also in March 2019, Polish fact-checkers verified a claim made by former prime minister Ewa Kopacz. While trying to explain why her party was dropping in the ratings, she said that, in prehistoric times, people without gunpowder would use rocks to fight. According to her, a single rock (scandal) couldn't do any harm to a dinosaur, but throwing many of them for over a month could eventually weaken the animal. Demagog published an interesting story saying that the last non-avian dinosaurs ceased to exist around 66 million years ago and that the Sahelanthropus, who could be considered a human ancestor, appeared on Earth 6 million years ago. It was a reminder that dinosaurs and man didn't coexist.

These Fact-Checks Are Just Unbelievable

Agencia Lupa (Brazil): A photo of an obese white man went viral in Brazil, claiming the guy was being tried in the United States for being a cannibal. According to the fake post, he had eaten 31 people in the last seven years: 23 pizza delivery boys, some Jehovah's Witnesses who had knocked at his door and a couple of mailmen. Lupa's team found the story was based on a satirical article published in Canada.

GhanaFact (Ghana): In November 2019, the platform fact-checked an absurd claim from the American actress Lisa Raye McCoy, who said she had been crowned Queen Mother of Ghana. Ghana is not a monarchy. It doesn't have a king or queen.

Decrypteurs (Canada): A false story claimed that the mayor of Dorval, a small city just outside of Montreal, refused to ban pork in school cafeterias after Muslim parents asked for it. The story is not only false but impossible. Mayors in Quebec have no say in what goes on in schools. Even though the story has been debunked and even though a Google search for "Dorval Mayor" in French returns two fact-checking articles, the falsehood keeps circulating. Décrypteurs has counted over 400,000 shares on this story—when Quebec has only 8 million inhabitants.

The Quint (India): Old and unrelated images of Indian former prime minister Jawaharlal Nehru come and go in the misinformation world in different contexts—some of them are simply unbelievable. Fact-checkers at The Quint have created a list of false images so you are not fooled.

RMIT ABC Fact Check (Australia): Is a person torn to pieces by a crocodile every three months in north Queensland? Hell, no! Please read RMIT ABC fact check on this.

Print Citations

CMS: Tardaguila, Cristina. "Fact Checkers Say These Are the Best Fact-Checks They Did during This Decade." In *The Reference Shelf: Propaganda & Misinformation,* edited by Annette Calzone, 157–160. Amenia, NY: Grey House Publishing, 2020.

MLA: Tardaguila, Cristina. "Fact Checkers Say These Are the Best Fact-Checks They Did during This Decade." *The Reference Shelf: Propaganda & Misinformation,* edited by Annette Calzone, Grey House Publishing, 2020, pp. 157–160.

APA: Tardaguila, C. (2020). Fact checkers say these are the best fact-checks they did during this decade. In Annette Calzone (Ed.), *The reference shelf: Propaganda & misinformation* (pp. 157–160). Amenia, NY: Grey House Publishing.

Bibliography

Anderson, Janna, and Lee Rainie. "The Future of Truth and Misinformation Online." Pew Research Center. Oct 19, 2017. https://www.pewresearch.org/internet/2017/10/19/the-future-of-truth-and-misinformation-online/.

Applebaum, Anne. "Regulate Social Media Now: The Future of Democracy Is at Stake." *Washington Post*. Feb 1, 2019. https://www.washingtonpost.com/opinions/global-opinions/regulate-social-media-now-the-future-of-democracy-is-at-stake/2019/02/01/781db48c-2636-11e9-90cd-dedb0c92dc17_story.html.

Arendt, Hannah. "Truth and Politics." *New Yorker*. Feb 18, 1967. https://www.newyorker.com/magazine/1967/02/25/truth-and-politics.

Badsey, Stephen. "Propaganda: Media in War Politics." International Encyclopedia of the First World War. https://encyclopedia.1914-1918-online.net/article/propaganda_media_in_war_politics.

Bernays, Edward. "The Engineering of Consent." First published Mar 1, 1947. https://journals.sagepub.com/doi/10.1177/000271624725000116.

Branson, Ken. "President Trump and the Art of Spin." *Rutgers Today*, Feb 23, 2017. https://news.rutgers.edu/qa/president-trump-and-art-spin/20170222#.XksTmIpKiM8.

Bruinius, Harry. "Who Made You an Expert? Is America's Distrust of 'Elites' Becoming More Toxic?" *Christian Science Monitor*. Aug 27, 2018. https://www.csmonitor.com/USA/Politics/2018/0827/Who-made-you-an-expert-Is-Americas-distrust-of-elites-becoming-more-toxic.

Chan, Melissa. "Conspiracy Theories Might Sound Crazy, But Here's Why Experts Say We Can No Longer Ignore Them." *Time*. Aug 15, 2019. https://time.com/5541411/conspiracy-theories-domestic-terrorism/.

Conner-Simons, Adam. "Detecting Fake News at Its Source." MIT Computer Science and Artificial Intelligence Lab (CSAIL). Oct 4, 2018. http://news.mit.edu/2018/mit-csail-machine-learning-system-detects-fake-news-from-source-1004.

Connolly, Kate. "Joseph Goebbel's 105-Year-Old Secretary: 'No One Believes Me Now, But I Knew Nothing.'" *The Guardian*. Aug 15, 2016. https://www.theguardian.com/world/2016/aug/15/brunhilde-pomsel-nazi-joseph-goebbels-propaganda-machine.

Coppins, McKay. "The Billion Dollar Disinformation Campaign to Reelect the President." *The Atlantic*. Mar 2020. https://www.theatlantic.com/magazine/archive/2020/03/the-2020-disinformation-war/605530/.

Coppins, McKay. "What if the Right-Wing Media Wins?" *Columbia Journalism Review*. Fall 2017. https://www.cjr.org/special_report/right-wing-media-breitbart-fox-bannon-carlson-hannity-coulter-trump.php.

Daly, Christopher B. "How Woodrow Wilson's Propaganda Machine Changed American Journalism." *The Conversation*. Apr 27, 2017. https://theconversation.com/how-woodrow-wilsons-propaganda-machine-changed-american-journalism-76270.

"Digital Literacy and Citizenship." National Conference of State Legislatures. Feb 8, 2017. https://www.ncsl.org/research/education/digital-literacy.aspx.

Domonoske, Camila. "Students Have 'Dismaying' Inability to Tell Fake News from Real, Study Finds." *NPR*, Nov 23, 2016. https://www.npr.org/sections/thetwo-way/2016/11/23/503129818/study-finds-students-have-dismaying-inability-to-tell-fake-news-from-real.

Doshi, Rush. "China Steps Up Its Information War in Taiwan." *Foreign Affairs*. Jan 9, 2020. https://www.foreignaffairs.com/articles/china/2020-01-09/china-steps-its-information-war-taiwan.

Doubek, James. "18-Year-Old Testifies about Getting Vaccinated Despite Mother's Anti-Vaccine Beliefs." *NPR*. Mar 6, 2019. https://www.npr.org/2019/03/06/700617424/18-year-old-testifies-about-getting-vaccinated-despite-mothers-anti-vaccine-beli.

Dubois, Elizabeth, and Grant Blank. "The Myth of the Echo Chamber." *The Conversation*. Mar 8, 2018. https://theconversation.com/the-myth-of-the-echo-chamber-92544.

"Echo Chambers May Not Be as Dangerous as You Think, New Study Finds." *Science Daily*. May 13, 2019. https://www.sciencedaily.com/releases/2019/05/190513155629.htm.

Figueira, Álvaro Figueira, and Luciana Oliveira. "The Current State of Fake News: Challenges and Opportunities." *ScienceDirect*. 2017. https://reader.elsevier.com/reader/sd/pii/S1877050917323086?token.

Fox, Jo. "World War One Atrocity Propaganda." British Library. https://www.bl.uk/world-war-one/videos/world-war-one-atrocity-propaganda.

Freeman, James. "Clinton Backer at Facebook Debunks Clinton Claims." *Wall Street Journal*. Jan 7, 2020. https://www.wsj.com/articles/clinton-backer-at-facebook-debunks-clinton-claims-11578437355?mod=djemBestOfTheWeb.

Fried, Carla. "The Malleability of Who Falls for Conspiracy Theories." *UCLA Anderson Review*. Mar 6, 2019. https://www.anderson.ucla.edu/faculty-and-research/anderson-review/prevention-promotion.

"Genocide Timeline." Holocaust Encyclopedia, U.S. Holocaust Memorial Museum. https://encyclopedia.ushmm.org/content/en/article/genocide-timeline.

Glader, Paul. "Real Facts Rather Than Alternative Facts." *Forbes*, Feb 1 2017. https://www.forbes.com/sites/berlinschoolofcreativeleadership/2017/02/01/10-journalism-brands-where-you-will-find-real-facts-rather-than-alternative-facts/#1312eac5e9b5.

"'The Great Moon Hoax' Is Published in the *New York Sun*." History.com. https://www.history.com/this-day-in-history/the-great-moon-hoax.

Grimes, David Robert. "Echo Chambers Are Dangerous—We Must Try to Break Free of Our Online Bubbles." *The Guardian*. Dec 4, 2017. https://www.

theguardian.com/science/blog/2017/dec/04/echo-chambers-are-dangerous-we-must-try-to-break-free-of-our-online-bubbles.

Grynbaum, Michael M. "Trump Discusses Claims of 'Fake News,' and Their Impact, with New York Times Publisher." *New York Times*. Feb 1, 2019. https://www.nytimes.com/2019/02/01/business/media/donald-trump-interview-news-media.html?campaignId=7JFJX.

Gunderman, Richard. "The Manipulation of the American Mind: Edward Bernays and the Birth of Public Relations." *The Conversation*. July 9, 2015. https://theconversation.com/the-manipulation-of-the-american-mind-edward-bernays-and-the-birth-of-public-relations-44393.

Heitin, Liana. "Digital Literacy: An Evolving Definition." *Education Week*. Nov 8, 2016. https://www.edweek.org/ew/articles/2016/11/09/what-is-digital-literacy.html.

Hofstadter, Richard. "The Paranoid Style in American Politics," *Harper's Magazine*. Nov 1964. https://harpers.org/archive/1964/11/the-paranoid-style-in-american-politics/.

Howard, Philip N. "How Political Campaigns Weaponize Social Media Bots." *IEEE Spectrum*, Oct 18, 2018. https://spectrum.ieee.org/computing/software/how-political-campaigns-weaponize-social-media-bots.

Hung Ng, Sik, and Fei Deng. "Language and Power." *Oxford Research Encyclopedia of Communication*. Aug 2017. https://oxfordre.com/communication/view/10.1093/acrefore/9780190228613.001.0001/acrefore-9780190228613-e-436.

Illing, Sean. "America's Misinformation Problem Explained." *Vox*. Nov 6, 2017. https://www.vox.com/2017/11/6/16504454/misinformation-fake-news-media-trump.

Kavanagh, Jennifer, and Michael D. Rich. "Truth Decay: An Initial Exploration of the Diminishing Role of Facts and Analysis in American Public Life." Santa Monica, CA: RAND Corporation, 2018. https://www.rand.org/pubs/research_reports/RR2314.html.

Kessler, Glenn, Salvador Rizzo, and Meg Kelly. "President Trump Made 16,241 False or Misleading Claims in His First Three Years." *Washington Post*. Jan 20, 2020. https://www.washingtonpost.com/politics/2020/01/20/president-trump-made-16241-false-or-misleading-claims-his-first-three-years/.

Koltay, Tibor. "The Media and the Literacies: Media Literacy, Information Literacy, Digital Literacy." *Media, Culture & Society*, vol. 33. doi10.1177/0163443710393382.

Kreps, Sarah, and Miles McCain. "Not Your Father's Bots: AI Is Making Fake News Look Real." *Foreign Affairs*. Aug 2, 2019. https://www.foreignaffairs.com/articles/2019-08-02/not-your-fathers-bots.

Levine, Alexandre S., Nancy Scola, Steven Overly, and Cristiano Lima. "Why the Fight Against Disinformation, Sham Accounts and Trolls Won't Be Any Easier in 2020." *Politico*. Dec 1, 2019. https://www.politico.com/news/2019/12/01/fight-against-disinformation-2020-election-074422.

Lichfield, Gideon. "21st-Century Propaganda: A Guide to Interpreting and Confronting the Dark Arts of Persuasion." *Quartz*. May 13, 2017. https://qz.com/978548/introducing-our-obsession-with-propaganda/.

Lizza, Ryan. "The Hidden Menace Threatening Democrats' Bid to Beat Trump in 2020." *Politico*. Oct 15, 2019. https://www.politico.com/news/2019/10/15/dnc-election-strategy-disinformation-046839.

Lorenz, Taylor. "The Political Pundits of TikTok." *New York Times*. Feb 27, 2020. https://www.nytimes.com/2020/02/27/style/tiktok-politics-bernie-trump.html?action=click&module=moreIn&pgtype=Article&region=Footer&action=click&module=MoreInSection&pgtype=Article&region=Footer&contentCollection=Style.

MacDonald, Eve. "The Fake News That Sealed the Fate of Antony and Cleopatra." *The Conversation*. Jan 13, 2017. https://theconversation.com/the-fake-news-that-sealed-the-fate-of-antony-and-cleopatra-71287.

Madison, Ed, and Ben DeJarnette. "Journalism's Gatekeepers Lost Control of Their Gates." *Medium*. June 21, 2017. https://medium.com/s/how-journalism-became-a-dirty-word/journalisms-gatekeepers-lost-control-of-their-gates-8548f1bec0a3.

Marson, James. "Zuckerberg Pitches How Facebook Should Be Regulated Over Content." *Wall Street Journal*. Feb 15, 2020. https://www.wsj.com/articles/zuckerberg-pitches-how-facebook-should-be-regulated-over-content-11581794890.

Martineau, Paris. "Why People Keep Falling for Viral Hoaxes." *Wired*. Aug 22, 2019. https://www.wired.com/story/why-people-keep-falling-viral-hoaxes/.

Memmot, Mark. "75 Years Ago, 'War of the Worlds' Started a Panic. Or Did It?" *NPR*. Oct 30, 2013. https://www.npr.org/sections/thetwo-way/2013/10/30/241797346/75-years-ago-war-of-the-worlds-started-a-panic-or-did-it.

Mudde, Cas. "Why the Hysteria around the 'Fake News Epidemic' Is a Distraction." *The Guardian*. Feb 7, 2018. https://www.theguardian.com/commentisfree/2018/feb/07/hysteria-fake-news-epidemic-distraction.

"Nazi Propaganda." Holocaust Encyclopedia, U.S. Holocaust Memorial Museum. https://encyclopedia.ushmm.org/content/en/article/nazi-propaganda.

"Not Just Funny: Satirical News Has Serious Political Effects." *Science Daily*. Jan 23, 2017. https://www.sciencedaily.com/releases/2017/01/170123115741.htm.

Orlando, Joanne. "How to Help Kids Navigate Fake News and Misinformation Online." *The Conversation*. June 25, 2017. https://theconversation.com/how-to-help-kids-navigate-fake-news-and-misinformation-online-79342.

Otis, Cindy L. "Americans Could Be a Bigger Fake News Threat Than Russians in the 2020 Presidential Campaign." *USA Today*. July 19, 2019. https://www.usatoday.com/story/opinion/2019/07/19/disinformation-attacks-americans-threaten-2020-election-column/1756092001/.

Phillips, Whitney. "Disinformation Is Polluting Our Media Environment: Facts Won't Save Us." *Columbia Journalism Review*. Fall 2019. https://www.cjr.org/special_report/truth-pollution-disinformation.php.

Polumbo, Brad. "Criminalizing Free Speech Online? Elizabeth Warren Has a Plan for That." *Washington Examiner*. Jan 29, 2020. https://www.washingtonexaminer.com/opinion/elizabeth-warren-unveils-dystopian-fighting-disinformation-plan-criminalizing-free-speech-online.

"Powers of Persuasion." National Archives. https://www.archives.gov/exhibits/powers-of-persuasion.

Schetzer, Alana. "Governments Are Making Fake News a Crime—But It Could Stifle Free Speech." *The Conversation*. July 7, 2019. https://theconversation.com/governments-are-making-fake-news-a-crime-but-it-could-stifle-free-speech-117654.

Shedden, David. "Today in Media History: Edward R. Murrow Challenged the Broadcast Industry in His 1958 RTNDA Speech." Poynter. Oct 15, 2014. https://www.poynter.org/reporting-editing/2014/today-in-media-history-edward-r-murrow-challenged-the-broadcast-industry-in-his-1958-rtnda-speech/.

Smith, B.L. "Propaganda Analysis and the Science of Democracy." *Public Opinion Quarterly*, vol. 5, no. 2 (1941): 250–59. Quoted in Hobbs, Renee, and Sandra McGee. "Teaching about Propaganda: An Examination of the Historical Roots of Media Literacy." *Journal of Media Literacy Education*, vol. 6, no. 2: 56–67. https://digitalcommons.uri.edu/jmle/vol6/iss2/5/.

Soares, Isa. "The Fake News Machine." *CNN Money*. https://money.cnn.com/interactive/media/the-macedonia-story/.

Stecula, Dominik. "The Real Consequences of Fake News." *The Conversation*. July 26, 2017. http://theconversation.com/the-real-consequences-of-fake-news-81179.

Sullivan, Margaret. "Facebook's Role in Trump's Win Is Clear: No Matter What Mark Zuckerberg Says." *Washington Post*. Sept 7, 2017. https://www.washingtonpost.com/lifestyle/style/facebooks-role-in-trumps-win-is-clear-no-matter-what-mark-zuckerberg-says/2017/09/07/b5006c1c-93c7-11e7-89fa-bb822a46da5b_story.html.

Tardaguila, Cristina, and Susan Benkelman. "Factually: Fact-Checking on Coronavirus Far Exceeds That of Zika." *American Press Institute*. Feb 20, 2020. https://www.americanpressinstitute.org/fact-checking-project/factually-newsletter/factually-fact-checking-on-coronavirus-far-exceeds-that-of-zika/.

Taylor, Adam. "Before 'Fake News,' There Was Soviet 'Disinformation.'" *Washington Post*. Nov 26, 2016. https://www.washingtonpost.com/news/worldviews/wp/2016/11/26/before-fake-news-there-was-soviet-disinformation/.

Thomson, Ian. "Umberto Eco Obituary." *The Guardian*. Feb 20, 2016. https://www.theguardian.com/books/2016/feb/20/umberto-eco-obituary.

Tye, Larry. *The Father of Spin*. New York: Henry Holt, 1998. https://www.google.com/books/edition/The_Father_of_Spin/GarJLYMm3A0C?hl=en&gbpv=1&printsec=frontcover.

"US 2020: Another Facebook Disinformation Election?" *Avaaz*. Nov 5, 2019. avaaz-images.avaaz.org.

"U.S. Congress Passes Espionage Act." History.com. https://www.history.com/this-day-in-history/u-s-congress-passes-espionage-act.

U.S. Holocaust Memorial Museum. "What Is Propaganda?" https://www.ushmm.org/propaganda/resources/.

Webster's Dictionary. "Propaganda." https://www.merriam-webster.com/dictionary/propaganda.

"Why the Government Should Not Regulate Content Moderation of Social Media." Policy Analysis No. 865. Cato Institute. Apr 9, 2019. https://www.cato.org/publications/policy-analysis/why-government-should-not-regulate-content-moderation-social-media.

Woolley, Samuel. "We're Fighting Fake News AI Bots by Using More AI: That's a Mistake." *MIT Technology Review*. Jan 8, 2020. https://www.technologyreview.com/s/614810/were-fighting-fake-news-ai-bots-by-using-more-ai-thats-a-mistake/.

Websites

AllSides
www.allsides.com

AllSides is not a fact-checking site, but collects news from different political perspectives as way of highlighting contrasting coverage and bias. Focusing on political coverage, AllSides links to stories on a topic from sources that are left, center, and right as well as viewpoints generally missed by the mainstream media. Founded by CEO John Gable, who leans right according to AllSides, the site is funded by Gable and donations. AllSides also provides media bias ratings for news sources based on crowd-sourcing, surveys, and internal research, though some media outlets dispute the system's accuracy.

American Press Institute (API)
www.americanpressinstitute.org

Founded in 1946, the American Press Institute is an educational non-profit group supporting media studies through research, training, and industry leader conventions. Refocusing efforts from traditional newspaper training to encompass modern media outlets, initiatives include the Media Insight Project, Metrics for News, and Thought Leadership Summits. The API also provides education on media literacy and journalism and publishes academic studies on the industry.

Center for Responsive Politics
OpenSecrets.org

The Center for Responsive Politics is a nonprofit, nonpartisan Washington, D.C.-based research group that maintains a public online database tracking federal campaign contributions and lobbying by firms, individuals, and industries. OpenSecrets.org also contains personal financial disclosures of U.S. Congress members, the president, and key presidential administration officials. CRP was launched in 1983 by retired Senators Frank Church and Hugh Scott to track spending in congressional elections and has developed into a data resource to track money in politics. Major donors to CRP include the Sunlight Foundation, the Pew Charitable Trusts, the Carnegie Corporation of New York, Open Society Institute, the Joyce Foundation, and the Ford Foundation.

Center for Media Literacy
www.medialit.org

The Center for Media Literacy was founded in 1989 as a nondenominational, nonpartisan organization to raise awareness of media literacy both in the United States and internationally. The CML promotes research in the field and has helped to define media literacy and set a standard for education in the field. CML provides resources for teaching media literacy as well as training, and through its website provides resources and a media tool kit on the history of media literacy as well as current topics.

FactCheck
www.factcheck.org

FactCheck.org, devoted primarily to highlighting false and inaccurate claims made by politicians, is owned and operated by the University of Pennsylvania's Annenberg Public Policy Center. Started in 2003 by former Associated Press, *Wall Street Journal*, and *CNN* reporter Brooks Jackson, FactCheck is a non-partisan website that has received multiple awards for its efforts to reduce deception and confusion in U.S. politics and is used by journalists and other authors.

National Association for Media Literacy Education
www.namle.org

The National Association for Media Literacy Education is a non-profit professional association for educators, academics, activists, and students promoting literacy in all forms of media. NAMLE is dedicated to making media literacy a basic life skill, and provides resources for educators and others and sponsors the annual national "Media Literacy Week" program held in November. The organization publishes the *Journal of Media Literacy Education* and is a primary sponsor of the national "Media Literacy Week" program held in November.

Politifact
www.politifact.com

Politifact is a nonprofit fact-checking concern operated by the Florida-based Poynter Institute for Media Studies. Politifact was started in 2007 by *Tampa Bay Times* reporters and editors primarily to report on the accuracy of elected officials and political candidates. Politifact also reports on the progress made by elected officials in keeping campaign promises. Sister site Punditfact, established by the same group, fact-checks claims made by political pundits. Politifact has been criticized for bias by both liberals and conservatives, but articles on the website link back to original sources. Claims rated on Politifact receive ratings from "True" to "Pants on Fire."

Poynter Institute

www.poynter.org

The Florida-based nonprofit Poynter Institute for Media Studies was established in 1975 by Nelson Poynter, then editor and chairman of the *St. Petersburg Times* (now the *Tampa Bay Times*) as a small journalism school. The Institute has developed into an important center for media studies. In 2015 Poynter started the International Fact-Checking Network to set a code of ethics and provide certification for fact-checkers. In 2019 the institute compiled a list of news websites and other media outlets it considers unreliable. The institute offers information on media legitimacy, fact-checking, and media literacy for general readers.

Society of Professional Journalists (SPJ)

www.spj.org

The Society for Professional Journalists, formerly known as Sigma Delta Chi, is the oldest journalism organization in the United States. Established in 1909, the SPJ provides resources for professional journalists as well as maintaining a code of ethical standards to guide journalism practices that are voluntarily adhered to by many media outlets. The SPJ defends First Amendment rights through its Legal Defense Fund, and its Project Sunshine campaign focuses on freedom of information. It publishes the national magazine *Quill*, and hosts the annual Sigma Delta Chi Awards honoring excellence in journalism.

Index

4chan, 50
9/11 attacks, 4
2016 election, xii, 17, 36, 54, 67, 112, 116, 117, 123
2018 midterms, 112, 115
2020 election, ix, 50, 53, 100, 110

ABC News, 61, 92, 156
Abramowitz, Elkan, 57
Adali, Sibel, 120
advertising, xii, 3, 5, 14, 15, 16, 30, 31, 34, 68, 99, 101, 113, 130, 131, 144
Afghanistan, 4, 5
Agapashvili, Girgi, 159
AIDS, 3, 11
Alexandrov, Dimitar, 120
algorithm, 107, 108, 109, 119, 123, 130
al-Qaeda, xii
alternative facts, ix, 22, 152, 156
Amazon, 49, 57, 154
American Media Inc., 56
anarchism, 20
Andersen, Kurt, 150
anonymity, 33, 142
anti-intellectualism, 149, 150
anti-vaccinators, 149
anti-vaxxers, 4
Apple, 49, 100
Arendt, Hannah, xiii, 73
artificial intelligence, xiii, 6, 73, 101, 104, 112, 122, 123, 126
Australia, 29, 32, 35, 160
authoritarian, 70, 86

Baldwin, Brooke, 60
Ball, James, 150
ballots, 55
Baly, Ramy, 101, 119
Barrett, Paul, 110
BBC, 32, 41, 152, 154
Becker, Joshua, 94

Bell-Pottinger, 25
Bergstrom, Carl, 149
Bernays, Edward L., 3, 16, 137
Bezos, Jeff, 57, 154
bias, xi, 6, 57, 58, 60, 71, 73, 101, 102, 108, 120, 138, 150, 152, 167, 168
Biden, Joe, 50, 53, 113
bin Salman, Mohammed, 56
Black Lives Matter, 68
Blumenthal, Jesse, 113
Booch, Grady, 126
Bosworth, Andrew, 67, 99
bots, xiv, 5, 6, 12, 30, 35, 41, 73, 101, 103, 106, 110, 112, 122, 123, 124, 125, 126, 127
Brazil, 34, 47, 158, 159
Breitbart, 48, 92, 135
Brexit, 30, 36, 40, 43, 85, 101, 122
Buttigieg, Pete, 101, 110

Cambridge Analytica, 25, 36, 43, 67, 99, 122
Canada, 90, 92, 159
Caplan, Arthur, 64
Carlson, Tucker, 60
Carpini, Michael X. Delli, 95
CBS News, 156
censorship, ix, x, 13, 70, 99
Centers for Disease Control and Prevention (CDC), 63, 100
Centola, Damon, 78, 94
China, 12, 16, 47, 53, 63, 102, 103, 158
Churchill, Winston, 48
CIA, xii, 5, 11, 32, 50
climate change, 5, 78, 82, 83, 94
Clinton, Bill, 50, 78
Clinton, Hillary, 30, 50, 67, 72, 77
Cloots, Anacharsis, 20
CNN, 31, 32, 39, 41, 48, 50, 51, 60, 61, 62, 72, 139, 156
code of ethics, 139, 145, 152

Cold War, 12, 27, 38
collective intelligence, 78, 94
Committee on Public Information, 3, 13, 32, 137
Communications Decency Act, 115, 128
communism, 20, 21, 27
computational propaganda, 24, 100, 115, 116, 122, 123, 124, 125, 126
configuration, 104
conservatism, 20, 153
conspiracy theories, 47, 63, 64, 65, 77, 78, 83, 108, 109, 149, 157
content moderation, 99, 101, 128, 129, 132, 133
context collapse, 99, 101, 128, 129, 132, 133
coronavirus, 5, 47, 51, 63, 64, 65, 66, 139
Coulter, Ann, 65, 79
credibility, xiii, 5, 32, 78, 105, 106, 144, 158
Creel, George, 3, 14
Crimea, 122
critical thinking, 126
Currie, Willie, 49
cyberbullying, 130
cybersecurity, 30, 112, 116, 123
cyberwar, 73

D'Ancona, Matthew, 150
data collection, 67
debunked stories, 101, 124
deepfakes, 117
democracy, 13, 14, 16, 40, 54, 71, 88, 90, 95, 100, 102, 111, 117, 118, 122, 142
Democrats, 51, 52, 53, 54, 55, 78, 82, 94, 95, 101, 110, 113, 114
de Sales, St. Francis, 18
digital literacy, 102, 133, 137, 138, 139
digital viruses, 122
Dingell, Debbie, 63
Dionne, E. J., 20

disinformation, ix, x, xiii, xiv, 5, 6, 11, 12, 17, 18, 24, 25, 26, 28, 30, 31, 32, 34, 35, 36, 42, 43, 47, 50, 51, 53, 54, 55, 63, 70, 72, 73, 80, 86, 100, 101, 102, 103, 104, 105, 106, 110, 111, 112, 113, 114, 116, 117, 122, 123, 124, 125, 126, 137
diversity, 35, 89, 143
Donald J. Trump Foundation, 57
Donohue, Bill, 18
Dostoyevsky, Fyodor, 20
Douthat, Ross, 20
Duncan Hunter, 58
Durant, Kevin, 60

echo chamber, 78, 88, 89, 90
Eco, Umberto, xiii, xv
education, xi, 84, 137, 138, 140
election interference, 53, 54, 55, 102, 112
Electoral College, 54
emails, 60
England, 15
Epstein, Jeffrey, 78
ethical journalism, 142, 144, 153
EU, 40, 42, 71
European Commission, 70, 130
evangelicals, 150

Facebook, x, xii, xiv, xv, 5, 27, 29, 30, 31, 32, 33, 34, 35, 36, 37, 38, 40, 41, 49, 50, 51, 61, 63, 64, 65, 67, 68, 69, 71, 72, 78, 79, 80, 85, 86, 88, 89, 93, 99, 100, 101, 103, 110, 111, 112, 113, 114, 115, 116, 117, 119, 122, 124, 125, 130, 132, 133, 138, 146, 147, 159
fact-checkers, 31, 71, 119, 120, 157, 159
fact-checking, 30, 39, 51, 78, 89, 101, 113, 119, 120, 124, 125, 139, 157, 158, 159, 160
fake accounts, 100, 101, 110, 112, 113, 138

fake news, ix, x, xi, xii, 5, 8, 9, 10, 11, 17, 18, 19, 22, 24, 25, 27, 28, 29, 30, 31, 32, 33, 34, 35, 36, 37, 38, 39, 40, 41, 42, 43, 47, 48, 49, 50, 55, 61, 70, 71, 72, 73, 79, 80, 82, 83, 84, 85, 86, 87, 91, 92, 93, 97, 99, 101, 105, 119, 120, 121, 127, 137, 138, 139, 147, 148, 152
Fallows, James, 18
fascism, 20
FBI, 32, 50, 62, 77
Federal Election Commission, 58
Federal Trade Commission, 67
Feigenbaum, Ed, 126
Feinstein, Dianne, 72
films, 3, 4, 36, 137, 152
filter bubbles, x, 88
Final Solution, 4
First Amendment, 71, 72, 101, 144
Flagg, James Montgomery, 1, 14
Fonville, Javon, 139
foreign interference, 55
Foster, Lee, 112
Foucault, Michel, 71
Fox News, 60, 91, 92, 107, 113, 119, 146
France, ix, 3, 15, 33, 71, 91, 124
Frankfurt, Henry, 149
Franklin, Ben, 8
free speech, ix, 43, 70, 71, 72, 73, 101, 115
French Revolution, 20
Freud, Sigmund, 3, 16

G+, 116
gatekeeper, xii, 99
Gates, Bill, 64
German, 4, 14, 26, 33, 41, 43, 70, 79
Germany, ix, x, xii, 4, 13, 15, 26, 33, 35, 36, 41, 43, 91
Ghebreyesus, Tedros Adhanom, 64
Gilded Age, x, 8
Glass, James, 120

Goebbels, Joseph, xii, 4, 26, 79, 81
Google, 5, 20, 30, 32, 41, 49, 64, 68, 93, 99, 101, 107, 108, 109, 110, 112, 113, 124, 125, 130, 138, 159
Great Depression, x, 137
Greenberg, David, xi
gun control, 60, 83
gun violence, 60

Haab, Colton, 60
hackers, 31
Hannity, 60, 62
Hanson, Victor Davis, 20
harassment, 25, 30, 35, 36, 125, 130, 132, 133, 134
Harris, Kamala, 101, 110, 118
hate speech, 70, 99, 101, 125, 130, 133
Hearst, William Randolph, 8
Hicks, Troy, 137
Hinton, Geoff, 126
Hitler, Adolf, xii, 4
hoaxes, 5, 6, 8, 18, 24, 25, 31, 40, 47, 67, 99, 116, 152, 158
Hofstadter, Richard, 77, 150
Holder, Eric, 50
Howard, Phil, 85
Hunter, Margaret, 58
Huxley, Aldous, 152
hype houses, 139

immigration, 70
impeachment, 53, 79, 80
India, 34, 36, 43, 124, 157, 159, 160
information disorder, 24, 25
information ecosystem, 116, 117
information literacy, 35, 137
information war, 29, 102, 115, 116, 118
InfoWars, 48, 135
Ingraham, Laura, 60
Instagram, 30, 63, 64, 65, 116
intermediaries, 129, 131

internet, ix, x, 9, 24, 34, 40, 42, 48, 49, 50, 78, 101, 108, 111, 115, 123, 129, 132, 137, 138
Iran, 12, 33
Iraq, 4, 28, 38
ISIS, 117, 130
Italy, 11, 58, 91

Jacoby, Susan, 150
James, LeBron, 60
Jayapal, Pramila, 114
Jews, xii, 4, 26, 27, 79
Johnson, Hiram, 13
journalism, x, xi, xiv, 3, 6, 8, 9, 13, 16, 18, 25, 27, 30, 32, 35, 37, 48, 49, 56, 60, 71, 86, 100, 109, 137, 140, 142, 143, 144, 152, 153, 154, 155, 156
journalist, 14, 36, 43, 56, 58, 139, 142
junk news, 85

Kahan, Dan, 82
Kahn, Gabriel, 61
Kaplan, Alex, 65
Karadzhov, Georgi, 120
Kavanagh, Jennifer, 150
Kennedy, John F., 5, 11
Khashoggi, Jamal, 56, 58
King George III, 8
Kopacz, Ewa, 159
Kurtz, Howard 61

Laddis, Dimitri, 53
Lee, Ivy, 16
Leetaru, Kalev, 123
Lewis, Sterling Cade, 139
liberalism, 20
Library of Congress, 1, 14, 15, 134, 135
Lieu, Ted, 104, 107
Lindenberger, Ethan, 100
linguists, 101, 119, 120, 138
Liqiang, Wang, 158
Littlewood, Jesse, 112

Livingstone, Sonia, 49
Loesch, Dana, 60
Lofgren, Zoe, 107
Lyons, Tessa, 124

Macedonia, 30, 50
Macron, Emmanuel, 71
mainstream media, xi, 48, 62, 70, 72, 86, 116, 139, 147, 152
Malaysia, ix, x, 35, 36, 43, 70
Marchal, Nahema, 111
Marcos, Ferdinand, 158
Martin, Joel, 53
Martin, Trayvon, 109
McClure, S.S., 14
McConnell, Mitch, 20
McCoy, Lisa Raye, 159
McGurn, Bill, 154
McIntyre, Lee, 150
media literacy, xiii, 49, 71, 80, 89, 93, 137, 153
media manipulation, 72, 102
Medium, x, xiv, 116
memes, 11, 50, 112, 122
Merkel, Angela, 70
Merkley, Eric, 92
microtargeting, 12, 67, 99
millennials, 79
Miller, Clyde, xiii
Miringoff, Lee, 53
misinformation, ix, x, xii, 5, 10, 11, 12, 16, 19, 23, 24, 25, 28, 29, 31, 32, 33, 36, 37, 43, 47, 48, 49, 50, 51, 55, 59, 62, 63, 64, 65, 66, 67, 69, 73, 77, 79, 80, 82, 83, 84, 87, 90, 91, 92, 93, 95, 99, 100, 106, 109, 110, 114, 115, 116, 118, 119, 121, 127, 133, 134, 139, 140, 145, 146, 148, 150, 151, 156, 157, 160
Modigliani, Amedeo, 159
Modi, Narendra, 159
Mosley, Oswald, 70
Motta, Matt, 47
MSNBC, 62, 119

Mueller, Robert, 62, 110
Murdoch, Rupert, 153
Muslim, 5, 33, 120, 157, 159
Mussolini, Benito, 56
MySpace, 130

Nadler, Jerry, 68
Nakov, Preslav, 120
nationalism, 20, 26, 37
National Rifle Association, 60
Nazi propaganda, ix, 4, 26, 27
NBC News, 61, 65, 152, 156
Nehru, Jawaharlal, 160
Nichols, Tom, 150
Nietzsche, Friedrich, 21
nihilism, 20, 21
Nixon, Richard, 154
Noble, Safiya U., 109
Noonan, Peggy, 154
Norris, Chuck, 60
North Korea, 104, 105
Nougayrède, Natalie, 24
Nunes, Devin, 62
Nyhan, Brendan, 65, 83, 86

Obama, Barack, 94, 157
objective facts, xi, 150
Ochs, Adolph, 9
O'Connor, Cailin, 150
Orwell, George, 152

Pacepa, Ion Mihai, 5
Pakistan, 12, 31, 33, 40, 42
Pallone, Frank, Jr., 63
paranoia, 77
Pareene, Alex, 20
Parscale, Brad, 67
partisan content, 68
partisan news, x, 9
Pasquale, Frank, 131
PBS NewsHour, 53
Pearl Harbor, 11, 53
Pecker, 57
peer learning, 94

Pentagon Papers, 9
Philippines, 30, 32, 37, 158
Phillips, Whitney, 5, 47
phishing, 50, 101, 123
Pichai, Sundar, 68, 107
Pinterest, 116
polarization, ix, x, xi, 53, 78, 82, 89, 92, 94, 95, 106, 126
political ads, 100, 101, 110, 111, 113, 114
political discourse, 54, 150
political views, 83, 84, 88
politicians, xi, 60, 67, 71, 72, 101, 111, 113, 114, 152, 158
Pomsel, Brunhilde, 79
Pomsel, Kate Connolly, 79
Ponder, Stephen, 14
Pope Francis, 17, 18
Pope Gregory XV, 3
Pope Pius XII, 11
Porter, Ethan, 95
Post, David, 132
post-truth, ix, 85, 149, 150, 151, 153
propaganda, ix, x, xi, xii, xiii, xv, 3, 4, 5, 6, 8, 9, 11, 12, 13, 15, 16, 24, 25, 26, 27, 28, 32, 33, 34, 35, 36, 37, 38, 40, 42, 48, 56, 59, 77, 79, 80, 82, 100, 102, 109, 115, 116, 117, 119, 122, 123, 124, 125, 126, 130, 137, 138, 140, 149
public speech, 128
publishers, 9, 18, 49, 124, 129

Queen Elizabeth, 158

radio, ix, xiii, 4, 5, 14, 24, 26, 35, 38, 72, 88, 137, 154
Rajapaksa, Gotabaya, 158
rationalization, 82, 83, 84
Reagan, Ronald, 158
Reddit, x, 34, 42, 116, 147
Reifler, Jason, 83
Reines, Philippe, 50

Republicans, 48, 53, 54, 55, 78, 82, 94, 95, 101, 107, 110, 113, 154
revenge porn, 130
Rich, Michael, 150
Risch, James, 115
Robertson, Phil, 60
Rock, Kid, 60
Roof, Dylann, 109
Roosevelt, Franklin D., 4
Rosenberg, Simon, 111
Rosen, Jay, 18
Rosenthal, Tom, 48
Rove, Karl, 154
Russia, x, 11, 12, 21, 29, 30, 32, 39, 40, 41, 42, 53, 54, 62, 67, 68, 99, 104, 110

safe harbor, 129, 130, 131, 132, 133
Sanders, Bernie, 117, 139
Saudi Arabia, 12, 57
Scarpulla, Saliann, 58
Schamp, Scott, 49
Schiff, Adam, 67
Schneiderman Eric, 57
Section 230, 115, 128, 129, 130, 131, 132, 133, 134
"Seven Propaganda Devices," 137
sex trafficking, 78, 130
Silicon Valley, 68, 71, 101, 107, 110, 113, 128, 132
Singapore, ix, 36, 70
social media, ix, x, xi, xii, 5, 11, 12, 18, 24, 25, 29, 30, 31, 32, 33, 34, 36, 40, 41, 50, 54, 61, 63, 64, 65, 67, 70, 71, 73, 73, 79, 82, 83, 84, 85, 88, 89, 90, 91, 92, 94, 99, 100, 101, 102, 104, 105, 106, 110, 111, 112, 113, 114, 115, 116, 117, 122, 123, 125, 128, 129, 130, 131, 133, 134, 137, 139, 146, 147, 149, 150, 155, 159
Society of Professional Journalists, 142, 145
sock-puppet networks, 24
Soll, Jacob, 8, 13

sources, x, 5, 6, 25, 28, 29, 37, 39, 41, 42, 50, 63, 64, 65, 78, 79, 86, 88, 89, 91, 92, 100, 101, 119, 120, 137, 138, 139, 142, 143, 144, 146, 147, 150, 152, 153
South Africa, 26, 27, 34, 35, 38, 42, 124
Soviet Union, 16
Sri Lanka, 158
Stalin, Josef, 5, 11
Stein, Jill, 117
Stelter, Brian, 62
Streep, Meryl, 152
Strothmann, Frederick, 15
Sulzberger, A.G., xi
Supreme Court, 58, 129
Swoffard, Larry, 55
synthetic disinformation, 104, 105

Taiwan, 102, 103, 158
Tarbell, Ida, 14
tech companies, xii, 5, 49, 54, 55, 99, 100, 101, 110, 111, 113, 114, 130
television, ix, 24, 28, 47, 49, 72, 88, 102, 113, 116, 137, 139
terrorism, xii, 30, 80, 130, 132
Thorson, Emily, 48
TikTok, 63, 64, 65, 139, 140, 141
Times, xi, xiii, xv, 9, 11, 26, 28, 29, 30, 33, 36, 37, 38, 39, 40, 42, 43, 48, 61, 67, 82, 105, 106, 135, 139, 140, 152, 153, 154, 155, 156
totalitarianism, 12, 20
transparency, xii, 35, 71, 100, 112, 134
trending, 33, 131
troll, 5, 12, 24, 25, 29, 30, 33, 37, 39, 40, 106, 111, 116, 122
troll armies, 25, 29
troll farm, 30, 106, 111, 116
trolling, 101, 102, 125, 126, 130
Trump, Donald, xi, xii, 5, 29, 30, 31, 33, 34, 36, 41, 48, 50, 54, 56, 57, 67, 68, 72, 79, 91, 99, 107, 108, 111, 139, 150, 152, 159
Trump, Donald, Jr., 111

Trump, Eric, 92
truth decay, xi
Tumblr, 34, 116
Turgenev, Ivan, 21
Twitter, x, 5, 25, 29, 30, 32, 33, 34, 39, 41, 61, 63, 64, 71, 78, 85, 86, 88, 89, 100, 101, 110, 111, 112, 113, 116, 122, 125, 133, 146
Tworek, Heidi, 18
Tzu, Sun, 11

U.K., 11, 90
Ukraine, 11, 29, 53, 80, 111, 113
Underwood, Barbara, 57
unethical conduct, 144
urban myths, 79
U.S. Congress, 1, 3, 6, 13, 14, 15, 37, 71, 100, 107, 111, 123, 129, 134, 135
U.S. Justice Department, 4, 56, 104

vaccinations, 3
Venezuela, 31, 32, 34, 41, 42, 157
Vietnam War, x, 4, 27, 38
Vine, 116
Vitriol, Joseph, 78
Vlachos, Andreas, 120
voter suppression, x, 55, 112
voting, 5, 33, 55, 139

Wardle, Claire, 37
Warner, Mark, 115
Warren, Elizabeth, x, xiv, xv, 101, 110
Watergate, 9, 154
Weatherall, James Owen, 150
websites, 24, 30, 31, 35, 49, 50, 85, 92, 120, 129
Weisselberg, Allen, 57
Welles, Orson, 5
West, Jevin, 149
Wikipedia, 35, 120
Wilson, Woodrow, 3, 4, 6, 7, 13, 14, 15, 16, 42
Woods, James, 111
World Health Organization (WHO), 63
Wu, Irene, 49
WWI, 4, 13, 16
WWII, 4, 13
Wyden, Ron, 115

Yahoo, 39, 91, 92, 129
yellow journalism, 8, 9
YouTube, 30, 32, 63, 110, 113, 116, 130, 132

Zuckerberg, Mark, xiv, xv, 31, 40, 99, 114, 123